My 60
Memorable Games

Selected and fully annotated
by Bobby Fischer

with Introductions to the games

by International Grandmaster Larry Evans

A Fireside Book Published by
SIMON AND SCHUSTER / NEW YORK

SBN 671-21483-7

CONTENTS

(B and W refer to Black and White)

Preface

PAGE

Opponent

The 60 games annotated in this volume were all played during 1957 through '67 and, with the exception of nos. 44 and 50, under strict tournament conditions. The notes frequently include references to additional games, occasionally presenting them in full. An interested reader will find 34 of my earlier efforts in Bobby Fischer's Games of Chess (*Simon and Schuster, 1959*).

All of the 60 here offered contain, for me, something memorable and exciting—even the 3 losses. I have tried to be both candid and precise in my elucidations in the hope that they would offer insights into chess that will lead to fuller understanding and better play.

Finally, I wish to express my gratitude to Larry Evans, friend and colleague, for his invaluable aid in the preparation of the text as well as for his lucid introductions.

ROBERT J. FISCHER
New York City

On the chessboard lies and hypocrisy do not survive long. The creative combination lays bare the presumption of a lie; the merciless fact, culminating in a checkmate, contradicts the hypocrite.

—EMANUEL LASKER

I Fischer - Sherwin *[U.S.A.]*

SICILIAN DEFENSE

Too little, too late

Although Sherwin makes no serious errors in the opening, he misses several equalizing opportunities. Demonstrating the technical virtuosity that is to become his hallmark, Fischer, with astonishing maturity, gradually strengthens his grip by accumulating small advantages: the better center and the two Bishops. Sherwin, meanwhile, attempts to consolidate his position—only to see his 14-year-old opponent shatter it with a thunderbolt (18 N×RP). It brings to mind Alekhine's combinations, which also seemed to spring from nowhere. Sherwin, lashing back, refuses to fall. However, his defense finally disintegrates under a series of acute blows to his wobbly King.

1	P – K4	P – QB4
2	N – KB3	P – K3
3	P – Q3	. . .

This used to be my favorite. I thought it led to a favorable variation of the King's Indian reversed, particularly after Black has committed himself with . . . P – K3.

3	. . .	N – QB3
4	P – KN3	N – B3

Fischer – Ivkov, Santa Monica 1966 continued; *4* . . . P – Q4; *5* QN – Q2, B – Q3; *6* B – N2, KN – K2; *7* O – O, O–O; *8* N–R4! with chances for initiative.

5	B – N2	B – K2
6	O – O	O – O

More usual is *6* . . . P – Q4; but Black has purposely delayed placing his center Pawns. Has he a new idea in mind?

7 QN – Q2   . . .

After 7 P – K5, N – Q4; 8 QN – Q2, P – B3; 9 P × P, N × P; 10 R –
K1 gives White an edge.

7 . . .   R – N1

Sherwin slid the Rook here with his pinky, as if to emphasize the
cunning of this mysterious move. 7 . . . P – Q4; 8 R – K1, P –
QN4; 9 P – K5, N – Q2 ; 10 N – B1, P – N5; 11 P – KR4, P – QR4;
12 B – B4, P – R5; 13 P – R3! Fischer – Mjagmarsuren, Sousse
Interzonal 1967, leads to double-edged play where Black's chances
on the Q-side countervail White's K-side attack—but White
usually comes first.

8 R – K1   P – Q3
9 P – B3   P – QN3

Not bad. But I had expected 9 . . . P – QN4; 10 P – Q4, P × P!
(if 10 . . . P – N5; 11 P – K5! P × BP? [11 . . . P × KP; 12
P × KP, N – Q2; 13 P – B4 holds the advantage]; 12 P × N, P × N;
13 N × P! wins a piece); 11 P × P, P – Q4, with equality.

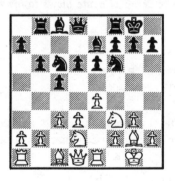

SHERWIN

Position after 9 . . .
P – QN3

FISCHER

10 P – Q4   Q – B2?

This leads to trouble. Black should strive for counterplay by
opening the QB file: 10 . . . P × P; 11 P × P, P – Q4; 12 P – K5,
N – Q2, etc.

11 P – K5!   N – Q4

Worse is 11 . . . N – Q2; 12 P × QP, B × P; 13 N – K4, P × P;
14 N × B, Q × N; 15 B – B4, P – K4; 16 N × KP!, N/2 × N; 17 P × P
winning a Pawn. The best try is 11 . . . P × KP; 12 P × KP,

N – Q2; *13* Q – K2, B – N2; *14* P – KR4 with a bind, but Black's game may be tenable.

12 P×QP	B×P
13 N – K4!	P – B5

An unpleasant choice, since it releases the pressure in the center and gives White a free hand to start operations on the K-side. However, other moves lose material:

A] *13* . . . B – K2; *14* P – B4, N – B3; *15* B – B4, etc.

B] *13* . . . P×P; *14* N×B, Q×N; *15* P – B4!, N – B3; *16* B – B4 and again the lineup on this diagonal is unfortunate.

14 N×B	Q×N
15 N – N5!	QN – K2?

A bad mistake. Black's game is still tenable after *15* . . . P – KR3; *16* N – K4, Q – Q1.

16 Q – B2!	N – N3

On *16* . . . P – B4?; *17* Q – K2 picks off a Pawn. Had Sherwin seen what was coming, however, he might have chosen *16* . . . P – N3; *17* N – K4, Q – B2; *18* B – R6, R – Q1; though *19* Q – Q2 prepares to exploit his weakened dark squares.

17 P – KR4	N – B3

Apparently everything's defended now. Unappetizing is *17* . . . R – Q1 (*17* . . . P – KR3; *18* P – R5, P×N; *19* P×N, P – B3?; *20* Q – K2 – R5); *18* N×RP!, K×N; *19* P – R5, P – B4; *20* P×N+, K×P; *21* R – K5! with a bind.

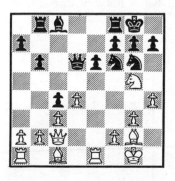

SHERWIN

Position after 17 . . .
N – B3

FISCHER

18 N×RP!	. . .

Throwing a monkey wrench into Black's carefully contrived setup! As usual, tactics flow from a positionally superior game.

                    18 . . .   N × N

Not *18 . . . K × N?; 19* B – B4.

                    19 P – R5   N – R5!

The best fighting chance. Not *19 . . .* N – K2; *20* B – B4 wins a clear exchange.

                    20 B – B4   Q – Q1
                    21 P × N   . . .

21 B × R?, N × B; *22* K × N, B – N2+ ; *23* P – B3, Q × B.

                    21 . . .   R – N2!
                    22 P – R6!   . . .

He's hoping for *22* B × R, B × B and, suddenly, the initiative passes to Black despite his material deficit.

                    22 . . .   Q × P

Once again, time-pressure had Sherwin burying his thumbs in his ears. Instead of trying to mix it up, Black should keep his King sheltered as long as possible with *22 . . .* P – N3; *23* P – R5!, P – N4 (if *23 . . .* P × P; *24* Q – K2); but *24* B – K5 stays a pawn ahead with two Bishops. It might still be a fight, though.

                    23 P × P   K × P?

Suicidal. The last hope would have been *23 . . .* R – Q1; *24* B – N3, Q – R3; though *25* Q – K2 is hard to meet (if *25 . . .* P – N4; *26* P – R4, P – R3; *27* P × P, P × P; *28* R – R8).

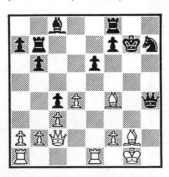

SHERWIN

Position after 23 . . .
K × P

FISCHER

24 R – K4!   . . .

Threatening B – K5+.

24 . . .   Q – R4
25 R – K3!   . . .

Now the Rook joins the King hunt—and it's murder. The immediate threat is *26* R – R3, Q – N3; *27* R – N3.

25 . . .   P – B4
26 R – R3   Q – K1

26 . . . Q – N3?; 27 R – N3.

27 B – K5+   . . .

White can pick off a couple of exchanges with *27* B – R6+, K – N1; *28* B × KR, Q × B; *29* B × R, etc. But by now I felt there was more in the offing.

27 . . .   N – B3

27 . . . K – N1?; 28 R – N3+, K – B2; 29 R – N7 mate.

28 Q – Q2!   K – B2
29 Q – N5   Q – K2

On *29 . . . K – K2; 30* R – R7+ is devastating.

30 B × N   Q × B
31 R – R7+   K – K1
32 Q × Q   R × R

On *32 . . . R × Q; 33* B × R nets a whole Rook.

33 B – B6+   Black resigns

If *33 . . . B – Q2; 34* Q × P+.

SHERWIN

Final Position after 33
B – B6+

FISCHER

2 Fischer - Larsen [Denmark]

PORTOROZ 1958

SICILIAN DEFENSE

Slaying the dragon

Although the Sicilian, as a whole, is still the best fighting defense at Black's disposal, much of the steam has been taken out of the time-honored Dragon Variation. This is one of the key games which helped to batter its reputation.

In a laudable attempt to create complications, Larsen deviates from the book on move 15. That proves to be disastrous, since his counterattack never gets started. Mechanically, routinely, Fischer pries open the KR-file, sacrificing first a Pawn and then the exchange. There is an aura of the inevitable about the outcome. Here the notes are as instructive and lucid as the text, which is an object lesson in how to mount an assault against the fianchettoed King.

1 P – K4	P – QB4
2 N – KB3	P – Q3
3 P – Q4	P × P
4 N × P	N – KB3
5 N – QB3	P – KN3

Larsen was one of the diehards who refused to abandon the Dragon until recently. White's attack almost plays itself . . . weak players even beat Grandmasters with it. I once thumbed through several issues of *Shakhmatny Bulletin*, when the Yugoslav Attack was making its debut, and found the ratio was something like nine wins out of ten in White's favor. Will Black succeed in reinforcing the variation? Time will tell.

6 B – K3	B – N2

6 . . . N – N5? still loses to 7 B – N5+.

7 P – B3	O – O
8 Q – Q2	N – B3
9 B – QB4	. . .

This refinement supersedes the old O – O – O. The idea is to prevent . . . P – Q4.

9 . . .   N×N

Just how Black can attempt to thread his way to equality is not clear. Interesting is Donald Byrne's *9 . . . P – QR4.* The strongest reply is *10* P – KN4 and if N – K4; *11* B – K2, P – Q4?; *12* P – N5! wins a Pawn.

10 B×N   B – K3

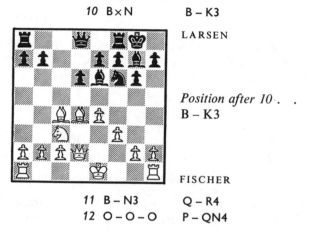

LARSEN

Position after 10 . . .
B – K3

FISCHER

11 B – N3   Q – R4

12 O – O – O   P – QN4

After *12 . . . B×B; 13* BP×B! Black cannot make any attacking headway against this particular Pawn configuration. White is lost in the King and Pawn ending, it's true, but Black usually gets mated long before then. As Tarrasch put it: "Before the endgame the gods have placed the middle game."

13 K – N1   P – N5

14 N – Q5   . . .

Weaker is *14* N – K2, B×B; *15* BP×B, KR – Q1.

14 . . .   B×N

Bad judgment is *14 . . . N×N?; 15* B×B, K×B; *16* P×N, B – Q2; *17* QR – K1 with a crushing bind. (Suetin–Korchnoi, USSR Championship prelims 1953.)

15 B×B   . . .

Stronger is *15* P×B!, Q – N4; *16* KR – K1, P – QR4; *17* Q – K2! (Tal–Larsen, Zurich 1959) where White abandons the attack and plays for pressure along the K-file instead.

15 . . .   QR – B1 ?

The losing move. After the game Larsen explained he was
playing for a win, and therefore rejected the forced draw with
*15 . . . N×B; 16 B×B, N – B6+; 17 P×N (17 B×N, P×B;
18 Q×BP, Q×Q; 19 P×Q, KR – B1 renders White's extra Pawn
useless), QR – N1!; 18 P×P, Q×NP+!; 19 Q×Q, R×Q+; 20
B – N2, KR – N1*, etc. After *15 . . . N×B*, however, I intended
simply *16 P×N, Q×P; 17 Q×P*, keeping the game alive.

16 B – N3!   . . .

He won't get a second chance to snap off the Bishop! Now I
felt the game was in the bag if I didn't botch it. I'd won dozens of
skittles games in analogous positions and had it down to a science:
pry open the KR-file, sac, sac . . . mate!

16 . . .   R – B2

This loss of time is unfortunately necessary if Black is ever to
advance his QRP. *16 . . . Q – QN4?* is refuted by *17 B×P*.

17 P – KR4   Q – QN4

There's no satisfactory way to impede White's attack. If *17
. . . P – R4; 18 P – N4!, P×P (18 . . . KR – B1; 19 QR – N1,
P×P; 20 P – R5!, P×RP; 21 P×P, N×KP; 22 Q – B4, P – K4;
23 Q×N, P×B; 24 P×P, K– R1; 25 P – R6, B – B3; 26 R – N7!
wins); 19 P – R5!, P×RP (on 19 . . . N×RP; 20 B×B, K×B;
21 P×P, N – B3; 22 Q – R6+ mates); 20 P×P, N×KP (on 20
. . . P×P; 21 QR – N1, P – K4; 22 B – K3, R – Q1; 23 B – R6,
or 20 . . . N×NP; 21 QR – N1, B×B; 22 R×N+!, P×R; 23
Q – R6 leads to mate); 21 Q – K3, N – B3 (21 . . . B×B; 22
Q×N, B – N2; 23 R×RP); 22 P×P, P – K4; 23 P – R6 wins.*

LARSEN

Position after 17 . . .
Q – QN4

FISCHER

Now Black is threatening to get some counterplay with . . . P – QR4 – 5.

       18 P – R5!   . . .

There's no need to lose a tempo with the old-fashioned P – N4.

       18 . . .   KR – B1

On *18* . . . P × P; *19* P – N4!, P × P; *20* P × P! N × KP; *21* Q – R2, N – N4; *22* B × B, K × B; *23* R – Q5, R – B4; *24* Q – R6+, K – N1; *25* R × N+, R × R; *26* Q × P mate.

       19 P × P   P × P
       20 P – N4   . . .

Not the impatient *20* B × N ?, B × B; *21* Q – R6, P – K3! (threatening . . . Q – K4) and Black holds everything.

       20 . . .   P – R4

Now Black needs just one more move to get his counterattack moving. But for want of a nail the battle was lost . . .

       21 P – N5   N – R4

Vasiukov suggests *21* . . . N – K1 as a possible defense (not *21* . . . P – R5?; *22* P × N, P × B; *23* P × B!, P × BP+; *24* Q × P!, P – K4; *25* Q – R2 wins); but White crashes through with *22* B × B, N × B (*22* . . . K × B?; *23* Q – R2); *23* R – R6!, P – K3 (if *23* . . . P – R5; *24* Q – R2, N – R4; *25* R × P+); *24* Q – R2, N – R4; *25* B × P!, P × B (if *25* . . . Q × P; *26* R × P+!, Q × R; *27* B × R, threatening R – N1); *26* R × P+, N – N2; *27* R – R1, etc.

LARSEN

Position after 21 . . .
N – R4

FISCHER

       22 R × N!   . . .

Fine wrote: "In such positions, combinations are as natural as a baby's smile."

$$22 \ldots \quad\quad\quad P \times R$$

No better is 22 . . . B×B; 23 Q×B, P×R; 24 P – N6, Q – K4 (if 24 . . . P – K3; 25 Q×QP); 25 P×P+, K – R2 (if 25 . . . K – B1; 26 Q×Q, P×Q; 27 R – N1, P – K3; 28 B×P, K – K2; 29 B×R, R×B; 30 R – N5 wins); 26 Q – Q3! (intending P – KB4) should be decisive.

$$23 \ P - N6 \quad\quad\quad P - K4$$

On 23 . . . P – K3; 24 P×P+, K×P (if 24 . . . R×P; 25 B×P); 25 B×B, K×B; 26 R – N1+, K – R2; 27 Q – N2, Q – K4; 28 Q – N6+, K – R1; 29 R – N5, R – N2; 30 R×P+, K – N1; 31 B×P+, K – B1; 32 R – B5+, K – K2; 33 R – B7+ wins.

$$24 \ P \times P+ \quad\quad\quad K - B1$$
$$25 \ B - K3 \quad\quad\quad P - Q4!$$

A desperate bid for freedom. On 25 . . . P – QR5 (if 25 . . . R – Q1; 26 B – R6); 26 Q×P+, R – K2; 27 Q – Q8+!, R×Q; 28 R×R+, R – K1; 29 B – B5+ mates.

$$26 \ P \times P! \quad\quad\quad \ldots$$

Not 26 B×P, R×QBP!

$$26 \ldots \quad\quad\quad R \times KBP$$

On 26 . . . P – QR5; 27 P – Q6!, P×B; 28 P×R wins.

$$27 \ P - Q6 \quad\quad\quad R - KB3$$

On 27 . . . R – Q2 White can either regain the exchange with 28 B – K6 or try for more with 28 B – R6. And on 27 . . . R×KBP; 28 P – Q7, threatening Q – Q6 mate.

$$28 \ B - N5 \quad\quad\quad Q - N2$$

Or 28 . . . Q – Q2; 29 Q – Q5!, Q – KB2 (if 29 . . . R – KB2; 30 B – K7+!); 30 B×R wins material.

$$29 \ B \times R \quad\quad\quad B \times B$$
$$30 \ P - Q7 \quad\quad\quad R - Q1$$
$$31 \ Q - Q6+ \quad\quad\quad \ldots$$

A mistake! 31 Q – R6+! forces mate in three.

$$31 \ldots \quad\quad\quad \text{Black resigns}$$

3   Petrosian *[U.S.S.R.]* - Fischer

PORTOROZ 1958

KING'S INDIAN DEFENSE

Bear hug

In what appear to be perfectly equal positions, Petrosian consistently finds seemingly innocuous moves which gradually overwhelm his opponent. He accomplishes his objective simply by exchanging pieces and maneuvering for victory without taking unnecessary risks. This essentially defensive technique has the virtue, when it doesn't utterly succeed, of producing a draw. Fischer, by contrast, generally chooses the sharpest course, however precipitous it may become. Occasionally he overreaches himself, but it makes for interesting chess.

In this game, replete with errors on both sides, Petrosian succeeds in pinning his opponent for a time to a static endgame. But Fischer manages to burst his bonds, only to blunder on the very next move (51 . . . K – Q3). Petrosian, however, by blundering in his turn, restores the balance. The ensuing Rook and Pawn ending produces a thrilling draw.

1	P – QB4	N – KB3
2	N – QB3	P – KN3
3	P – KN3	B – N2
4	B – N2	O – O
5	N – B3	P – Q3
6	O – O	N – B3
7	P – Q3	. . .

On 7 P – Q4 I intended P – K4. Petrosian is striving for an English Opening formation, a slow system for which he is temperamentally suited.

7	. . .	N – KR4
8	P – Q4	. . .

Reckoning he can afford this loss of time in view of Black's misplaced KN. On *8* R – N1, P – B4!; *9* Q – B2, P – R4; *10* P – QR3, P – B5 (Petrosian–Vasiukov, Moscow 1956) Black obtains an excellent aggressive setup. I was as impressed by that game as Petrosian must have been, since he got crushed.

> *8* . . .   P – K4
> *9* P – Q5   . . .

9 P × P, P × P; *10* Q × Q, R × Q; *11* N – Q5, R – Q2; *12* B – R3, P – B4; *13* P – KN4, N – B3! If *14* P × P (*14* N × N+, B × N; *15* P × P, P × P; *16* B × P??, R – N2+ wins), N × N; *15* P × N, R × P.

> *9* . . .   N – K2
> *10* P – K4   . . .

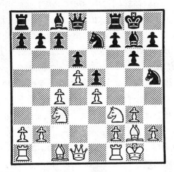

FISCHER

Position after 10 P – K4

PETROSIAN

This is the right time to get in *10* . . . P – QB4! Petrosian–Boleslavsky, USSR Championship prelims 1957, continued: *11* N – K1, K – R1; *12* N – Q3, P – B4; *13* R – N1, N – KB3=.

> *10* . . .   P – KB4
> *11* P × P   P × P

Tempting but unsound is *11* . . . N × BP; *12* P – KN4, N – Q5; *13* P × N, B – N5; *14* N × N!, B × Q; *15* N – K6, etc. And on *11* . . . B × P; *12* N – KN5, Q – Q2; *13* N – K6!, B × N; *14* P × B, Q × P; *15* B × P, QR – N1; *16* B – N2, Q × P; *17* N – Q5! White comes out on top.

> *12* N × P!   N × NP

A "desperado" combination: this Knight (which is doomed anyway) sells its life as dearly as possible.

> *13* RP × N   . . .

Simple and good. I had expected *13* BP × N, but Petrosian eschews the K-side attack and plays for control of the center squares instead. His judgment turns out to be right.

> *13* . . .   B × N?

13 . . . P × N, keeping a fluid Pawn center, offers more play. I was unduly worried about White's passed QP after *14* P – B5.

> *14* P – B4!   B – N2
> *15* B – K3   B – Q2
> *16* B – Q4   . . .

Forcing the trade of Black's most active piece. White soon obtains a firm grip on the position.

> *16* . . .   N – N3
> *17* R – K1?   . . .

A careless transposition. Now by *17* . . . B × B+; *18* Q × B, P – KR4!, followed by . . . P – R5, Black could exchange his isolated KRP for White's NP and the game would be dead equal. Correct was *17* B – B3.

> *17* . . .   R – B2?
> *18* B – B3!   . . .

Black doesn't get a second chance.

FISCHER

Position after 18 B – B3

PETROSIAN

> *18* . . .   Q – KB1
> *19* K – B2   R – K1
> *20* R × R   Q × R
> *21* B × B   R × B
> *22* Q – Q4   P – N3
> *23* R – R1   . . .

White has effortlessly achieved a plus and now he wants to improve his position before embarking on a committal course. *23* P – QN4!, threatening P – B5, is much sharper, and poses more immediate problems.

$$23 \ . \ . \ . \qquad \text{P – QR4}$$

My first free breath!

$$24 \ \text{N – Q1} \qquad \text{Q – KB1}$$
$$25 \ \text{N – K3} \qquad . \ . \ .$$

Petrosian keeps building without getting sidetracked—even by good moves. I was more afraid of *25* B – R5! tying me up completely. Then the Rook can't move because of B × N followed by a check on KR8.

$$25 \ . \ . \ . \qquad \text{R – B2!}$$
$$26 \ \text{P – N3} \qquad \text{Q – N2}$$

The exchange of Queens eases the cramp. White can't afford to retreat and cede this important diagonal.

$$27 \ \text{Q × Q+} \qquad \text{K × Q}$$
$$28 \ \text{P – R3} \qquad \text{R – B1}$$
$$29 \ \text{B – K2} \qquad . \ . \ .$$

White constantly finds ways to improve his position. Not *29* P – QN4, P × P; *30* P × P, R – QR1 and Black seizes the open file.

$$29 \ . \ . \ . \qquad \text{N – K2}$$
$$30 \ \text{B – Q3} \qquad \text{P – R3}$$
$$31 \ \text{R – R5} \qquad \text{B – K1}$$

FISCHER

Position after 31 . . .
B – K1

PETROSIAN

$$32 \ \text{R – R2} \qquad . \ . \ .$$

Avoiding a little trap: *32* N×P+? (or *32* R×BP?, R – R1!),
N×N; *33* R×N, R – R1! followed by . . . B – N3 winning the
exchange.

32 . . .	B – Q2
33 R – R1	R – KR1
34 N – B2!	. . .

Headed for an even stronger post on Q4. I was amazed during
the game. Each time Petrosian achieved a good position, he
managed to maneuver into a better one.

34 . . .	K – B3
35 N – Q4	K – N2
36 B – K2	. . .

Feigning an invasion with B – R5 and R – K1 and N – K6.
White has two wings to operate on: Black must be flexed to react
appropriately, and this requires alertness.

36 . . .	N – N1?

Panicking and giving him the opportunity he's been waiting for
to sneak P – QN4 in at a moment when Black can't counter with
. . . P×P and . . . R – QR1. Petrosian likes to play cat-and-
mouse, hoping that his opponents will go wrong in the absence of a
direct threat. The amazing thing is—they usually do! Witness a
case in point. I should just have ignored his "threat" with, say,
36 . . . R – R1; *37* B – R5, R – QB1; *38* R – K1, K – B3; and
if *39* N – K6, P – B3.

37 P – QN4!	N – B3
38 B – Q3!	

38 P×P, N – K5+; *39* K – N2, P×P; *40* R – QN1, N – B4 holds.

FISCHER

Position after 38 B – Q3

PETROSIAN

38 . . .   P × P

38 . . . N – K5+ ?; *39* B × N, P × B; *40* P × P, P × P (if *40* . . . R – R1; *41* P × P, P × P; *42* R – QN1); *41* R – QN1 followed by R – N7 wins easily. White also invades after *38* . . . K – N3; *39* P × P, P × P; *40* R – QN1.

39   P × P   K – N3

40   R – R1!   . . .

White has finally achieved his ideal setup, but Black's game is still tenable.

40   . . .   N – N5+

41   K – K2   R – K1+

42   K – Q2   N – B3

43   R – R6   . . .

43 R – R7, R – QB1 transposes to the game.

43   . . .   R – QN1

44   R – R7   R – QB1

45   P – B5!   . . .

This Pawn sac caught me completely by surprise. It's the only line that gives Black any trouble.

45   . . .   NP × P

Not *45* . . . N × P?; *46* P – B6.

46   P × P   P × P

47   N – B3!   K – B2!

47 . . . N × P loses to *48* N – K5+.

48   N – K5+   K – K2

49   N × B   N × N

50   B × P   R – B1!

51   P – N4   . . .

51 B × N, K × B; *52* K – K3 (if *52* R – R6, R – KN1), K – Q3; *53* R – R6+, K × P; *54* R × P, R – K1+; *55* K – B3, P – B5 should draw.

FISCHER

Position after 51 P – N4

PETROSIAN

51 . . .	K – Q3 ?

Should be the losing move! Correct is *51 . . . N – B3!; 52 B – K6, N×QP!; 53 B×N, R×P (53 . . . R – Q1 also draws)* winning the last Pawn and forcing a draw.

52 B×N!	K×B
53 K – K3	R – K1+

On *53 . . . P – B5; 54 R – R6* wins. The idea is to force his King to the K-side, away from the passed QBP.

54 K – B3	. . .

Not *54 K – Q3, R – KN1.*

54 . . .	K – Q3
55 R – R6+	K×P
56 R×P	P – B5

FISCHER

Position after 56 . . . P – B5

PETROSIAN

57 R – R1 ?	. . .

As Petrosian points out in the Russian bulletins of the tournament, White can win with the following line: "*57 R – R7!, P – B3;*

58 R – Q7+, K – B4; *59* R – Q1, P – B6; *60* P – N5, K – B5; *61* P – N6, P – B7; *62* R – QB1, K – B6; *63* P – B5, R – KN1; *64* K – B4, K – Q7; *65* R × P+, K × R; *66* K – N5, P – B4; *67* P – B6, P – B5; *68* P – B7, R × P+; *69* K × R, P – B6; *70* P – N8 = Q."
White is a tempo ahead of the game, where Black's Pawn succeeds in reaching B7, instead of B6 (as here).

What if Black tries to improve? For example, after *57* R – R7, P – B4; *58* R – Q7+, K – K3; *59* R – Q1, R – QN1. Now there are two main lines:

A] *60* P – N5?, P – B6; *61* K – N4 (if *61* R – QB1, K – B4; *62* R × P, P – B5!; *63* R × P, R – N6+ with a draw by blockade although two Pawns down), R – N5!; *62* R – K1+, K – B2; *63* K – B5, P – B7; *64* R – QB1, R – B5; *65* P – N6+, K – N2; *66* K – N5, R – B6 draws.

B] *60* P – B5+!, K – K4; *61* R – K1+, K – Q5 (after *61* . . . K – B3; *62* K – B4, P – B6; *63* P – N5+, K – N2; *64* P – N6, P – B7; *65* K – N5, R – N8; *66* P – B6+ wins); *62* P – N5, P – B6; *63* P – B6, P – B7; *64* R – QB1! (*64* P – B7?, R – N8! draws), K – K4; *65* K – N4! snuffs out Black's resistance.

57 . . .	P – B6
58 P – N5	P – B4
59 R – Q1+	. . .

It's tough right down the line. After *59* P – N6, R – KN1; *60* P – B5, K – K4!; *61* K – N4, K – B3; *62* R – QB1, P – B5!; *63* R × P, R – QB1! White can make no headway. Or on *59* K – N4, R – K7!; *60* P – N6, K – K5!; *61* K – N5, R – N7+; *62* K – B6, K × P, etc., as the Russian bulletins also point out.

59 . . .	K – B5
60 P – N6	P – B7
61 R – QB1	. . .

On *61* R – KN1, R – Q1! the threat of . . . R – Q8 forces *62* R – QB1 (not *62* P – N7?, R – KN1! followed by . . . R × P and wins).

61 . . .	K – Q6
62 P – B5	R – KN1!
63 K – B4	K – Q7
64 R × P+	K × R
65 K – N5	P – B5

66 P – B6	P – B6
67 P – B7	

Drawn

FISCHER

Final Position after 67
P – B7

PETROSIAN

I offered the draw, not realizing it was bad etiquette. It was Petrosian's place to extend the offer after *67* . . . R × P+ (if Black wants to get melodramatic *67* . . . R – QB1; *68* P – N7, K – N8; *69* P – B8 = Q, R × Q; *61* P × R = Q, P – B7 reaches the same position); *68* K × R, K – N8; *69* P – B8 = Q, P – B7 with a book draw.

4 Pilnik [*Argentina*] - Fischer

MAR DEL PLATA 1959

SICILIAN DEFENSE

Tact and tactics

The presence in Argentina of Pilnik, Najdorf, and Eliskases, who chose to remain there after participating in the Buenos Aires chess Olympic of 1939, created a chess renaissance, as attested by the annual event at Mar del Plata which, though not lavish with prizes, offers an exotic vacation and attracts the world's best. Fischer tied for 3 – 4 with Ivkov, a mere half point behind Pachman and Najdorf in a strong field of fifteen.

After a lackluster opening by both sides, and a middle game that, with the exception of 26 . . . P × P, can scarcely be described as more than routine, Fischer pilots the game into an even ending. Both he and Pilnik then proceed to complicate; but the latter is drawn into making a false lead, which Fischer exploits by obtaining a passed center Pawn. From this point on, although Pilnik does all that can be done to stave off the inevitable, Fischer is not gulled into making a single wrong step.

1	P – K4	P – QB4
2	N – KB3	P – Q3
3	P – Q4	P × P
4	N × P	N – KB3
5	N – QB3	P – QR3
6	B – K2	. . .

For 6 P – KR3 see games 35, 40, 43. For 6 B – QB4 see games 17, 55, 58.

6	. . .	P – K4
7	N – N3	B – K2

For 7 . . . B – K3 see game 42.

8 O – O   . . .

Another try is *8* B – N5, O – O! (*8*. . . QN – Q2?; *9* P – QR4! gives a powerful bind); *9* N – Q2, N × P!; *10* B × B, N × QN; *11* B × Q, N × Q;   *12* B – K7, R – K1;   *13* N – B4, N × NP!;   *14* N – N6, R × B; *15* N × R, N – R5; *16* O – O – O (Fischer–Ghitescu, Leipzig 1960), R – Q2! with the better game.

8 . . .   O – O
9 B – K3   B – K3
10 P – B3   . . .

A sharper alternative is *10* P – QR4, Q – B2; *11* P – R5, QN – Q2; *12* N – Q5, N × N; *13* P × N, B – B4; *14* P – QB4, B – N3; *15* K – R1, QR – B1;   *16* Q – Q2, Q – Q1;   *17* QR – B1, P – R3;   *18* P – B4, P × P;   *19* B × P, B – N4=. (Smyslov–Gligorich, Havana 1962.)

10 . . .   Q – B2

Premature is *10*. . . P – Q4; *11* P × P, N × P; *12* N × N, Q × N; *13* Q × Q, B × Q; *14* KR – Q1 with a slight edge in the ending.

FISCHER

Position after 10 . . .
Q – B2

PILNIK

11 Q – K1   . . .

Once popular, this whole system is now known to give White nothing. It hinders neither Black's development nor his Q-side expansion.

11 . . .   QN – Q2
12 R – Q1   . . .

On *12* P – QR4, P – Q4 is strong.

                  12 . . .   P – QN4
                  13 R – Q2   . . .

13 P – QR3 is met by N – N3; *14* B × N!, Q × B+ =.

                  13 . . .   N – N3

More direct is *13* . . . P – N5; *14* N – Q5, N × N; *15* P × N,
B – B4; *16* Q – B2, P – QR4 with good play against White's backward QBP.

                  14 Q – B2?   . . .

Careless. *14* B × N is necessary.

                  14 . . .   QR – N1 ?

I figured if he didn't take it off last move he wouldn't take it
now; so I wanted to build a little more and keep the option of
moving the Knight to R5 as well as B5. But Black should pounce
on the chance to play *13* . . . N – B5!; *14* B × N, P × B; *15*
B – N6 (if 15 N – R1, QR – N1; *16* R – N1, R – N2 is strong; or
if *15* N – B1, QR – N1; *16* N – R4, P – B6!; *17* P × P?, Q – B3;
18 N – N6, B – Q1), Q – B1; *16* N – R5, N – Q2! and White's in
trouble. E.g., *17* N – Q5 (or if *17* B – K3, B – Q1; *18* N – Q5,
B × N; *19* R × B, N – B3 winning at least the exchange), B × N; *18*
R × B (if *18* P × B, N × B; *19* Q × N, B – Q1; *20* Q – N4, R – N1;
21 Q – R3, B × N; *22* Q × B, R × P), R – N1 winning at least a
Pawn.

                  15 B × N!   . . .

Pilnik hastens to make amends for his omission. Not *15* N – R5?,
P – Q4! wins material.   (STAHLBERG)

                  15 . . .   R × B
                  16 N – Q5   N × N
                  17 P × N   B – Q2
                  18 P – KB4   B – KB3

I didn't want to weaken my K3 square with *18* . . . P – B4; *19*
P – B3, B – KB3; *20* P × P, P × P (if *20* . . . B × P; *21* N – Q4);
21 N – B5 =.

                  19 P – B3   R/3 – N1
                  20 P × P   B × P

On *20 . . . P×P; 21 P – Q6* gives White active play. Black's advantage of the Bishop pair is neutralized by the weakness of his QB3, which White can later occupy with his Knight.

| 21 | N – Q4 | P – N3 |
| 22 | P – QR3 | . . . |

More to the point was *22 B – B3, P – N5; 23 P×P, R×P; 24 N – B6=.*

| 22 | . . . | P – QR4 |
| 23 | K – R1 | . . . |

23 B – B3 should again be played. White starts drifting.

| 23 | . . . | P – N5 |
| 24 | BP×P | . . . |

On *24 RP×P, P×P; 25 P – B4, P – N6!* holds the initiative.

| 24 | . . . | P×P |
| 25 | R – B2 | . . . |

On *25 B – B3, P×P; 26 P×P, R – R1* presents its problems.

| 25 | . . . | Q – N3 |
| 26 | N – B6 | . . . |

FISCHER

Position after 26 N – B6

PILNIK

This is the position White was playing for. A draw now looks secure.

| 26 | . . . | P×P! |
| 27 | Q×Q | . . . |

27 P×P is also adequate. But not *27 N×R?, Q×Q; 28 R×Q, P – R7; 29 R – KB1* (if *29 R – QB1, B×NP*), *B – B4; 30 R/2 – B1, R×N* wins.

27 . . .	R×Q
28 P×P	R – R1
29 N×B?	. . .

This gives Black a strong passed KP. Correct is *29* R – R2, R – N7; *30* R×R, B×R; *31* B – N5!, R×P (otherwise P – QR4); *32* N – K7+, K – B1; *33* N×P+ with a draw in view. On *33* . . . P×N; *34* B×B produces opposite colored Bishops. Or on *33* . . . K – K1; *34* R – K1+! (*34* B×B+, K×B; *35* R× P+?, K – Q1 wins a piece), K – Q1; *35* B×B, BP×N (if *35* . . . K×B; *36* N – B8+, any; *37* N×P)=.

29 . . .	P×N
30 R – QB3	. . .

30 R – B7 gets nowhere after R – Q3; and the sacrifice *31* B – N5?! is refuted by B×B; *32* KR×P, R – QB1! Or on *30* R – R2 (*30* R – R1?, R×P), R – R4; *31* B – B4 (if *31* R – Q1, B – R5), R – B4 and QP falls.

30 . . .	R – N7!
31 R – B7	. . .

Desperately striving for counterplay. On *31* B – B4 (to prevent . . . R – R7), K – N2; *32* P – Q6, P – B4; *33* B – Q5, R – R3 again wins the QP. Or *31* B – B3, P – B4; *32* R – B7, B – N4; *33* R – K1, P – K5 squelches White's play.

31 . . .	B – B4

FISCHER

Position after 31 . . .
B – B4

PILNIK

32 P – N4	. . .

A wild hope. Hopeless is *32* B – B4, R – QB7!; *33* P – Q6, R×B!; *34* R×R, B – Q6; *35* R/1 – B1, B×R; *36* R×B, R×P; *37* K – N1, K – N2! Black soon picks off the QP and wins easily.

32 . . .	B – K5+
33 B – B3	B – Q6
34 P – Q6	. . .

Or *34* R – K1, P – K5!; *35* B – N2 (if *35* B×P, R – K1 wins), R – Q1; *36* R – B5, K – N2!; *37* K – N1 (if *37* P – N5, P – R3; *38* P – KR4, P×P; *39* P×P, R – R1+; *40* K – N1, R – R5! wins), P – B4; *38* P×P, P×P and the two passed center Pawns should win (if *39* P – Q6, K – B3!).

34 . . .	R – Q1
35 R – K1	R×P

Najdorf chided me after the game for "missing" *35* . . . P – K5; *36* B×P!, R – N8!; *39* R×R, B×B+; *40* K – N1, B×R and wins.

36 R×P	. . .

Falling into the trap. *36* R – K7 holds out longer, but . . . R – KB3; *37* B – Q5, P – K5; *38* B×P, B×B+; *39* R/7×B, R/3 – B7 wins.

36 . . .	R – KB3!
37 R – K3	. . .

Forced. On *39* B – N2, R – N8+ is decisive.

37 . . .	R×B!
38 R×R	B – K5
39 R×P	R – KB7
40 R – B8+	K – N2
White resigns	

After *41* R – B7+, K – R3 wins. Or *41* R – B4, B – Q4 (*41* . . . B×R+; *42* K – N1, R – N7+; *43* K – B1, B – B3; *44* R – B4, B – N4! also wins) cooks White's goose.

5 Fischer - Rossetto [*Argentina*]

MAR DEL PLATA 1959

SICILIAN DEFENSE

The unpleasant obligation

This game exemplifies most dramatically the German
expression zugzwang.

Unable to achieve any workable advantage from the
opening or mid-game, Fischer embarks on an equally un-
promising ending. He manages, however, after 19 N – Q5, to
acquire a Bishop against a Knight. Subsequently he employs an
unusual Rook maneuver along the third rank (23 R – R3) in
order to make spatial inroads. Rossetto unwittingly co-
operates and soon is faced by a rare predicament: although
material is equal, any move he makes must disturb the
precarious balance and hasten his own disaster. That is
zugzwang—and, appropriately, Rossetto resigns.

1	P – K4	P – QB4
2	N – KB3	P – K3
3	P – Q4	P × P
4	N × P	P – QR3
5	P – QB4	Q – B2

Stronger is 5 . . . N – KB3; 6 N – QB3, B – N5 which theory
gives as equal for Black.

6	N – QB3	N – KB3
7	B – Q3?	. . .

Misplacing the Bishop. Right is 7 P – QR3! and if N – B3; 8
B – K3, etc. (if 8 . . . N – K4; 9 B – K2!, N × BP?; 10 B × N,
Q × B; 11 R – QB1 wins).

7 P – QR3!, by preventing . . . B – N5 once and for all, forces
Black to adopt a kind of Scheveningen formation that keeps him
desperately cramped. A Spielmann–Tartakover game proceeded:
7 . . . B – K2; 8 B – K2 O – O 9 O – O, P – Q3; 10 B – K3,

QN – Q2; *11* R – B1, P – QN3; *12* P – QN4!, B – N2; *13* P – B3, QR – B1; *14* Q – K1, Q – N1; *15* Q – B2 "with a beautiful position for White." (From *More Chess Questions Answered*.)

7 . . .	N – B3
8 B – K3	N x N?

Instead of trying to simplify, Black should select the aggressive *8* . . . N – K4!; *9* R – QB1 (not *9* O – O, QN – N5! or if *9* B – K2, N x BP; *10* B x N, Q x B; *11* R – QB1, Q – N5; *12* O – O, P – Q3; and if *13* N – N3?, N x P!; *13* P – QR3, N x N, etc.), KN – N5! with advantage.

9 B x N	B – B4
10 B – B2	P – Q3
11 O – O	B – Q2
12 N – R4	. . .

Forcing a series of exchanges which give White a microscopic edge, at best.

12 . . .	B x B
13 Q x B	R – Q1
14 KR – Q1	O – O
15 QR – B1	. . .

On *15* Q x P, Q x Q; *16* R x Q, B x N; *17* R x R, R x R; *18* B x B, N x P=.

15 . . .	Q – R4

15 . . . P – QN4?; *16* P x P, P x P; *17* N – B3 (not *17* P – K5?, P x P; *18* B x P+, N x B), and Black's QNP is weak. *15* . . . B – B3 is solid but cramped.

16 Q – N6	Q x Q

Unsound is *16* . . . Q – K4; *17* R x P, N – N5; *18* P – KN3, Q – KR4; *19* P – R4.

17 N x Q	B – B3
18 P – B3	N – Q2!

Black had relied on this move to get him out of trouble. Now *19* N x N (or *19* N – R4, N – K4; *20* B – N3, P – KN4! holds the balance), R x N; *20* R – Q2, R/1 – Q1; *21* R/1 – Q1, K – B1 is dead equal.

19 N – Q5! . . .

An unexpected reply which throws Black, unjustifiably, into a
state of confusion.

ROSSETTO

Position after 19 N – Q5

FISCHER

19 . . .   B × N

Caught by surprise, Rossetto fails to find the most accurate
reply: *19 . . . N – K4!* (also tenable is *19 . . . P × N; 20
KP × P, N – K4; 21 P × B, P × P; 22 P – QN3, P – QB4; 23 B – K4,
KR – K1); 20 N – K7+* (if *20 N – K3, P – KN4!*), *K – R1; 21
N × B, P × N; 22 B – R4, P – N4!* followed by *. . . K – N2 –
B3 – K2=.*

20 KP × B   P – K4

Safer is *20 . . . N – K4; 21 B – K4, P – QN3* (not *21 . . .
P – B4?; 22 P × P!*).

21 P – QN4 . . .

Playing for the big breakthrough on QB5.

21 . . .   P – KN3

On *21 . . . P – QR4; 22 P – QR3, P × P; 23 P × P, R – R1;
24 B – B5!* holds the advantage.

22 B – R4   P – N3

On *22 . . . N – N3; 23 B – N3* followed by P – B5.

23 R – Q3   P – B4?

Oblivious to the danger! The best defense is *23 . . . P – QR4;
24 P – QR3* (Black should hold after *24 B × N, R × B; 25 P × P,
P × P; 26 P – B5, P × P; 27 R × P, P – R5*), P – B4 and it's hard for

White to make progress. Black should never allow P – B5 without first forcing White to make the concession of exchanging the Bishop for the Knight.

24 R – R3!   . . .

The threat is simply *25* B × N. The veiled and seemingly insignificant attack on Black's QRP is the means of forcing him to drop the protection of his QB4 square.

24 . . .   N – N1

Forced. On *24* . . . N – B3; *25* B – B6 wins a Pawn. The only other try is *24* . . . P – QR4; *25* P × P, P × P; *26* B – B6!, N – B4 (on *26* . . . N – N1; *27* B – N5! or *26* . . . N – N3; *27* R – N1!, N × BP?; *28* R – B3, N – Q7; *29* R – N2 traps the Knight); *27* R × P and White should win.

25 P – B5!   NP × P

On *25* . . . P – QN4; *26* B – N3, R – B2; *27* P – B6, R – B2; *28* R – R5!, K – B2; *29* P – QR4, P × P; *30* R × P, K – K2; *31* B – B4 picks off the QRP.

26 P × P   P × P
27 R × P   K – N2

On *27* . . . N – Q2; (if *27* . . . R – B1; *28* R/3 – B3 keeps the bind); *28* R – B7, N – B3; *29* B – N3, K – R1; *30* R × P, N × P; *31* B × N, R × B; *32* R/6 – R7 wins. Black's game collapses once the heavy guns penetrate.

28 R – N3   R – B2
29 P – Q6!   N – Q2

The Pawn is obviously immune. So Black attempts to revive his Knight.

30 R – B7   N – B1

Also hopeless is *30* . . . N – B3; *31* R/3 – N7, R × R; *32* P × R, R – QB1; *33* B – N3, N – K1; *34* R – N8, N – Q3; *35* R × R, N × R; *36* B – K6, etc.

31 R/3 – N7   R × R
32 P × R   R – B1
33 B – N3!   . . .

Completely immobilizing Black. He is reduced to Pawn moves.

33	. . .	P – QR4
34	P – QR4	P – R3
35	P – R3	P – N4
36	P – N4	P×P
37	RP×P	Black resigns

ROSSETTO

Final Position after
37 RP×P

FISCHER

Zugzwang! Black has run out of satisfactory Pawn moves. On *37* . . . K – B3; *38* R – N8 wins a piece. On *37* . . . N – N3; *38* B – K6 wins. Or on any Rook move, say *37* . . . R – K1; *38* P – B8 = Q +.

6 Fischer - Shocron [Argentina]

MAR DEL PLATA 1959

RUY LOPEZ

A small oversight

*Fischer's opening repertoire has been less extensive than most
practicing Grandmasters', yet his contributions to theory have
been numerous. 20 P – N5!? is one of his innovations. However,
it is not responsible for Shocron's defeat. Neither is Shocron's
response; in retrospect, his system of defense seems sur-
prisingly adequate. Nevertheless, after defending sensibly,
Shocron outfoxes himself. Thinking he has seen one move
further than his adversary, he provokes a combination. But his
vision is one move short. In consequence, though otherwise it
had withstood all of Fischer's assaults, his game crumbles.*

1	P – K4	P – K4
2	N – KB3	N – QB3
3	B – N5	P – QR3
4	B – R4	N – B3
5	O – O	B – K2
6	R – K1	P – QN4
7	B – N3	P – Q3
8	P – B3	O – O
9	P – KR3	. . .

For an immediate 9 P – Q4!? see game 36.

9	. . .	N – QR4
10	B – B2	P – B4
11	P – Q4	Q – B2

For Keres' *11* . . . N – Q2 see game 38.

12	QN – Q2	B – Q2

Some alternatives are *12* . . . K – R1, . . . R – K1, . . . R – Q1, . . . N – B3, . . . B – N2, . . . N – Q2, . . . BP × P. I don't think there's any easy way for Black to achieve complete equality—but who knows?

13	N – B1	KR – K1
14	N – K3	P – N3

The Yugoslav System, popularized by Gligorich and Matanovich. The idea is to strengthen the position, and transfer the Bishop to KB1 while awaiting further developments. Black will undertake specific counteraction only after White commits himself.

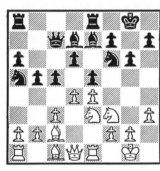

SHOCRON

Position after 14 . . .
P – N3

FISCHER

15 P × KP   . . .

This positional approach bares the hole on Q5, so that White may gain access to it with his Knight. Alternate plans ensue after *15* B – Q2, B – KB1 and now:

A] The quiet *16* QR – B1, B – N2? (after *16* . . . N – B3; *17* P – Q5!, N – QR4 [on *17* . . . N – Q1; *18* P – B4! robs Black of his normal counterplay with . . . P – QB5, Olafsson–Ivkov, Buenos Aires 1960, and now White can leisurely build up a strong attack with K – R2, P – KN4, R – KN1 and later the stock sac N – KB5]; *18* P – QN4, N – N2; *19* P – QR4 with a slight advantage); *17* P – QN4, N – B3; *18* N – Q5!, N × N; *19* P × N, N – K2; *20* QP × BP, N × P (if *20* . . . P × P; *21* B – K3, Q – Q3; *22* B × BP, Q × P; *23* B – N3!); *21* B – N3, N – B3 (if *21* . . . B – QB3; *22* B – N5!); *22* P × P, Q × QP; *23* N – N5!, R – KB1; *24* B – K3, Q × Q; *25* KR × Q, P – R3; *26* N – K4!, N × N; *27* R × B, QR – B1; *28* P – QB4, N – N4; *29* B × N, P × B; *30* P – B5, Black resigns. (Fischer–Rinaldo, US Open 1957.)

B] The sharp *16* P – QN4, P × NP; *17* P × NP, N – B5; *18* N × N, P × N; *19* R – QB1, P × P; *20* N × P, P – Q4 (not *20* . . . P – B6;

21 B – N3, N × P; *22* R × N!, R × R; *23* Q – B3, B – B3; *24* Q × P wins); *21* P × P, R × R+? (better is *21 . . .* Q – Q3); *22* B × R, Q – Q3. (Fischer–Matanovich, Bled 1961.) And now, as Keres pointed out, White can retain his extra Pawn with *23* N – B3! Not *23 . . .* Q × QP?; *24* B – B3! wins a piece. Or *23 . . .* N × P; *24* B – K4.

15 . . .	P × P
16 N – R2	. . .

When examined microscopically, Black has his problems. The hole on Q4 might be described as "gaping."

16 . . .	QR – Q1
17 Q – B3	B – K3

On *17 . . .* P – R4?; *18* N – Q5!, N × N; *19* P × N Black's K-side is weakened.

18 N/2 – N4	N × N
19 P × N	. . .

Black has a new burden: neutralizing the potential attack along the open KR-file.

19 . . .	Q – B3
20 P – N5!?	. . .

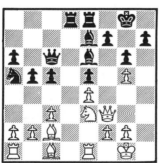

SHOCRON

Position after 20 P – N5

FISCHER

The old line *20* Q – N3, P – B3 (better is . . . B – B3); *21* P – N5! is good for White. (Boleslavsky–Tal, USSR 1957.) I'd always thought my line was an improvement (the idea is to clear KN4 for the Knight before Black can force an exchange with . . . N – B5) but a closer look at this game shows that Black may have resources.

20 . . .	N – B5

20 . . . B × NP puts White's concept to the crucial test. After
21 N – Q5!, B × B (*21* . . . B × N; *22* B × B wins the exchange);
22 N – B6+, K – R1! (if *22* . . . K – B1; *23* QR × B, R – K2;
24 N × P+, K – N1; *25* QR – Q1!, R – R1 [R × R; *26* N – B6+,
K – N2; *27* R × R, N – N2; *28* P – KN4! followed by P – N5 with
a strong attack]; *26* N – B6+, K – N2; *27* N – Q5, B × N; *28*
R × B White's better); *23* QR × B (if *23* N × R, B – N4; *24* N – B6,
N – B5! Black has good play for the exchange), R – KB1 (not *23*
. . . R – K2; *24* Q – N3 threatening either Q × KP or Q – R4);
24 Q – N3, Q – B2!; *25* Q – N5, K – N2; and now White can
force a draw with *26* N – R5+, etc., or try for more with either
26 P – KB4 or R – K3.

21 N – N4	B × N

Black can't allow N – B6+. As a consequence, White obtains the
Bishop pair and attacking prospects along the open KR-file.

22 Q × B	N – N3!

To prevent P – R4 and, as will be seen, to swing the Knight to
KB1 in order to defend the vulnerable KRP. For Unzicker's
22 . . . P – B3 see game 10.

23 P – KN3	P – B5!

The right timing. He's careful to see that P – R4 is restrained.
Wrong, for example, is *23* . . . N – Q2; *24* P – R4, P – N5; *25*
P × P, P × P; *26* B – N3! and this Bishop comes crashing back into
the game via the open diagonal.

24 K – N2	N – Q2
25 R – R1	N – B1

Phase one is over. Having seen his K-side threats neatly parried,
White is compelled to start some action on the opposite wing.

SHOCRON

Position after 25 . . .
N – B1

FISCHER

26 P – N4 . . .

26 P – N3 leads to trouble after P – N5!; *27* BP×P, P – B6; *28* P – R3?, N – K3; *29* Q – R3, P – KR4; *30* P×P e.p., N – Q5! and wins. On *26* P – R4, P – N5!; *27* P×P, B×QNP; *28* P – R5 (threatening B – R4), Q – B2 is satisfactory.

26 . . . Q – K3

Sharper is *26 . . .* P – QR4!; *27* P – R3 (if *27* P×P, Q – R3; *28* P – R4, Q×P), R – R1=.

Bad, however, is *26 . . .* P×P e.p.; *27* B×P, Q×P; *28* B – K3 (*28* B – N2!?, Q×QB; *29* Q – B3, N – K3; *30* B×N, R – KB1! holds. But not *30 . . .* P×B?; *31* R×P!, R – KB1; *32* QR – R1!, Q×P+; *33* Q×Q, R×Q+; *34* K×R, R – Q7+; *35* K – B3, B×P; *36* R – R8+ mates), R – Q2 (not *28 . . .* Q – B1?; *29* Q – B3, N – K3; *30* R×P! wins); *30* R×P! should win.

27 Q – K2 P – QR4
28 P×P Q – R3
29 B – K3 Q×P
30 P – R4 R – R1

30 . . . Q×BP!; *31* P×P leads to equal play.

31 P×P Q×NP

More active is *31 . . .* Q×BP! (if *32* QR – QB1, B – R6!). But not *31 . . .* Q×R?; *32* R×Q, R×R; *33* Q×P, resigns.

32 KR – QN1 Q – B3
33 R – N6! Q – B2
34 R/6 – R6 . . .

Obtaining control of the QR-file.

34 . . . R×R
35 R×R R – B1
36 Q – N4 N – K3

Bringing the Knight back into the game. Wrong would be an attempt to simplify with *36 . . .* B – B4; *37* B×B, Q×B; *38* B – R4! and Black has trouble finding a move. If *38 . . .* N – K3; *39* B – Q7. Or *38 . . .* R – Q1; *39* R – QB6, Q – R2; *40* R×P, R – Q7; *41* Q – B3 staying a Pawn ahead.

37 B – R4 R – N1
38 R – B6 Q – Q1?

Up to here Shocron has defended coolly, but now he makes a fatal miscalculation. Correct is *38 . . . Q – Q2!* and it's not clear how White can improve his position any further. If *39* K – R2 (not *39* R × P, Q – Q6!; *40* R – B6, R – N8 with a strong attack), R – N8!; *40* R – N6 (if *40* R × P, Q – Q6; *41* R – B8+, K – N2; *42* Q – R4, B × P!; *43* B × B, R – R8+!; *44* K × R, Q – B8+ with a perpetual), Q – Q6; *41* R × R (not *41* R × N?, Q – B8!), Q × R; *42* B – Q7, N – B2! (on *42 . . . N* – B4; *43* B – B6 followed by B – Q5 should win); *43* B – B6, Q – Q6! with drawing chances.

39 R × N!   Q – QB1!

Blow for blow! Apparently Shocron was prepared for this trick, having seen that *39 . . . P* × R?; *40* Q × P+, K – B1; *41* Q × KP is crushing.

SHOCRON

Position after 39 . . .
Q – B1

FISCHER

Now how does White avoid losing material?

40 B – Q7!   Black resigns

This is the shot he overlooked. On *40 . . . Q* × B; *41* R × P+ wins his Queen.

7 Olafsson [Iceland] - Fischer

ZURICH 1959

KING'S INDIAN DEFENSE

Pride goeth

Miscalculating, as he explains in his notes, Fischer rapidly gets into trouble and is thrown on the defensive. Olafsson quietly strengthens his attacking prospects and seems well on the road to victory. But he tries, prematurely, to force the issue (21 N – N1) and, as the game opens up, loses the initiative, although he seems to be blissfully unaware of it. He fails to foresee the power of the riposte to his 24 Q – Q2. Still blind to the danger, while seeking a forced win, he misses several opportunities to equalize. In extreme time pressure, he is compelled to exchange Queens under particularly unfavorable circumstances. The resulting endgame holds no further surprises.

1	P – QB4	N – KB3
2	N – QB3	P – KN3
3	P – Q4	B – N2
4	P – K4	P – Q3
5	N – B3	O – O
6	B – K2	P – K4
7	P – Q5	QN – Q2
8	B – N5	. . .

Steinitz automatically gave this pin a question mark. Since there is no real threat involved (because the Bishop is worth more than the Knight) Black can now gain time by kicking it around.

Petrosian has had some success with this treatment. The idea is to restrain . . . N – K1 and the subsequent . . . P – KB4.

| 8 . . . | P – KR3 |
| 9 B – R4 | P – R3 |

This slow system has never been refuted. But better is *9 . . .
P – KN4!*; *10* B – N3 (Black's break with . . . P – KB4 has now
been blunted, but on the other hand White's Bishop on KN3 is
deadwood), N – R4!; *11* P – KR4, the latest wrinkle (*11* N – Q2,
N – B5; *12* O – O, N × B+; *13* Q × N, P – KB4; *14* P × P, N – B3;
15 P – B5, B × P; *16* QR – B1, R – B2!; *17* N – B4, B – KB1 is
better for Black. Wexler–Reshevsky, Buenos Aires 1960), N × B!;
12 P × N, P × P!; *13* R × P (if *13* N × RP, Q – N4; *14* N – B5,
N – B3; or *13* P × P, P – KB4; *14* P × P, N – B3; *15* O – O, B × P),
P – KB4; *14* Q – B2, N – B4; *15* B – Q3, Q – B3 with advantage.
(Damyanovich–Hort, Sarajevo 1964.)

| 10 N – Q2 | Q – K1 |

FISCHER

*Position after 10 . . .
Q – K1*

OLAFSSON

The idea is to free the Knight and thus make possible the break
with . . . P – KB4. In some variations, the Queen may help to
support . . . P – QN4 also, particularly if White elects to castle
long.

11 P – KN4!? . . .

In the Candidates' Tournament, 1959, Tal essayed against me
the quieter *11* O – O, N – R2; *12* P – QN4, N – N4 (later I tried
. . . B – B3!? against him); *13* P – B3, P – KB4 with chances for
both sides. The text is risky and commits White to Q-side castling.

| 11 . . . | N – R2 |
| 12 Q – B2 | N – N4? |

Intending . . . N – R6 – B5, but White's simple reply brands
it as a mistaken plan. Correct is *12* . . . N – B4; *13* O – O – O
(*13* P – N4, N – Q2 leaves White with a shaky game), P – B4=.

13 P – KR3!   N – B4

14 O – O – O   B – Q2

Weak is *14 . . . P – B4; 15* B × N!, P × B; *16* NP × P, P × P; *17* QR – N1.

15 P – B3   N – R5

15 . . . P – N4!?; 16 P – N4, N – N2 may not be too bad.

16 N × N   B × N

17 P – N3   B – Q2

18 B – B2   P – QB4!

19 P – KR4   . . .

Black's game springs to life after *19* P × P e.p. ?, P × P; *20* N – N1, P – Q4!; *21* KP × P (or *21* B – B5, P – Q5; *22* B × R, B × B with a juicy position), P × P; *22* R × P, B – QB3, etc.

19 . . .   N – R2

20 B – K3   P – QN4

21 N – N1?   . . .

Intending Q – Q2. But correct is *21* B – Q3! (if *21* P – R5, N – N4), maintaining the bind by restraining . . . P – B4.

21 . . .   P – B4!

Ready or not—here we come! Olafsson was sure that this break was impossible, or he wouldn't have allowed it.

22 NP × P   KNP × P

23 P × BP   . . .

To prevent . . . P – B5 which would seal the K-side and neutralize White's attack.

23 . . .   B × P

24 Q – Q2   . . .

This is the position White played for.

24 . . .   P – K5!

The game turns on this shot. *24 . . .* R – B3 or P – KR4 cedes the initiative.

25 QR – N1   . . .

25 B × P loses to P – K6!; *26* B × P (if *26* Q × P, B × N!; *27* K × B, Q – N3+ wins a piece), B × N; *27* K × B, Q – K4.

| 25 . . . | P × KBP? |

Correct is *25 . . .* R – R2! and if *26* B × P, P × KBP transposing to the game.

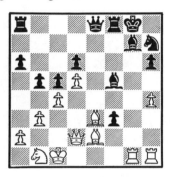

FISCHER

Position after 25 . . . P × KBP

OLAFSSON

| 26 B × RP? | . . . |

26 R × B+ ! (STAHLBERG), K × R; *27* B × P+, K – R1; *28* B × R, Q × QB; *29* B × P wins a pawn (if *29 . . .* B × N; *30* Q – B3+).

| 26 . . . | R – R2! |

Olafsson later told me he had underestimated the strength of this defensive move.

27 B × B	R × B
28 R × R+	K × R
29 B – Q3	. . .

An admission of defeat since Black's KBP now becomes dangerously potent. But not *29* B × P? (or *29* Q – B3+, Q – K4; *30* Q × P, B × N; *31* Q – N4+, B – N3), B × N; *30* K × B, R × B; *31* Q – N2+, Q – N3+ (the saving resource) and Black hangs on to his extra piece. My game hinges on this defense, on the fact that the KBP has such divine protection.

29 . . .	P × P
30 R – N1+	K – R1
31 Q – B3+	. . .

Now Black gets another passed center Pawn, but White's defense is difficult anyway. *31* P × P, P – B7; *32* R – B1, B × B; *33* Q × B, Q – K8+; *34* K – B2, N – B3; *35* N – Q2, N – N5 wins.

31 . . .	Q – K4
32 Q×Q+	. . .

After *32* B×B, R×B; *33* P×P, N – B3 White has nothing better than to transpose into the actual game with *34* Q×Q.

32 . . .	P×Q
33 B×B	R×B
34 P×P	. . .

34 P – Q6, N – B3; *35* N – Q2! offers no better: e.g., *35* . . . P×P; *36* P×P, P – K5; *37* N – B4!, P – B7; *38* R – B1, N – N5! (threatening P – K6); *39* K – Q1, N – R7!; *40* P – Q7, R – Q4+ is decisive.

34 . . .	N – B3
35 N – Q2	P – B7
36 R – R1	. . .

White must keep his KB1 square open for the Knight.

36 . . .	P – K5

FISCHER

Position after 36 . . .
P – K5

OLAFSSON

37 K – Q1	. . .

A better chance is offered by *37* N – B1, N – N5!; *38* K – Q2 (if *38* P – Q6, R – B3; *39* P – Q7, R – Q3), but R – B6! squelches all counterplay.

37 . . .	P – K6
38 N – B1	R – K4
39 K – K2	N – R4!
40 K – B3	P – K7
White resigns	

One of the black Pawns must reincarnate.

8 Fischer - Keres *[U.S.S.R.]*

ZURICH 1959

RUY LOPEZ

Meat and potatoes

> Alekhine said, in his prime, that to wrest a point from
> him it was necessary to win the same game three times:
> once at the beginning, once in the middle, once at the end. No
> less a tribute may be paid to Keres.
>   Each phase of this game is fascinating and hard-fought.
> Even the errors, and there are more than a few, contribute
> to making it an unusually complete exhibition of two
> master craftsmen using all the tools of their trade. While
> perhaps unglamorous, there is meat here, and potatoes too.
> And it is likely that as a result of this victory Fischer came to
> be regarded as a serious contender by the leading Soviet
> Grandmasters—this was the first time he had defeated one.

1	P – K4	P – K4
2	N – KB3	N – QB3
3	B – N5	P – QR3
4	B – R4	N – B3
5	O – O	B – K2
6	R – K1	P – QN4
7	B – N3	O – O
8	P – B3	P – Q3
9	P – KR3	N – QR4
10	B – B2	P – B4
11	P – Q4	Q – B2
12	QN – Q2	BP × P

Keres has abandoned *13* . . . R – Q1; *14* N – B1, P – Q4?;
15 P × KP!, P × P (if *15* . . . N × P; *16* Q – K2, B – N2; *17*
N – K3 threatening N × P); *16* N/1 – Q2!, P × N; *17* P × N, B × BP;
18 Q × P, B – K3; *19* N – K4 with a winning attack.

13 P×P	B – N2
14 N – B1	QR – B1
15 B – Q3	N – B3

Keres later played *15 . . . N – Q2* against Smyslov at the Candidates' 1959. The game continued *16* N – K3 (better is *16* P – Q5, P – B4; *17* N – K3!, P – B5; *18* N – B5, B – Q1; *19* B – Q2!), P×P; *17* N×P, B – KB3; *18* N/4 – B5, P – N3=.

16 N – K3	KR – K1

Black already has difficulties. On *16 . . .* N×QP; *17* N×N, P×N; *18* N – B5, KR – K1; *19* B – N5 is strong. Not *16 . . . N – QN5?*; *17* B – N1, B×P??; *18* B×B, N×B; *19* P – R3, N – QB3; *20* N – Q5, etc.

17 N – B5?	. . .

A superficial plan. Correct is *17* P – Q5!, N – QN5 (if *17 . . . N – N1*; *18* P – QR4!); *18* B – N1, P – QR4; *19* Q – K2!, N – Q2 (if *19 . . .* Q – N3; *20* N – B5!); *20* B – Q2, Q – N3; *21* P – R3, N – R3; *22* P – QN4 followed by B – Q3 with a bind.

17 . . .	B – B1
18 B – N5	N – Q2
19 R – QB1	Q – N1

To get out of the pin.

20 B – N1	N×P
21 N/3×N	R×R?

Overlooking White's follow-up. After *21 . . .* P×N; *22* R × R, Q × R; *23* Q × P, N – B4! White has precisely nothing.

22 B×R	P×N

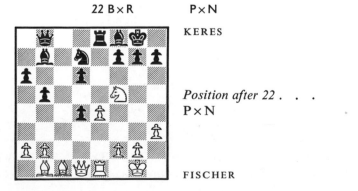

KERES

Position after 22 . . .
P × N

FISCHER

                    23 N – R6+!   . . .

Keres probably expected *23* Q × P, N – B4=.

                    23 . . .   P × N
                    24 Q – N4+   K – R1
                    25 Q × N   . . .

Regaining the piece. Black's extra Pawn is meaningless in view
of his mangled Pawn formation.

                    25 . . .   B – Q4!

An energetic maneuver! This Bishop is headed, if circumstances
permit, toward the defense of Black's weakened K-side.

                    26 Q – B5   R – K4!
                    27 Q – B3   P – B4!

Aggressive defense!

                    28 B – B4!   R – K1

On *28* . . . R – K2; *29* Q – Q1, B × KP; *30* B × B, P × B; *31*
Q × P+, B – N2; *32* Q – Q5! maintains pressure against the weak
Pawns.

                    29 Q – R5!   B × KP
                    30 P – B3   B – B3
                    31 R – QB1!   . . .

Not *31* R × R?, B × R; *32* Q × BP?, B – N3! and Black wins!

                    31 . . .   B – Q2
                    32 B × RP   . . .

A difficult choice. The alternative was *32* B × BP, B × B; *33*
Q × B with possibilities of probing his sick Pawns.

                    32 . . .   R – K3!
                    33 B × B   . . .

On *33* B – B4, Q – K1! looks tenable.

                    33 . . .   Q × B
                    34 Q – R4!   . . .

On *34* Q × P??, R – K8+ wins! Or *34* B × P??, R – R3 wins!
The text forces Black into an ending where his weak Pawns can't

be concealed by tactical tricks. On *34* R – B7, Q – K2 holds; e.g., *35* B×P?, R – K8+; *36* K – R2 (or *36* K – B2, Q – K6+; *37* K – N3, Q – K4+), Q – K4+ wins.

34 . . .	Q – B3

Not *34* . . . Q – N2; *35* R – B7, R – K7?; *36* Q – Q8+, R – K1; *37* R×B!, R×Q; *38* R×R+ wins.

35 Q×Q+	R×Q

KERES

Position after 35 . . .
R×Q

FISCHER

36 K – B2?	. . .

Losing a vital tempo, which gives Black time to rush his King toward the center. At the time I rejected *36* R – B7 because I couldn't see a winning continuation after . . . R – B2 (if *36* . . . B – K3; *37* P – QN3! squelches all counterplay). But I underestimated the strength of *37* R – R7! (*37* B×P, R×B; *38* R×B, R – Q4; *39* K – B2, P – Q6; *40* K – K1, R – K4+; *41* K – Q1, R – K7 should draw), B – K3; *38* R×P, R – B2; *39* K – B2, R – B8; *40* B – Q3 and Black's Pawns are hopelessly weak.

36 . . .	K – N2!
37 R – B7	R – B2
38 K – K2	. . .

Now *38* R – R7 loses all of its effectiveness after the reply . . . B – B1.

38 . . .	P – B5!?

A risky selection in time-pressure, aimed against *39* K – Q3??, B – B4+. Best is simply *38* . . . K – B3 (on *38* . . . B – K3; *39* R – B6 is strong); *39* R – R7 (not *39* P – B4, B – K3; *40*

R – B6?, R – KN2;   *41* K – B2, R × P + !),   B – B1;   *40* R × R +,
K × R =.

	39 R – R7	K – B3

Not *39* . . . B – B1; *40* R × R +, K × R; *41* B × P.

	40 R × P	R – K2+
	41 K – B2	. . .

41 K – Q2 is refuted by R – N2.

	41 . . .	B – K3!

Sacrificing a second Pawn for counterplay on the open QB-file.
On *41* . . . K – K4; *42* R – R7 keeps Black tied up.

	42 R × P	K – K4
	43 R – B6	. . .

On *43* R – N6, B – B5; *44* P – QN3, P – Q6!; *45* P × B, P × P
and Black's passed Pawns should be sufficient to draw.

	43 . . .	B – Q4

KERES

Position after 43 . . .
B – Q4

FISCHER

	44 R – KR6	. . .

On *42* R – B5, K – Q3; *43* R × P?, B – B5 is menacing. *44*
R – B1 is too passive to yield any real winning chances.

	44 . . .	R – QB2
	45 R – R5+	K – Q3
	46 R – R6+	K – K4
	47 R – R5+	. . .

Not *45* R – QN6, R – B8; *46* B × P?, B – B5.

	47 . . .	K – Q3
	48 R – B5?	. . .

No better is *48* R×P (if *48* B×P, R – B8 threatening B – B5), R – B8; *49* B – Q3, B – B5. The winning line is *48* P – QN3! (to shut him out from QB5). If *48 . . .* R – B8; *49* B – K4!, B×B; *50* P×B, etc.

48 . . .	R – B8
49 B – Q3	R – Q8

Not *49 . . .* B – B5?; *50* R×P!, B×B; *51* R×P+, etc.

50 K – K2	R – KN8
51 K – B2	R – Q8
52 K – K2	R – KN8
53 R – N5	B×P?

Keres later claimed that *53 . . .* R – QR8 would have drawn easily: e.g., *54* B×RP, B – B5+; *55* K – Q2, R×P; *56* K – B2, R – R8.

54 B×NP	R – N8
55 K – Q3	P – R3?

55 . . . R×P; *56* K×P, B – N8! should hold the draw.

56 R – R5	R×P
57 K×P	R×P
58 R×P+	. . .

The second adjournment. There are two technical obstacles facing White:

1] He cannot exchange Bishops; the ending where he is two Pawns ahead remains a theoretical draw with Rooks on the board.

2] He cannot exchange Rooks so long as Black's King has access to KB3; the ending (even with two extra Pawns) is still a draw with Bishops on the board.

58 . . .	K – K2
59 K – K4	R – N4
60 B – R6?	. . .

Keres thought *60* B – B1! was the winning chance. If *60 . . .* R – N8; *61* B – R6! and Black no longer has the defense mentioned in the next note. Wrong is the immediate *60* B – Q3 owing to B – B2!; *61* K×P, R – R4; *62* R×R, B×R followed by . . . B×P.

KERES

Position after 60 B – R6

FISCHER

60 . . .   B – B2?

This slip is fatal. Keres told me he had reached this position in his adjournment analysis, but had forgotten his drawing line over-the-board. Right is *60 . . . B – N8+!; 61* K × P, R – B4+; *62* K – N4, R – B3; *63* R × R, K × R with the aforementioned blockade.

61 B – B8!   . . .

Headed for KN4. Not *61* K × P?, R – KR4 draws.

61 . . .   R – N3

After *61 . . .* R – QB4; *62* B – N4, R – B5+; *63* K – K5 White's penetration is decisive, even though he doesn't win a second Pawn immediately.

62 R – R7   K – B1
63 B – N4   R – N2

Not *63 . . .* R × B?; *64* R × B+!

64 R – R6   . . .

White still can't afford to trade.

64 . . .   R – N3
65 R × R!   B × R+
66 K × P   K – N2
67 K – N5!   . . .

This makes all the difference. Black's King can no longer set up a blockade on KB3.

67 . . .   B – Q6
68 P – B4   B – K5
69 P – R4   . . .

Of course not *69* P – B5?, B × P! and White is left with what Hans Kmoch calls "the impotent pair."

69	. . .	B – Q6
70	P – R5	B – K5
71	P – R6+	K – R1

On *71* . . . K – B2; *72* B – R5+, K – N1; *73* B – N6 makes progress.

72	B – B5	B – Q4
73	B – N6	B – K3
74	K – B6	B – B5
75	K – N5	B – K3
76	B – R5	. . .

Back on the right track.

76	. . .	K – R2
77	B – N4!	B – B5

On *77* . . . B × B; *78* K × B, K × P; *79* K – B5 wins.

78	P – B5	. . .

Finally the BP is free to advance.

78	. . .	B – B2
79	B – R5	B – B5
80	B – N6+	K – N1
81	P – B6	Black resigns

KERES

Final Position after 81 P – B6

FISCHER

On *81* . . . B – N6; *82* K – B4, K – R1; *83* K – K5, B – B5; *84* K – Q6, B – N6; *85* K – K7, B – B5; *86* B – B7, B – Q6; *87* B – K8!, B – B5; *88* B – Q7, B – N1; *89* B – K6, B – R2; *90* P – B7 and queens.

9 Walther *[Swiss]* - Fischer

ZURICH 1959

SICILIAN DEFENSE

Betwixt the cup and the lip

Here, against a minor European master, Fischer appears to be busted after seventeen moves, and admits he was ready to resign on move 36. Nevertheless, he extracts a miraculous draw from a hopeless ending, two Pawns down. Time and again Walther fumbles, allowing Fischer to prolong the struggle until he gets his break on move 54.

What makes this game memorable is the demonstration it affords of the way in which a Grandmaster redeems himself after having started like a duffer; and how a weaker opponent, after masterfully building a winning position, often lacks the technique required to administer the coup de grâce. As Capablanca remarked, "The good player is always lucky."

1	P – K4	P – QB4
2	N – KB3	P – Q3
3	P – Q4	P × P
4	N × P	N – KB3
5	N – QB3	P – QR3
6	B – N5	P – K3
7	P – B4	B – K2

Sharper is 7 . . . Q – N3; *8* Q – Q2, Q × P; *9* R – QN1, Q – R6 which I tried with success later in my career.

8	Q – B3	QN – Q2

More exact is *8* . . . Q – B2 to prevent *9* B – B4.

9	O – O – O	. . .

Sharper is *9* B – B4!, O – O (*9* . . . Q – B2?; *10* B × P!, P × B;

11 N×P, Q – N3; *12* N×P+, K – B2; *13* N – B5 with a crushing attack); *10* O – O – O. The text gives Black a chance to repair his earlier inaccuracy.

9 . . .   Q – B2
10 B – Q3   . . .

For *10* B – K2 see game 14. For *10* P – KN4 see games 12 and 15.

10 . . .   P – N4
11 B×N   . . .

Pointless. Better is *11* P – QR3.

11 . . .   N × B

Only not *11* . . . B × B?; *12* B × P!, P × B; *13* N/4 × P wins.

12 KR – K1   . . .

12 P – QR3 is necessary. Black comes out all right after *12* P – K5, B – N2; *13* Q – N3, P × P; *14* P × P, N – Q2; *15* KR – K1, O – O – O! (Paoli–Tolush, Balatonfüred 1958.)

12 . . .   B – N2

As I learned (see game 15), Black should avail himself of . . . P – N5! (followed by . . . B – N2 and . . . P – Q4) the instant he has the opportunity.

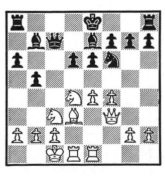

FISCHER

Position after 12 . . . B – N2

WALTHER

13 K – N1   . . .

At the risk of repeating myself, *13* P – QR3 is mandatory.

13 . . .   R – QB1?

The disadvantage of this move is that Black loses his option of

Q-side castling. Right is *13 . . . P – N5; 14 N/3 – K2, P – N3!; 15 P – N4, P – K4; 16 N – QN3, P – Q4; 17 N – Q2, O – O* with initiative.

           14 P – KN4   . . .

14 P – QR3 is still correct. We both suffered from the *idée fixe* that . . . P – N5 was unplayable.

           14 . . .   **N – Q2**
           15 P – N5   **N – N3?**

15 . . . P – N5!; 16 N/3 – K2, N – B4 still makes a fight of it.

           16 P – B5!   **P – K4**

Now on *16. . . . P – N5?; 17 P × P!* splatters Black.

Not *16 . . . B × NP?; 17 B × P+!, K – K2; 18 P × P, P × P; 19 N × KP!*, etc. But I still thought Black was all right. Walther's next move quickly disabused me of that notion.

           17 P – B6!   **P × P**

I'd overlooked that on *17 . . . P × N; 18 N – Q5!* is deadly.

           18 P × P   **B – B1**
           19 N – Q5!   . . .

Black's busted.

           19 . . .   **N × N**
           20 P × N   **K – Q1**

FISCHER

Position after 20 . . .
K – Q1

WALTHER

           21 N – B6+!   . . .

A wise investment. The Pawn sac is insignificant compared to the opening of the center files against Black's King.

21 . . .	B × N
22 P × B	Q × P
23 B – K4	Q – N3
24 Q – R5	K – B2
25 B – B5!	R – Q1
26 Q × P+	K – N1
27 Q – K6	Q – B2
28 R – K3!	B – R3
29 R – QB3	Q – N2
30 P – B7	. . .

Very business-like. Not *30* R × P??, Q – R8+.

30 . . .	B – N2
31 R/3 – Q3	B – B1
32 Q × P!	. . .

Should be decisive. "Any resemblance to chess is purely coincidental."

32 . . .	P × Q
33 R × R+	K – R2
34 R/1 – Q7	P – KR4
35 R × Q+	K × R
36 P – B3	K – B2

Ordinarily the curtain would be drawn here, but I just wanted to see what he'd do next.

37 R – R8(?)	. . .

The wrong track. On *37* R – K8! Black resigns.

37 . . .	K – Q3

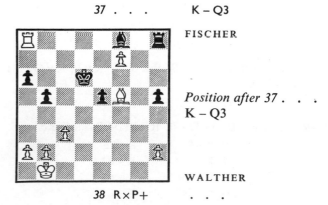

FISCHER

Position after 37 . . .
K – Q3

WALTHER

38 R × P+	. . .

I was still prepared to resign after *38* R – K8! Black has absolutely no moves. White simply strolls his King to K4, creating *zugzwang*.

38	. . .	K – K2
39	R – K6+	. . .

Even simpler is *39* R – R7+, K – B3; *40* B – Q3.

39	. . .	K × P
40	R × P	P – N5

The game was adjourned. Strangely enough, I began to feel the position contained some swindling prospects.

41	P × P	B × P
42	P – KR3	K – B3
43	R – N5	B – Q3
44	B – K4	. . .

On *44* P – QR4, R – QN1! forces the exchange of Rooks (if *45* R – Q5?, B – K4). The pure opposite-colored-Bishop ending is Black's best chance to draw.

44	. . .	R – K1

My first threat in the entire game!

45	R – B5+	K – N2
46	B – B3	R – K8+
47	K – B2	R – B8!
48	R – Q5	. . .

The threat was *48* . . . R – B7+; *49* K – N1 (if *49* K – N3?, K – N3 wins a piece), R – B8+ with a draw.

48	. . .	R – B7+
49	R – Q2	. . .

49 K – N1, B – R6!; *50* P × B, R × B; *51* R × P, R × QRP is also hopeless for Black.

49	. . .	R × R+

On *49* . . . R × B; *50* R × B, R × P; *51* P – R4, etc.

50	K × R	P – R5
51	K – Q3	K – B3
52	K – B4	K – K2
53	K – N5	K – Q2

FISCHER

Position after 53 . . .
K – Q2

WALTHER

54 P – R4?   . . .

This natural push throws away the win! The Swiss endgame composer, Fontana, pointed out the proper method: *54* P – N4!, K – B2; *55* K – R5!, K – N1; *56* P – N5, B – R6; *57* P – N6, K – B1; *58* K – R6, K – N1; *59* B – N2! and Black is in *zugzwang*. If *59* . . . K – B1 (or *59* . . . B – B4; *60* P – R4); *60* K – R7, B – Q5; *61* P – R4, etc.

The theme underlying Black's defense is this: once he succeeds in sacrificing his Bishop for both the Q-side Pawns, then White will be left with the "wrong Bishop" for his KRP.

54 . . .	K – B2
55 P – N4	K – N1
56 P – R5	K – R2
57 K – B4	B – N6
58 P – N5	B – B7
59 B – K2	. . .

59 P – N6+ is met by B×P!

59 . . .	B – K6
60 K – N3	B – Q7

60 . . . B – B7 also draws.

61 P – N6+	K – N2
62 K – R4	K – B3
63 B – N5+	K – B 4
Drawn	

White's Pawns are stymied. On *64* P – N7, B – B5; *65* P – R6, K – N3=.

Fischer - Unzicker *[W. Germany]*

ZURICH 1959

RUY LOPEZ

Milking the cow

The Ruy Lopez has been so extensively analyzed that often
both players reel off their first twenty moves in two minutes
flat. Nevertheless, it gives rise to situations that call for tact
and patience. As Bronstein remarked, "When you play the
Ruy, it's like milking a cow." Fischer, here, milks the cow to a
fare-thee-well.

The first twenty-two moves are identical with game number
6. Unzicker then varies with the dubious . . . P – B3,
which undermines his KP and leaves him with weak squares.
Retribution, though not swift, is sure. Creating simultaneous
threats on both wings, Fischer finally infiltrates on the
QR-file. Black is so tied up that he cannot defend one of his
Pawns when attacked—making defeat imminent.

1	P – K4	P – K4
2	N – KB3	N – QB3
3	B – N5	P – QR3
4	B – R4	N – B3
5	O – O	B – K2
6	R – K1	P – QN4
7	B – N3	P – Q3
8	P – B3	O – O
9	P – KR3	N – QR4
10	B – B2	P – B4

10 . . . P – B3; *11* P – Q4, Q – B2 is an interesting alternative. (ROSSOLIMO)—Black avoids weakening his Q4.

11	P – Q4	Q – B2
12	QN – Q2	B – Q2

13 N – B1	KR – K1
14 N – K3	. . .

Tal and Geller recommend *14* P – QN3 and if P – N3; *15* B – N5.

14 . . .	P – N3
15 P×KP	P×P
16 N – R2	QR – Q1
17 Q – B3	B – K3
18 N/2 – N4	N×N
19 P×N	. . .

Against Matanovich, at Portoroz 1958, I tried the inferior *19* N×N, B×N; *20* P×B, P – B5; *21* P – KN3, N – N2; *22* K – N2, N – B4; *23* R – R1, P – B3=. Black's Knight is already prepared to parachute to Q6.

UNZICKER

Position after 19 P × D

FISCHER

19 . . .	Q – B3

White gets an edge after *19* . . . N – B5; *20* N – Q5, B × N; *21* P × B.

20 P – N5!?	N – B5
21 N – N4	B×N
22 Q×B	P – B3?

For analysis of this position see game 6. Unzicker prefers active defense. He eliminates the potential pressure along the KR-file, it is true, but at the cost of weakening his KP.

23 P×P	B×P
24 P – R4!	N – N3
25 P×P	P×P
26 B – K3	. . .

Because both flanks are fluid, White, with his two Bishops, is better able to penetrate and exploit the "loose" Pawns.

26 . . .   R – R1

26 . . . N – B5 is met by *27 B – N3* instituting an awkward pin.

27 KR – Q1   . . .

If he swaps, White gains the R-file; if he doesn't, White keeps the Q-file.

27 . . .   K – R1
28 P – QN3   B – N2

Black should ease the pressure by *28 . . . R × R; 29 R × R, R – R1; 30 R × R+, N × R;* though *31 Q – Q1!* followed by *Q – R1!* forces an invasion on the Q-side.

29 Q – R4   B – B3
30 B – N5!   B × B
31 Q × B   . . .

Now White must penetrate on either the R- or Q-file. Black's KP has clearly been exposed as a weakling.

31 . . .   R × R

The threat was *32 R × R, N × R; 33 R – Q5.*

32 R × R   N – Q2

Apparently defending everything. *33 R – R7* can be met by *Q – Q3.*

UNZICKER

Position after 32 . . .
N – Q2

FISCHER

33 B – Q1!   . . .

Bringing the Bishop into the game puts additional pressure on Black's overburdened pieces.

$$33 \ldots \quad N-B3$$

Not *33 . . .* Q×P; *34* B – B3, Q – KB5 (if *34 . . .* Q – B7; *35* R – R7 with a winning attack); *35* Q×Q, P×Q; *36* B – B6, R – K2 (or *36 . . .* R – Q1; *37* R – Q1); *37* R – R8+!, K – N2; *38* R – R7 wins a piece.

$$34 \ R-R7 \quad \ldots$$

Infiltration!

$$34 \ldots \quad Q-Q3$$

On *34 . . .* N×P?; *35* Q – R6 forces mate.

$$35 \ B-K2! \quad \ldots$$

Simply attacking a Pawn. Curiously, Black is in too much of a straitjacket to do much about it.

UNZICKER

Position after 35 B – K2

FISCHER

$$35 \ldots \quad R-K2$$

How can Black defend the Pawn? (a) *35 . . .* P – N5?; *36* R – R6, N×P; *37* Q – R4, Q – Q4; *38* B – B3, Q – Q6; *39* R – R7 wins. (b) *35 . . .* N×P?; *36* Q – R6, R – K2; *37* Q – B8 mate. (c) *35 . . .* Q – N3; *36* R – KB7, N – N1; *37* Q – R4, P – R3; *38* Q – N4, R – Q1; *39* B×P! wins. (d) *35 . . .* R – QN1; *36* R – KB7, N – N1; *37* R – Q7!, Q – KB3 (if *37 . . .* Q×R; *38* Q×P+, Q – N2; *39* Q×R, Q×P; *40* Q×P); *38* Q – K3, Q – B3; *39* R – Q5 when one of Black's hanging Pawns must fall.

$$36 \ R×R \quad Q×R$$
$$37 \ B×P \quad K-N2$$

                    38 B – K2   . . .

The win is still far from clear. White's major technical problem is
creating a passed Pawn on the Q-side while sheltering his King
from a perpetual check.

                    38 . . .   Q – QB2

Threatening . . . N × P.

                    39 Q – K3   Q – R4
                    40 P – N3   Q – R6

Black should wait around with *40* . . . Q – B2.

                    41 K – N2   . . .

Sharper and possibly immediately decisive is *41* P – QN4!, P × P;
42 Q – B5!

                    41 . . .   Q – R4

On *41* . . . Q × P; *42* Q × P, N × P; *43* Q × P+, N – B3; *44*
P – QB4 should win.

                    42 Q – Q3   Q – N3
                    43 Q – B4   Q – B3
                    44 B – Q3   . . .

It's better to refrain from *44* P – B3 which weakens the K-field.

                    44 . . .   Q – N3
                    45 P – QN4   P × P
                    46 P × P   . . .

Step one is completed: White has a passed QNP.

                    46 . . .   N – N5
                    47 Q – B5   Q × Q

Forced. *47* . . . Q – Q1 ? loses a second Pawn after *48* B – K2.

                    48 P × Q   K – B2
                    49 P – B4   . . .

The idea is to create another passed Pawn in the centre.

                    49 . . .   K – K2
                    50 K – B3   N – B3

On *50* . . . P – R4; *51* B – B4 maintains the bind (if *51* . . .
K – Q2; *52* B – B7).

51 B – N5   . . .

Not *51* P × P?, N – Q2 draws.

51 . . .   K – K3

Striving to keep the blockade as long as possible.

52 B – B4+   K – K2
53 P – B6!   . . .

UNZICKER

Position after 53 P – B6

FISCHER

53 . . .   N – K1

Makes it easy. The best defense was *53 . . .* P × P (if *53 . . .*
K – Q3?; *54* P × P+, K × KP; *55* P – B7); *54* P × P, N – K1; *55*
P – K5, N – B2; *56* K – K4, N – K1 (if *56 . . .* P – R4; *57*
K – B3 wins); *57* B – N8, K – B1; *58* B × P, K – N2; *59* B × P,
K × B; *60* P – B5+, K – N4; *61* P – B6, K – N3; *62* K – Q5, K –
B2; *63* K – B5, K – K3; *64* K – N6 wins.

54 P × P   P – R3
55 K – K3   N – B2
56 K – Q4   P – R4
57 K – K3!   P – N4
58 B – K2   P – R5
59 P × P   P × P
60 B – B4   N – K1
61 K – B4   K – Q1
62 K – N4   K – B2
63 B – B7   N – N2
64 K × P   K × P
65 K – N5   Black resigns

After *65 . . .* K – Q2; *66* K – B6, N – K1+; *67* B × N+ leads
to an elementary win.

I I Fischer - Benko *[U.S.A.]*

SICILIAN DEFENSE

Unheard melodies

> *Paul Morphy is the idol of all the romantics who pine for the swashbuckling chess of yesteryear; but it is rarely possible to succeed with that kind of flamboyance any longer since players now are more evenly matched. A rise in the standard of defense has necessitated a corresponding adjustment in the character of attack. In modern chess most of the beauty resides in the annotations. Brilliancies often exist only as grace notes—because the opposition anticipates and thwarts them with appropriate rejoinders. To the uninitiated, some of the most hard-fought struggles seem devoid of all bravura. That is the situation in this game.*
>
> *Confronted with a dozen beautiful outlandish losing variations, Benko chooses what appears to be a prosaic one. Is this "ugliness" not a by-product of skill? Though the reader may feel cheated, and the winner frustrated, does it not argue for the perspicacity of the loser who sidestepped those seductive invitations?*

1	P – K4	P – QB4
2	N – KB3	N – QB3
3	P – Q4	P × P
4	N × P	N – B3
5	N – QB3	P – Q3
6	B – QB4	Q – N3

For 6 . . . B – Q2 see game 13. By putting immediate pressure on the center, Black forces the Knight to a passive post.

7	KN – K2	. . .

For 7 N – N3 see game 58, note to Black's sixth move. No good is 7 N/4 – N5, P – QR3; 8 B – K3, Q – R4; 9 N – Q4, N × P, etc. And 7 N × N!?, P × N only helps Black strengthen his center, but after 8 O – O White has promising tactical chances.

7	. . .	P – K3
8	O – O	B – K2
9	B – N3	O – O
10	K – R1	. . .

If *10* B – K3, Q – B2; *11* P – B4, N – KN5!

10	. . .	N – QR4
11	B – N5	Q – B4!

A finesse aimed at provoking *12* B – K3, Q – B2 after which White's initiative is blunted.

12	P – B4	P – N4

Another virtue of Black's last move was that it freed this Pawn.

13	N – N3	P – N5?

Gligorich suggests simply *13* . . . B – N2. Also satisfactory is *13* . . . N×B!; *14* RP×N, B – N2 (or . . . P – N5); *15* N – R5, K – R1 =.

The text exposes Black to a vicious attack.

14	P – K5!	. . .

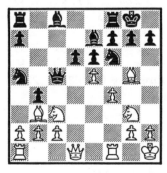

BENKO

Position after 14 P – K5

FISCHER

14	. . .	P×P

A] It's too late now for *14* . . . N×B; *15* P×KN, P×P (if *15* . . . B×P; *16* QN – K4); *16* B – R6, etc.

B] *14* . . . P×N; *15* P×N, B×P (if *15* . . . P×BP; *16* B – R6, P – B4; *17* N – R5 threatening to bring the Queen to KN3); *16* B×B, P×B; *17* N – K4!, Q – B4; *18* N×QP, Q – N3; *19* R – B3 with a decisive attack (UDOVICH). If now *19* . . . K – R1; *20* R – N3, Q – R3; *21* Q – N4 (threatening Q – N8+!), Q – N3; *22* Q – R4.

15 B×N   P×B

A] On *15 . . . B×B; 16* QN – K4, Q – K2 (if *16 . . .*
Q – Q5; *17* N×B+, K – R1; *18* Q – N4+, K – R1; *19* QR – Q1,
Q×NP; *20* N – R5, R – KN1; *21* Q×R+!, K×Q; *22* R – Q8
mate); *17* N – R5!, K – R1 (if *17 . . . B* – R5; *18* P×P followed
by Q – N4 GLIGORICH); *18* N/4×B, P×N; *19* P×P, P×P; *20*
N – B6 threatening Q – R5 and wins.

B] The best chance is *15 . . . P×N!; 16* N – K4, Q – N5; *17*
Q – N4, B×B; *18* N×B+, K – R1; *19* Q – R4, P – KR3; *20* N –
N4 threatening N × RP with a strong attack.

16 QN – K4   Q – Q5

Benko gave this move a lot of thought. On the alternative
16 . . . Q – B2; *17* N – R5! (Black holds after *17* Q – N4+,
K – R1; *18* Q – R4, R – KN1; *19* N×P, R – N2; *20* Q – R6, B –
N2!), P – B4; *18* N/5 – B6+!, K – N2; *19* Q – R5!, B×N (not
19 . . . P – KR3; *20* R – B3, R – R1 [*20 . . . P×P; 21* R –
R3, R – R1; *22* N – K8+!]; *21* R – N3+, K – B1; *22* Q×RP+!);
20 N×B, P – KR3 (if *20 . . . R* – R1; *21* Q – N5+, K – B1;
22 Q – R6+, K – K2; *23* Q – R4, K – B1; *24* N×P+ wins the
exchange); *21* R – B3!, R – R1 (not *21 . . . K*×N; *22* Q – R4+,
K – N2; *23* R – N3+, K – R2; *24* R – R3 wins); *22* N – K8+!,
R×N; *23* R – N3+, K – B1; *24* Q×RP+, K – K2; *25* Q –R4+,
K – Q3 (if *25 . . . K* – B1; *26* R – R3!, Q – Q1; *27* Q – R6+,
K – K2; *28* Q – N5+ wins the Queen); *26* R – Q3+, K – B3 (if
26 . . . K – B4; *27* B – R4! threatens Q – B2+); *27* B – R4+,
K – N2; *28* B × R wins material.

17 Q – R5!   . . .

Already Black is without a satisfactory defense.

BENKO

Position after 17 Q – R5

FISCHER

17 . . .	N × B

A] On *17* . . . K – R1; *18* Q – R6, R – KN1 (if *18* . . . P × P; *19* N – R5 wins); *19* N × P, etc.

B] *17* . . . P × P; *18* N – B5!, P × N; *19* R × P, Q × N (otherwise R – R4); *20* R × Q, P × R; *21* Q × N wins. (This key line wouldn't work had Black interpolated *13* . . . N × B earlier!)

C] *17* . . . K – N2 (LOMBARDY); *18* QR – Q1, Q × P; *19* Q – R4, B – N2; *20* N × P!

18 Q – R6!	P × P

On *18* . . . P – B4; *19* P – B3! is devastating: e.g., *19* . . . P × QBP; *20* P × BP, Q – any; *21* N – R5 forces mate.

19	N – R5	P – B4
20	QR – Q1!	Q – K4
21	N/4 – B6+	B × N
22	N × B+	Q × N
23	Q × Q	. . .

Now it's skin and bones.

23	. . .	N – B4
24	Q – N5+	K – R1
25	Q – K7!	B – R3
26	Q × N	B × R
27	R × B	Black resigns

I 2 Gligorich *[Yugoslavia]* - Fischer

CANDIDATES' TOURNAMENT 1959

SICILIAN DEFENSE

Castling into it

Although not perfect, this is perhaps the most bitterly
contested game in this book. Fischer chooses a difficult
variation which requires Olympian judgment. He submits his
King to an attack which, on the face of it, can only be described as irresistible. Why did he do it? Because, we are told,
it was strategically justified.

Gligorich, too, must be given equal credit for his courage
and restraint. His continuation, despite intensive post-mortem
analysis, has yet to be improved upon. The complexity of each
phase of this tumultuous struggle must be studied to be
believed. Curiously, in the "barren" Rook and Pawn ending,
Gligorich somehow missed a win—a fact which he is
probably unaware of to this day.

1	P – K4	P – QB4
2	N – KB3	P – Q3
3	P – Q4	P×P
4	N×P	N – KB3
5	N – QB3	P – QR3
6	B – N5	P – K3
7	P – B4	B – K2
8	Q – B3	Q – B2
9	O – O – O	QN – Q2
10	P – KN4	P – N4

Gligorich and I have a standing feud with this position, which
we've reached no less than three times. I've lost twice and drawn
once (this one).

11 B×N   . . .

Interesting is *11* B – N2, B – N2; *12* KR – K1, P – N5; *13* N – Q5!?, P×N; *14* P×P, K – B1; *15* N – B5, R – K1 and Black won. (Bernstein–Fischer, US Championship 1957–8.)

11. . .	P×B!?

For *11* . . . N×B see game 9.

12 P – B5	. . .

Giving up K5 in order to exert pressure on K6. Our game at Zurich 1959 continued: *12* B – N2, B – N2; *13* KR – K1, O – O – O; *14* P – QR3, N – N3=.

In the US Championship 1959–60, Mednis played *12* P – QR3 against me. The game went *12* . . . B – N2 (. . . R – QN1 is sharper); *13* P – B5, P – K4; *14* N/4 – K2, N – N3; *15* N – Q5, B×N; *16* P×B, R – QB1; *17* N – B3, N – B5; *18* B×N, P×B; *19* K – N1, R – QN1; *20* K – R2 with a better game for White.

12 B – Q3, B – N2; *13* K – N1, N – B4; *14* P – B5, P – N5; *15* QN – K2, P – Q4; *16* BP×P, QP×P; *17* P×P+, K – B1; *18* B × KP, B×B; *19* Q×B, N×Q; *20* N – K6+, K×P; *21* N×Q, R – R2 is exciting but equal. (Padevsky-Evans, Havana Olympic 1966.)

12 . . .	N – K4

Simagin gave this a " ?" and proceeded to analyze the alternative *12* . . . P – N5; *13* P×P, P×N (if *13* . . . N – K4; *14* N – Q5!); *14* P×N+, B×P; *15* P – K5, etc. By this logic, the whole variation is unsound for Black. We shall see.

13 Q – R3	O – O!

Not *13* . . . B – Q2; *14* P – N5!, P×NP (if 14 . . . P×BP; *15* N – Q5); *15* P×P, P×P; *16* N×KP and Black's game collapses.

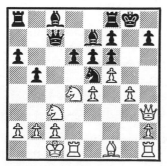

FISCHER

Position after 13 . . .
O – O

GLIGORICH

Petrosian and Tal both happened to stroll by the board at this instant. Petrosian made a wry face which looked to me like "Can Black do this and live?"

Black's "ugly" defense is based on sound positional considerations: once he can consolidate, there is a strong potential in the two Bishops coupled with his beautifully posted Knight and compact Pawn mass. These assets, in the long run, hopefully, should outweigh the temporary weakness of his King and the immobile target on K3.

14 QN – K2!　　. . .

The consistent strategical plan. Grigorich intends N – B4, bringing additional pressure to bear on K6. Simagin gave the offhand *14* Q – R6, K – R1; *15* P – N5! and "wins." It is incredibly naïve to imagine that a player of Gligorich's caliber could overlook such a simple refutation. In this line simply *15* . . . R – KN1! refutes White's strategy *16* P – N6 (if *16* P × BP, N – N5 regains the Pawn with advantage), BP × P; *17* N × KP (weaker is *17* P × KP, B – N2), B × N; *18* P × B, QR – B1; *19* Q – Q2 (if *19* P – QR3, P – Q4!; *20* P × P, B × P), N – B5; *20* B × N (if *20* Q – Q4, Q – R4), Q × B; *21* Q – Q5, KR – K1 threatening. . . B – B1 (or . . . P – N5).

In a sense my judgment was vindicated when Bronstein (as Black) reached the diagram against Kholmov in the 1964 USSR Championship. The continuation was *14* P – N5!?, P – N5? (Kholmov gives the best defense: "*14* . . . P × NP!; *15* P × P, P × P; *16* N × KP, Q – Q2; *17* N – Q5, Q × N; *18* Q × Q+, B × Q; *19* N × B+, K – B2; *20* N – B5="); *15* P × BP, B × P; *16* R – N1+, K – R1; *17* Q – R6, Q – K2; *18* N – B6!!, N × N; *19* P – K5!! and White won brilliantly.

14 . . .　　　　K – R1

14 . . . Q – N2 also comes into serious consideration.
　　Unsound is *14* . . . B – Q2; *15* N – B4, Q – B1; *16* Q – R6, K – R1; *17* N – R5, R – KN1; *18* N × BP, R – N2; *19* B – K2, Q – Q1; *20* P – N5, etc.

15 N – B4　　　　R – KN1
16 R – N1　　　　. . .

Gligorich gives *16* B – K2 as correct. After *16* . . . Q – N2; *17* P × P, P × P it's anybody's game. On *16* P × P, P × P; *17*

N/Q×KP, B×N (or . . . Q – R4 or . . . Q – N2); *18* N×B,
Q – B1=.

> *16* . . .   P – Q4!

Suddenly the game opens up! But more prudent is *16* . . . Q –
N2; and if *17* R – K1, Q – N3!

> *17* P×KP   . . .

Weak is *17* P×QP?, P×BP! and White can't recapture because
of the pin on the KN file.

> *17* . . .   QP×P
> *18* N – Q5   Q – B4

Black's game hangs by a hair. *19* P×P, N×BP; *20* N×B, Q×
N/2 is roughly even.

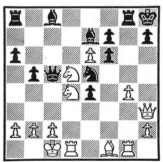

FISCHER

Position after 18 . . .
Q – B4

GLIGORICH

> *19* N×B   . . .

Weird complications result from the key line *19* N – B5!:

A] *19* . . . B – Q1; *20* Q – R6! (not *20* R – N3, P×P; or *20*
P – K7, B×N; *21* P×B=Q, QR×Q), R – N3; *21* N – B4!, N –
Q6+; *22* R×N! wins.

B] *19* . . . Q×R; *20* N/B×B, B×P (if *20* . . . Q×NP; *21*
Q×Q, R×Q; *22* N – B7, R – QN1; *23* R – Q8+, K – N2; *24*
N – B5+, K – N3; *25* P – K7 wins); *21* N×R (if *21* N×P, R – N2),
B×P; *22* Q – R6, B×R; *23* N/8×P, Q – N3; *24* Q×Q, RP×Q;
25 K×B with winning chances.

> *19* . . .   Q×N/2
> *20* N – B5   . . .

If *20* Q – K3, B – N2; *21* P×P, Q×P Black wins a Pawn.

> *20* . . .   Q×P
> *21* Q – R6   . . .

Possibly Gligorich had originally intended *21* R – Q6?, Q × P; *22* Q – R6 overlooking that Black can win with *22 . . .* Q – R8+ (if *22 . . .* B × N; *23* Q × BP+, R – N2; *24* R – Q8+ leads to a draw by perpetual); *23* K – Q2, N – B6+; *24* K – K3 (if *24* K – K2??, Q – K8 mate; or *24* K – B3?, Q – R4+; *25* K – N3, Q – R5+; *26* K – B3, P – N5+; *27* K – B4, B – K3+ leads to mate), Q × P! wins.

21 . . .   B – Q2!

Defending against the powerful threat of R – Q8! Not *21 . . .* N × P?; *22* R × N!, R × R; *23* R – Q8+, R – N1; *24* Q – N7 mate.

22 R – Q6   . . .

White has no choice. Black threatened *. . .* R – N3 followed by *. . .* Q × P. Or on *22* K – N1, N × P.

22 . . .   N × P!
23 R × N   . . .

Forced. *23* R × Q?, N × Q wins a piece.

23 . . .   Q × N
24 R × R+?   . . .

Handing Black the game on a silver platter. Correct is *24* R – B4, Q – N4; *25* Q × BP+, Q × Q; *26* R/6 × Q, P – K6!; *27* R × BP, R – N8!; *28* R × B, P – K7; *29* R – Q1!, P × R = Q+; *30* K × Q, K – N2; *31* K – K1, R – KB1; *32* R × R, R × R; *33* K – B2 with good drawing prospects.

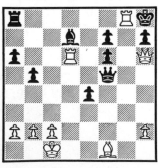

FISCHER

Position after 24 R × R+

GLIGORICH

Black has two ways to recapture: which one is correct?

24 . . .   R × R?

Returning the compliment! The winning line is *24 . . .* K × R!;

25 R×BP, Q – K4 with an extra Pawn and a dominating position (if *26* R×RP?, R×R; *27* Q×R, Q – B5+ wins a piece).

25	R×BP	Q – Q4
26	R – Q6!	Q – KB4

On *26* . . . Q – N2?; *27* Q – B6+, R – N2; *28* Q – Q8+, R – N1; *29* Q×B wins.

27	R – KB6	Q – N4+

I should have contented myself with the draw now by *27* . . . Q – Q4; *28* R – Q6, etc.

28	Q×Q	R×Q
29	R×BP	B – N5
30	K – Q2	B – B6
31	K – K3	R – N8
32	B – R3	. . .

Not *32* K – B2?, R – R8.

32	. . .	R – K8+
33	K – B4	B – Q8

Playing, as Dr. Tarrasch wryly put it, "for the loss." Nowadays I would know better than to try to squeeze a win out of such a simplified ending.

34	K – K5!	. . .

Gligorich is also playing to win—by cashing in on my inexperience. Simply *34* R – K7, B×P; *35* B – B5 holds the draw. But he is purposely inviting me to overextend myself.

34	. . .	P – K6
35	B – B5	R – N8
36	R×P+	K – N1
37	R – QB7	B – N5?

Still chasing the chimera of the missed win. Black should simply force a draw with *37* . . . P – K7; *38* K – B6, K – R1; *39* R – R7+, K – N1; *40* R – QB7, K – R1, etc.

38	B×B	R×B
39	R – B3	P – K7
40	R – K3	R – N7

FISCHER

Position after 40 . . .
R – N7

GLIGORICH

In my excitement I had originally intended *40 . . . R – N2?* overlooking the simple reply *41* K – Q4 (among others). Fortunately, Black can still hold the draw.

    41   K – Q4   P – K8 = Q!

After *41 . . .* R × P?; *42* K – Q3 Black is really lost!

    42   R × Q   R × BP
    43   R – N1   K – B2!

Not *43 . . .* R × RP?; *44* K – B5 with a fatal penetration on the Q-side.

    44   P – QR3   K – K3
    45   P – N3   . . .

On *45* P – KR4, K – Q3 holds the balance. The threat now is R – KR1.

    45   . . .   R × P
    46   K – B5   K – Q2
    47   K – N6   R – R7
    48   K × P   R × P+
    49   K – N7   . . .

Trying to finagle. *49* K × P, K – B2 leads to an easy book draw.

    49   . . .   K – Q3

Crisper is *49 . . .* P – N5; *50* R – Q1+ (on *50* K – N6, K – B1 the Black King gets in front of the Pawn), K – K3; *51* R – Q3, K – K4; *52* K – N6, K – K5; *53* R – R3, K – Q5; *54* K – N5, R – R1; *55* K × P, R – N1+; *56* K – R5, R – R1+; *57* K – N6, R – N1+; *58* K – B6 (if *58* K – R6, K – B4=), R – N5; *59* R – N3, R – N1 with an impenetrable blockade.

50 K – N6	K – Q2
51 P – N4	R – R6
52 R – QB1	R – R1 ?

After the game Olafsson scolded me: "How can you play an ending like this so fast?" (I'd only been taking a few seconds a move for the last dozen moves or so.) "Because there's no danger. It's a dead draw," I replied. Had I known then what I know now, I would have selected *52 . . . R – R4* and if *53 R – B5, R × R; 54 K × R, K – B2; 55 K × P, K – N2* holding the opposition, with a book draw.

FISCHER

Position after 50 . . .
R – R1

GLIGORICH

     53 K × P?   . . .

Now it's Gligorich's turn to let me out. As Olafsson showed me, White can win with *53 R – B7 + !* It's hard to believe. I stayed up all night analyzing, finally convincing myself and, incidentally, learning a lot about Rook and Pawn endings in the process. Gligorich failed to point it out in his notes to the Bled tournament book. The main point is Black cannot get his King in front of the Pawn.

A sample line is *53 R – B7+ !, K – Q3* (if *53 . . . K – Q1; 54 R – B5, K – Q2; 55 K – N7!, K – Q3; 56 R × P); 54 R – B6+, K – Q2* (if *54 . . . K – Q4; 55 K × P, R – N1+; 56 R – N6); 55 K × P, R – N1+* (if *55 . . . R – R5; 56 R – B1, R – R1; 57 K – R6); 56 R – N6, R – KR1; 57 R – N7+, K – B1; 58 K – R6, R – R3+; 59 K – R7* with a book win.

53 . . .	R – N1+
54 K – R4	R – R1+

The game was adjourned again. But the crisis has passed.

55 K – N3   R – QB1
56 R × R   K × R
57 K – B4   K – N1!
                    Drawn

Black holds the "distant opposition." For example, *58* K – B5 (or *58* K – Q5, K – N2), K – B2; *59* K – N5, K – N2, etc.

FISCHER

Final Position after 57 . . .
K – N1

GLIGORICH

I 3 Fischer - Gligorich *[Yugoslavia]*

CANDIDATES' TOURNAMENT 1959

SICILIAN DEFENSE

Something new

During the mid-fifties, Gligorich, Reshevsky, and Najdorf were considered the strongest non-Soviet Grandmasters. Within a few years Fischer managed to surpass them. However, in so doing, he succeeded in beating Gligorich only once—up to 1966 (see game 56).

On the occasion of this first win, Fischer employs a novel attacking system (13 Q – K2) against the Dragon Variation. Gligorich fails to react vigorously enough and makes the mistake of castling too soon, thereby exposing himself to the same type of sacrificial combination that demolished Larsen in game 2.

1	P – K4	P – Q B 4
2	N – KB3	N – QB3
3	P – Q4	P×P
4	N×P	N – B3
5	N – QB3	P – Q3
6	B – QB4	B – Q2

For Benko's 6 . . . Q – N3 see game 11.

Recently in a skittles game someone tried 6 . . . P – KN3!? against me. The game continued: 7 N×N, P×N; 8 P – K5, N – R4? (correct is 8 . . . N – N5. Not 8 . . . P×P??; 9 B×P+ winning the Queen—that was another skittles game!); 9 Q – B3!, P – K3 (if 9 . . . P – Q4; 10 N×P!); 10 P – KN4, N – N2; 11 N – K4, Q – R4+ (if 11 . . . P – Q4; 12 N – B6+, K – K2; 13 Q – R3+); 12 B – Q2, Q×KP; 13 B – B3, Black resigns.

7	B – N3	. . .

7 B – K3 is met by N – KN5! On *7* B – KN5, P – K3; *8* B×N?, Q×B; *9* N/4 – N5, O – O – O; *10* N×QP+, K – N1 with a winning attack (GLIGORICH). Also strong is *7* O – O, P – KN3; *8* N×N!, B×N (or *8* . . . P×N; *9* P – B4); *9* B – KN5, B – N2; *10* N – Q5!

| 7 . . . | P – KN3 |
| 8 P – B3 | . . . |

The only other try for any advantage is *8* B – K3, N – KN5; *9* N×N, P×N (*9* . . . N×B?; *10* B×P×!); *10* Q – B3 (not *10* B×P?, P – QB4), N – K4; *11* Q – N3.

| 8 . . . | N – QR4 |

Releasing the central tension this way is wrong. Correct is *8* . . . N×N; *9* Q×N, B – N2; but after *10* B – N5! White still keeps control.

| 9 B – N5 | B – N2 |
| 10 Q – Q2 | P – KR3 |

A concession. But on *10* . . . O – O; *11* B – R6 followed by P – KR4 – 5 produces a strong and almost mechanical attack.

11 B – K3	R – QB1
12 O – O – O	N – B5
13 Q – K2!?	. . .

A totally new idea at the time. *13* B×N, R×B; *14* P – KN4 was the usual, and good, procedure. The text permits Black to capture what was considered, then, to be the more important of the White Bishops.

GLIGORICH

Position after 13 Q – K2

FISCHER

Bronstein was so impressed with this concept that he enthusiastically gave my thirteenth move "!!" claiming it was virtually the winning line. Alexander Kotov, the commissar of chess criticism in the Soviet Union, wrote, with more sober restraint: "It is difficult to agree with this."

13 . . .   N × B

Not *13 . . . Q – B2?; 14* N/4 – N5.

14 Q × N   O – O

Reminiscent of game 12, it is now Gligorich who castles into it! At Mar del Plata 1960, Merini played against me the stronger *14 . . . Q – N3* (threatening *. . . P – K4); 15 Q – Q2, Q – B4; 16 P – B4, P – KR4?* (better is *16 . . . P – QN4* or *. . . O – O); 17 N – B3, B – R3; 18 P – K5!* with a powerful attack.

Kotov recommends *14 . . . Q – R4; 15 K – N1* (he gives only *15 P – N4?, Q – KN4!), Q – QB4; 16 Q – Q3, P – R3* and Black's all right. So best is probably *15 P – B4* (after *14 . . . Q – R4), O – O; 16 P – KR3, P – K3* but Black's two Bishops may offset the weakness of the QP.

15 P – N4   . . .

Timing is important. On *15 P – KR4, P – KR4* locks it up.

15 . . .   Q – R4
16 P – KR4   P – K3

On *16 . . . P – KR4; 17 P – N5, N – K1; 18 P – KB4 – 5* gives White a strong game.

17 N/4 – K2!   . . .

Black holds out after *17 P – N5, P × P; 18 P × P, N – R4; 19 P – B4, Q – QB4* (threatening *. . . P – K4).*

17 . . .   R – B3
18 P – N5   P × P

On *18 . . . N – R4; 19 P × P, B – B3; 20 P – B4* continues the Pawn stampede.

19 P × P   N – R4
20 P – B4   KR – B1
21 K – N1   . . .

An important preparatory move. On the immediate *21* P – B5!?,
KP × P; *22* N – Q5, Q × P! gives Black good play.

Position after 21 K – N1

21 . . .		Q – N3
22 Q – B3		R – B4
23 Q – Q3!		. . .

Several Yugoslav chess journalists scurried toward the analysis
room, where Matanovich was explaining the game on a demonstration board. Apparently the feeling was that I had just blundered.

The more obvious *23* P – B5 looks good, but Black still has
defensive resources with *23* . . . KP × P; *24* R × N (if *24* N – Q5,
Q – Q1; *25* P × P, B × BP; *26* R × N?, R × P! wins for Black), P × R;
25 N – B4, R × N; *26* P × R, R × P; *27* Q × P, R × B+; *28* BP × R,
Q – K6, etc.

23 . . .		B × N

The threat against the QP is awkward to meet. On *23* . . .
R/4 – B3; *24* P – B5!, KP × P; *25* R × N!, P × R; *26* P × P is crush-
ing. Or if *23* . . . R/1 – B3?; *24* N – R4 wins the exchange.
Finally on *23* . . . B – B1; *24* P – B5!, KP × P; *25* N – Q5,
Q – Q1 (if *25* . . . P × P; *26* Q × P, B – B4; *27* Q × B wins a
piece); *26* R × N!, P × R (or *26* . . . R × N; *27* B × R, P × R; *28*
P × P); *27* N – B6+, K – N2; *28* Q – R3 releases an avalanche.

24 N × B		. . .

Not *24* P × B?, B – N4.

24 . . .		N × P

This is what the crowd thought I had overlooked.

25	Q – B3	N – R4

On *25 . . . P – K4; 26 N – K2!* is decisive.

GLIGORICH

Position after 25 . . .
N – R4

FISCHER

26	R × N!	. . .

I've made this sacrifice so often, I feel like applying for a patent!

26	. . .	P × R
27	Q × P	B – K1

The best defensive try. On *27 . . . K – B1; 28 Q – R8+, K – K2; 29 Q – B6+, K – K1; 30 R – R1, B – N4; 31 B × P!, P × B; 32 Q × P+, K – Q1* (or *32 . . . K – B1; 33 R – R8+, K – N2; 34 Q – B6 mate); 33 R – R8+, K – B2; 34 R × R mate.*

28	Q – R6!	R × N
29	P × R	. . .

On *29 R – R1, Q – Q5* holds out for a while.

29	. . .	R × P

White still retains a winning attack after *29 . . . Q – K6; 30 R – R1, Q × BP; 31 P – N6, Q – N2; 32 Q – R2!* (BRONSTEIN).

30	P – N6!	P × P
31	R – R1	Q – Q5
32	Q – R7+	. . .

Again a mistake! *32 B × P+* mates more quickly.

32	. . .	**Black resigns**

I4 Keres *[U.S.S.R]* - Fischer

CANDIDATES' TOURNAMENT 1959

SICILIAN DEFENSE

Too many cooks

*Professionals spend much of their spare time hunting for
"cooks" with which they hope to surprise future opponents. It
was rumored, for example, that Marshall waited for over ten
years before springing his famous gambit on Capablanca, at
New York, in 1918. But, as it happened, the wily Cuban refuted
it over-the-board!*

*Keres, in like manner, confronts Fischer with an innovation
which the latter, in all innocence, proceeds to destroy. Rather
than admit that his surprise Queen sacrifice is good for only
a draw at best, Keres presses for more, offering material
in order to sustain his initiative. Fischer continues to accept
everything, but—at the very moment when victory is within his
grasp (on move 31)—stumbles. Now he must win the game all
over again; and he manages to do so, with an assist from
Keres, in another twenty-two moves.*

1	P – K4	P – QB4
2	N – KB3	P – Q3
3	P – Q4	P×P
4	N×P	N – KB3
5	N – QB3	P – QR3
6	B – N5	P – K3
7	P – B4	B – K2

Sharp is 7 . . . Q – N3 which I've tried on several occasions.

8	Q – B3	Q – B2

8 . . . P – R3; *9* B – R4, P – KN4!?; *10* P×P, KN – Q2; *11*
N×P!?, P×N; *12* Q – R5+, K – B1; *13* B – N5!, R – KR2!

(Gligorich–Fischer, Portoroz 1958) is now considered a drawish variation!

```
 9 O – O – O      QN – Q2
10 B – K2         . . .
```

An innovation whose dubious merit appears on move 13. For *10* B – Q3 see game 9. For *10* P – KN4 see games 12 and 15.

```
10 . . .          P – N4
11 B × N          N × B
```

Not *11* . . . B × B?; *12* B × P! Or on *11* . . . P × B; *12* Q – R5, N – N3 (if *12* . . . O – O?; *13* R – Q3); *13* P – QR3 followed by P – B5 is strong.

```
12 P – K5!?       . . .
```

On *12* P – QR3, R – QN1! followed by . . . P – N5 gives good counterplay.

```
12 . . .          B – N2
```

FISCHER

Position after 12 . . .
B – N2

KERES

```
13 P × N!?        . . .
```

The crux of Keres' prepared line. After *13* Q – N3, P × P; *14* P × P, N – Q2; *15* Q × P, Q × P Black stands better.

```
13 . . .          B × Q
```

So I chopped it off!

```
14 B × B          B × P
```

Not *14* . . . R – QB1?; *15* P × B, Q × P; *16* N – B5! (BON-DAREVSKY).

```
15 B × R          P – Q4
```

So far, so forced. Now . . . O – O is threatened.

16 B×P   . . .

On *16* B – B6+, K – B1; *17* QN – K2, K – K2 followed by . . . R – QB1.

16 . . .   **B×N**

Not *16* . . . Q×P+; *17* K – N1, B×N; *18* B – B6+!, K – K2; *19* N – K2, etc. Larsen suggested *16* . . . P – N5; *17* B – B6+, K – K2; *18* N/3 – K2, R – Q1 but *19* R – Q2! (*19* P – KN3?, Q – N3!), B×N; *20* N×B, Q×P; *21* N – N3 holds for the time being.

17	R×B	P×B
18	N×QP	Q – B4
19	R – K1+	K – B1
20	P – B3	. . .

FISCHER

Position after 20 P – B3

KERES

White seems to have fair prospects. But a Queen is a Queen!

20 . . .   **P – KR4!**

A hard move to find—even somewhat risky—over-the-board. Probably Keres had expected *20* . . . P – N3; *21* P – KN4, K – N2; *22* P – N5, P – R3 (if *22* . . . R – Q1; *23* N – B6, R×R; *24* R – K8, R – Q1!; *25* R×R, Q – K6+ draws); *23* P – KR4, P×P; *24* BP×P, R – Q1; *25* N – B6, R×R; *26* R – K8, R – Q1!; *27* R × R, Q – K6+ with a draw by perpetual.

21 P – B5   . . .

To hinder . . . P – N3.

Kotov gives *21* N – N4, Q – B1? (simply *21* . . . P – N3 is more than sufficient; if then *22* N×P, Q – B3); *22* N – B6! and wins.

Zagoryansky also mistakenly thinks White has all the chances.

He gives "*21* R – K5!, P – N3 (more passive is *21* . . . Q – B1; *22* N – K7, Q – R1; *23* N – B6, P – B3; *24* R – K6, K – B2; *25* P – B5); *22* P – B5!" but *22* . . . K – N2; *23* P – B6+, K – R3 (if *24* P – KN4, P – N5!) is quite satisfactory for Black.

21 . . . .   R – R3!

The key to Black's defense: now the Rook sneaks into play via the side exit.

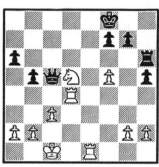

FISCHER

Position after 21 . . . R – R3

KERES

22 P – B6?   . . .

Throwing away a Pawn in an attempt to keep Black bottled up. Keres should just try to maintain the status quo with *22* KR – Q1, although Black retains some slight winning chances. But he seems to labor under the delusion that White has the initiative.

22 R/4 – K4, K – N1; *23* R – K8+, K – R2; *24* R – Q8, R – Q3 neutralizes all White's threats.

22 . . .   P × P
23 N – B4   P – R5
24 R – Q8+?   . . .

Continuing the "attack." The defensive *24* R – K2 was in order.

24 . . .   K – N2
25 R/1 – K8   Q – N8+
26 K – Q2   Q – B7+
27 N – K2   R – N3
28 P – KN3   . . .

28 R – N8+, K – R3; *29* R – R8+, K – N4 gets White nowhere.

28 . . .   P – B4
29 R – N8+   K – B3
30 R × R+   . . .

On *30* R – Q6+, K – K2; *31* R/6×R, P×R; *32* R×P, P – R6 wins (ZAGORYANSKY).

30 . . .   P×R
31 P×P   . . .

FISCHER

Position after 31 P×P

KERES

31 . . .   Q×P/7?

The winning method is *31* . . . Q×P/5!; *32* R – Q6+, K – B2; *33* P – KR3, Q – R3+! (if *33* . . . Q×P; *34* R×P!, K×R??; *35* N – B4+); *34* K – Q1 (if *34* K – K1, Q×P; *35* R×NP, Q – R5+!; *36* R – N3, P – B5 wins; or on *34* K – B2, Q×P; *35* R×NP, Q – R7 wins), Q×P; *35* R×NP, Q – B8+ and . . . K×R.

32 R – Q4!   . . .

Now Black has to win the game over again.

32 . . .   Q – R8
33 K – B2   . . .

33 N – B4? allows penetration with Q – QN8.

33 . . .   K – K4
34 P – R4   . . .

An even tighter defense is *34* N – B1! followed by N – Q3+ with a probable draw. But not *34* N – B4?, Q – R7+!; *35* K – Q1, Q×N!; *36* R×Q, K×R with a won King and Pawn ending: e.g., *37* K – K2 (if *37* P – N3, K – K6!), K – N6; *37* P – N3, K×P; *38* P – B4, P×P; *39* P×P, K – N4 and the King is "in the square."

34 . . .   Q – B8

Trying to capitalize on the disjointed state of White's **minor** pieces.

        35 N – B1   . . .

Forced. Not *35* K – Q2?, Q – QR8!; *36* K – B2, P×P, etc.

        35 . . .   Q – N7+

FISCHER

Position after 35 . . .
Q – N7+

KERES

        36 K – N3?   . . .

In time-pressure, Keres creates new losing chances for himself.
Also bad is *36* K – N1, P×P; *37* R×P, Q – B8; *38* K – B2,
K – B3! followed by . . . P – B5 (if *39* N – Q3?, Q – K7+).
    The right defense is *36* K – Q1!, P×P (not *36* . . . Q×P??;
37 N – Q3+); *37* N – Q3+, K – B3; *38* R×P, P – R4; *39* R – Q4
(not *39* R×P?, Q – N5+ and . . . Q×P) and Black can't make
any headway.

        36 . . .   P×P+
        37 K – R3   . . .

On *37* R×P (if *37* K×P, Q – B7+; *38* N – N3, Q×NP), Q –
Q7!; *38* N – R2, P – B5 is deadly.

        37 . . .   Q – QB7
        38 N – Q3+   K – B3
        39 N – B5   Q – B8!

Threatening . . . Q – R8+.

        40 R×P   . . .

40 N×P/4, P – B5; *41* N – B5, P – B6; *42* N – Q3, Q – K6 transposes into the note after White's 41st move.

        40 . . .   Q – K6

The game was adjourned and Keres sealed his move.

FISCHER

Position after 40 . . .
Q – K6

KERES

41 N×P? . . .

This makes it easy.

I had expected *41* R – Q4, P – B5; *42* N – Q3, P – B6. The win is hard, but eventually Black breaks through on QR6. For example, *42* K – N3 (*42* P – N4?, P – B7 wins), K – N2; *43* K – R3, Q – K7; *44* K – N3, Q – Q8+; *45* K – B4 (if *45* K – R3, P – R4; *46* K – R2, P – R5; *47* N – B2, Q – N6+; *48* K – R1, P – R6; etc.), P – R4; *46* K – N5, P – R5; *47* K – R5, Q – N6; *48* K – R6, P – R6; *49* P×P, Q×P+; *50* K – N5, Q×P; etc. Maybe White can improve, but Black should win because the blockade is not airtight.

41	. . .	P – B5
42	R – Q4	K – B4!

The move Keres missed when he sealed his forty-first. He had probably anticipated *42* . . . P – B6; *43* N – B5, P – B7; *44* N – K4+, Q×N; *45* R×Q, P – B8 = Q with a dead draw since Black can't create another passed Pawn.

43 N – N4 . . .

More resistance could have been offered by *43* N – B5, but it's still lost after Q – K2!; *44* P – N4, Q×P; *45* P – N5, Q – B3, etc.

43 . . . Q – K2!

This temporary pin is decisive. Now Black wins the RP and his two passed Pawns become irresistible.

44	K – N3	Q×P
45	N – Q3	P – N4
46	P – B4	Q – N6
47	P – B5	P – B6
48	K – B4	P – B7

49	N × P	Q × N
50	P – B6	Q × P
51	K – B5	Q – B6+

FISCHER

Position after 51 . . .
Q – B6+

KERES

52	K – Q5	. . .

On *52* R – B4, Q – R4+ ; *53* K – Q4, Q – B2 wins.

52	. . .	P – N5
53	R – B4	Q – K4 mate

15 Smyslov *[U.S.S.R.]* - Fischer

CANDIDATES' TOURNAMENT 1959

SICILIAN DEFENSE

A whopper

Here is Fischer's first win against Vassily Smyslov; and it is
hard to recall when the former world champion, conducting
White, has been so badly outplayed.

On move 13 of a crucial opening variation, Smyslov makes
what appears to be a "lapsus manus." Rather than fight a
prolonged uphill positional battle, he sacrifices a Pawn to try
to regain the initiative. This proves to be a piece of bad
judgment, since, basically, the loss of this Pawn alone brings
about his demise. Defending with deadly precision, Fischer
gradually consolidates—the shadow of his Pawn looming
larger with each approach to the endgame. Smyslov thrashes
about, striving desperately for complications, avoiding
exchanges like the plague. But he is unable to get off the hook.

1	P – K4	P – QB4
2	N – KB3	P – Q3
3	P – Q4	P×P
4	N×P	N – KB3
5	N – QB3	P – QR3
6	B – N5	. . .

For 6 B – K2 see games 4 and 42. For 6 B – B4 see games 17,
55, 58.

6	. . .	P – K3
7	P – B4	B – K2
8	Q – B3	Q – B2
9	O – O – O	QN – Q2

Weak is 9 . . . P – R3; *10* B – R4, QN – Q2; *11* B – Q3,
P – QN4; *12* P – K5!, B – N2; *13* N × KP!, P × N; *14* B – N6+,

K – B1; *15* P × N, B × Q (better is . . . N × P); *16* P × B +,
K – N1; *17* P × B, N – B3; *18* B × N, P × B; *19* P – K8 = Q +,
R × Q; *20* B × R, P – Q4 (Gligorich–Bobotsov, Hastings 1959–60);
21 P – B5! (*MCO*) wins.

10	P – KN4	P – N4
11	B × N	N × B

For *11* . . . P × B see game 12.

12	P – N5	N – Q2

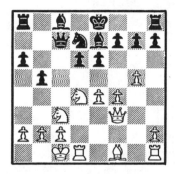

FISCHER

Position after 12 . . .
N – Q2

SMYSLOV

13 B – R3?   . . .

Innovation or omission? In either case, after this move White
throws away his theoretical advantage and even loses the initiative.
Necessary is *13* P – QR3, B – N2 (*13* . . . R – QN1! is in vogue)
and now there are two main lines:

A] *14* P – KR4, P – Q4; *15* P × P, N – N3; *16* P – B5, N × P; *17*
P × P, O – O – O; *18* B – N2, N × N; *19* Q × B +, Q × Q; *20* B ×
Q +, K × B; *21* P × N, B × RP +; *22* K – N1, P × P; *23* N × KP,
R – QB1; *24* R – R3, P – N3; *25* P – B4, KR – K1 and shortly
drawn. (Sherwin–Fischer, US Championship 1959–60.)

B] *14* B – R3, O – O – O; *15* P – B5!? (interesting is *15* B × P!?,
P × B; *16* N × KP, Q – B5 [Keres recommends . . . Q – N3];
17 N – Q5 with unclear complications, though White won. Tal–
Gligorich, Moscow 1963), B × P +; *16* K – N1, P – K4; *17*
N/4 × P, P × N; *18* N × P, Q – N3! (better than . . . Q – B4
which I played against Gligorich at the Candidates' 1959); *19*
N × P +, K – B2; *20* N × P, B – KB3 is roughly equal.

13	. . .	P – N5!

My game with Walther (9) had taught me this lesson well.

14	N/3 – K2	B – N2
15	K – N1?	. . .

In this sharp variation, White has no time for such amenities. *15 N – KN3* avoids incurring any severe disadvantage, while the speculative *15 B × P!?, P × B; 16 N × P, Q – B5; 17 N × P+* (better is N/2 – Q4), K – B1! favors Black.

15	. . .	N – B4
16	N – KN3	P – Q4!

FISCHER

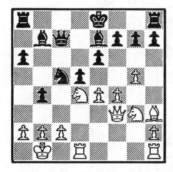

Position after 16 . . .
P – Q4

SMYSLOV

I could see from the expression on Smyslov's face that he already thought he was busted.

17	P – B5!?	. . .

On *17 P – K5, P – N3!; 18 R – QB1, Q – N3!* and if *19 P – B3, P – QR4* followed by . . . O – O with a powerful attack in the works. Smyslov's keen positional judgment tells him that such a course for White is lifeless. So he sacs a Pawn instead.

17	. . .	P × KP
18	Q – N4	P × P
19	N/4 × BP	P – N3!

Perhaps this simple retort had escaped him. Was he hoping for *19 . . . O – O?; 20 N – R5!, P – N3; 21 Q – N3!* winning material (if *21 . . . B – Q1; 22 R × B!, Q × R; 23 N – B6+,* etc.)? The rest of the game is, if one may use that hackneyed phrase, "a matter of technique." Black's a Pawn ahead with the better game to boot.

20	N × B	. . .

Not *20 N – R6?, B – QB1; 21 Q – R4, B × B; 22 Q × B, B × P+.*

20 . . .	Q × N
21 Q – B4	O – O
22 R – Q6	QR – Q1
23 R – KB6	. . .

Naturally Smyslov avoids swapping.

23 . . .	R – Q4
24 B – N4	N – Q2
25 R – KB1	. . .

A desperate attempt to complicate. On *25* N × P?, R – Q5; *26* B × N, Q × B wins a piece. Or *25* Q × P, R – Q8 + !; *26* R × R, B × Q; *27* R × N, Q – K4.

25 . . .	P – K6

Not *25* . . . N × R?; *26* P × N, Q – K4; *27* Q – R6 wins.

26 P – N3	R – Q7

Threatening *27* . . . N × R; *28* P × N, Q – B4!; *29* R – B1, Q – Q5. To avert further material loss, Smyslov is forced to indulge in the simplifications he has been trying so hard to forestall.

FISCHER

Position after 26 . . .
R – Q7

SMYSLOV

27 B × N	. . .

Forced, but now White's game rapidly deteriorates and the extra Pawn makes its presence felt.

27 . . .	R × B
28 R – K1	R – K1
29 P – KR4	Q – B4!
30 Q – B4	. . .

Horrible, but necessary, to meet the main threat of . . . Q – B6.

30	. . .	Q × Q
31	P × Q	R – Q5

Now Black hacks away unmercifully.

32	P – B5	R × P
33	P – B6	B – B1
34	R – Q6	R – QB5
35	K – N2	K – N2
36	K – N3	R – N5
37	N – K2	R – K3!
38	R/1 – Q1	. . .

On *32* R × R, B × R+; *39* K – N2, R – QB5, etc.

38	. . .	R – N7
39	N – B4	R × R
40	R × R	R – Q7
41	R – Q3	. . .

The only move. Smyslov might have resigned had we adjourned here. But we both were playing fast and, as a consequence, were still well in the first session, carried by sheer momentum.

41	. . .	R – B7
42	R – Q4	. . .

Again forced. On *42* N – Q5, P – K7; *43* R – K3, R – B6 wins.

42	. . .	P – K7
43	N – Q3	B – B4
44	P – B7	R – B6

Quicker is *44* . . . B × N; *45* P – B8 = Q, P – K8 = Q; *46* R × B, Q – N8+; *47* K – R4, R × P, etc.

45	P – B8 = Q	B × Q

Again *45* . . . P – K8 = Q was quicker, but I wanted to avoid "complications."

46	R – K4	B – B4
47	R × KP	B × N
48	P × B	R × P+

49	K×P	R – Q4
50	R – KN2	P – R3
51	P×P+	K×P
52	P – R4	P – N4
53	R – QB2	R – Q3
54	K – B5	R – K3

White resigns

FISCHER

Final Position after 54 . . .
R – K3

SMYSLOV

16 Fischer - Petrosian [U.S.S.R.]

CANDIDATES' TOURNAMENT 1959

CARO-KANN DEFENSE

Four Queens

> *Fischer extracted a slight minus score from the seven games in which he was called upon to face the Caro-Kann, prompting Botvinnik to note: "Fischer's both strong and weak point lies in that he is always true to himself and plays the same way regardless of his partners or any external factor."*
>
> *This variation is not only complex and critical—but perilous. After a single slip the edge passes to Black. But Petrosian overestimates his position and, somewhat recklessly, dissipates his advantage. In time-pressure he misses a forced draw and Fischer regains the upper hand. From this point on, with four marauding Queens roaming the board, the play becomes "rich and strange"—resulting in a tortuous draw.*

1	P – K4	P – QB3
2	N – QB3	P – Q4
3	N – B3	. . .

The purpose of this line is to exclude the possibility of . . . B – B4. For example, *3* . . . P × P; *4* N × P, B – B4?; *5* N – N3, B – N3 (if *5* . . . B – N5; *6* P – KR3); *6* P – KR4, P – KR3; *7* N – K5, B – R2; *8* Q – R5, P – KN3; *9* B – QB4!, P – K3; *10* Q – K2 (threatening N × KBP) and Black has a terrible game.

3	. . .	B – N5

3 . . . N – B3; *4* P – K5, N – K5; *5* N – K2!, Q – N3; *6* P – Q4, P – QB4; *7* P × P, Q × BP; *8* N/2 – Q4, N – QB3; *9* B – QN5, P – QR3; *10* B × N+, P × B; *11* O – O, Q – N3; *12* P – K6!, P × P; *13* B – B4 is good for White. (Fischer–Olafsson, Candidates' 1959.)

4	P – KR3	B × N

In our first-round game here, Smyslov played *4* . . . B – R4; *5* P × P, P × P; *6* B – N5+, N – B3; *7* P – KN4, B – N3; *8* N – K5, R – B1; *9* P – Q4, P – K3; *10* P – KR4 (correct is *10* Q – K2! to prevent . . . P – B3), P – B3; *11* N × B, P × N; *12* Q – Q3, K – B2; *13* P – R5, P × P; *14* P × P, KN – K2=.

5 Q × B   N – B3

The old *5* . . . P – K3; *6* P – Q4, P × P; *7* N × P, Q × P; *8* B – Q3 gives White a good attack for the Pawn. And on *5* . . . P × P; *6* N × P, N – Q2; *7* N – N5!? (better is simply *7* P – Q4), KN – B3; *8* Q – QN3, P – K3; *9* Q × P, N – Q4! Black gets good play. (Fischer–Cardoso, Portoroz 1958.)

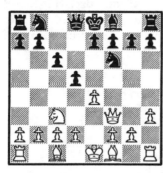

PETROSIAN

Position after 5 . . . N – B3

FISCHER

Inferior is *6* P – Q4, P × P; *7* N × P!? (*7* Q – K3, QN – Q2; *8* N × P, N × N; *9* Q × N, N – B3; *10* Q – Q3, Q – Q4! is equal Fischer–Keres, Bled 1961), Q × P; *8* B – Q3, QN – Q2 (threatening . . . N – K4).

On *6* P – K5, KN – Q2; *7* P – K6? (playable is *7* Q – N3, P – K3; *8* B – K2 Spassky–Reshko, Leningrad 1961), P × P; *8* P – Q4, P – K4!

Finally on *6* P – KN3, P × P; *7* N × P, N × N; *8* Q × N, Q – Q4!; *9* Q × Q, P × Q; *10* B – N2, P – K3 (if *11* P – QB4, N – B3; *12* P × P, N – N5!) gives Black an even ending (SUETIN).

6 P – Q3   P – K3
7 P – KN3   . . .

A recent try is *7* B – Q2 followed by O – O – O. Against Larsen, at Zurich 1959, I tried *7* P – R3, B – B4; *8* B – K2, O – O; *9* O – O, QN – Q2 and Black got a satisfactory game.

7 . . .   B – N5
8 B – Q2   . . .

Not *8* B – N2?, P – Q5; *9* P – R3, Q – R4.

8 . . .   P – Q5

Inferior is *8* . . . Q – N3; *9* O – O – O, P – Q5; *10* N – K2.

9 N – N1   B×B+

In this tournament Keres and Benko both tried *9* . . . Q – N3
forcing White to weaken the Q-side with *10* P – N3. But Black's
Queen is slightly misplaced after *10* . . . QN – Q2; *11* B – N2,
P – QR4; *12* P – R3, B×B+ (the retreat *12* . . . B – K2 seems
illogical—even though Keres beat me with it); *13* N×B, Q – B4;
14 Q – Q1, P – R4; *15* P – KR4! with an edge. (Fischer–Benko.)
Petrosian apparently didn't want to get involved with this line,
despite the fact that his countryman, Tal, accused me of "bad
judgment" for preferring White here.

10 N×B   P – K4
11 B – N2   P – B4
12 O – O   N – B3
13 Q – K2   . . .

PETROSIAN

Position after 13 Q – K3

FISCHER

The critical juncture. In our earlier game (round two) Petrosian
continued with *13* . . . P – KN4; *14* N – B3? (Simagin gives *14*
P – KB4, NP×P; *15* P×P, Q – K2; *16* N – B4, N – Q2; *17* Q – N4
"with advantage" but after . . . O – O – O; *18* P×P, K – N1
Black succeeds in planting his Knight on K4 where it cannot be
dislodged), P – KR3; *15* P – KR4, R – KN1; *16* P – R3, Q – K2;
17 P×P, P×P; *18* Q – Q2, N – Q2; *19* P – B3, O – O – O; *20*
P×P, KP×P with advantage for Black.

13 . . .   Q – K2

Fearing a prepared line, Petrosian deviates.

On *13*. . . P – KN4 I had intended *14* P – QB3!, Q – K2; *15* N – B3, P – KR3; *16* P×P!, KP×P (if *16*. . . N×QP; *17* N×N, BP×N; *18* QR – B1. Or *16*. . . BP×P; *17* P – KR4, R – KN1; *18* P×P, P×P; *19* KR – B1, O – O – O; *20* P – QN4!, K – N1; *21* P – N5, N – QR4; *22* Q – Q2 wins a Pawn); *17* P – K5!, O – O – O; *18* KR – K1. Now the Bishop diagonal is unblocked and Black can't set up a blockade on his K4, as in our first game.

After *13*. . . O – O; *15* P – KB4, K – R1; *16* P – B5, N – KN1; *17* P – KN4, P – B3 White has a tough nut to crack, but his initiative is permanent. The text indicates Petrosian's intention to castle long without trying to prevent P – KB4.

14	P – KB4	O – O – O
15	P – R3	N – K1

Also playable is *15*. . . N – Q2; *16* P – QN4, P – B3; and if *17* N – B4, P – QN4.

16	P – QN4	P×NP

Wide open! Safer is *16*. . . P – B3; *17* P – N5 (if *17* P×BP, Q×P; *18* P×P, N×P), N – R4; *18* N – N3, N×N; *19* P×N, K – N1; *20* P – QR4=.

PETROSIAN

Position after 16 . . . P × NP

FISCHER

17	N – B4?	. . .

Now Black has time to consolidate. Correct is *17* P×KP! with advantage in all variations:

A] *17*. . . Q×P; *18* R×P, Q×NP; *19* P – K5!, Q – K6+; *20* Q×Q, P×Q; *21* N – B4.

B] *17*. . . P×P; *18* N – B4, R – B1; *19* R×RP (if *19*. . . P – QN4; *20* Q – N4+!).

C] *17*. . . N×P; *18* P×P, K – N1; *19* N – B3, P – B3; *20*

Q – B2!, N × N+ (if *20 . . . Q × P; 21* N × N, P × N; *22* Q – B7 penetrates); *21* Q × N, N – Q3 (if *21 . . . Q × P; 22* P – K5!); *22* R – R5, P – QR3; *23* Q – B4, KR – K1; *24* R – Q5.

D] *17 . . .* K – N1; *18* P × P, N × NP (*18 . . .* N × KP; *19* N – B3 transposes to "C"); *19* N – B4, N – QB3 (if *19 . . .* N – B2; *20* N – Q6!, KR – B1; *21* KR – N1, N/2 – R3; *22* Q – Q2, Q × P; *23* N × NP!, K × N; *24* R × N! wins); *20* Q – B3, R – B1; *21* P – K6!, Q × P; *22* P – K5! followed by KR – N1 and White has a winning attack.

$$\text{17 . . .} \qquad \text{P – B3!}$$

I had expected *17 . . .* P × RP; *18* P × P transposing to "B" above.

18	P × KP	P × KP
19	P × P	N – B2

Black wants to secure a Q-side blockade. The QNP won't run away.

20	N – R5	N – N4!

I already knew I'd been outplayed. Petrosian didn't even consider *20 . . .* N × P, opening up the lines.

21	N × N	P × N
22	R – B2	P – N3

On *22 . . .* Q × P?; *23* Q – N4+, R – Q2; *24* R – B7, KR – Q1; *25* Q × P regains the Pawn.

23	P – R4	K – N2

Ordinarily one would expect Petrosian to simplify and simplify in order to reach a winning ending. *23 . . .* KR – B1! is strong.

24	P – R5	Q × P

Really risky! I was amazed he was allowing so much counterplay. *24 . . .* KR – B1 is still right. On *24 . . .* P × P; *25* Q × P, KR – B1; *26* R – B5!

25	R – B7+	K – N3

On *25 . . . K – N1; 26* Q – B2, KR – B1; *27* P – B4!, N – B2
(if *27 . . .* P × P e.p.?; *28* R/1 × P!, R × R; *29* Q – N6+); *28*
Q – B6 with good play.

26 Q – B2!   P – R4

Not *26 . . .* KR – B1?; *27* P – B4!, N – B6; *28* R/1 × P wins.

27 P – B4   N – B6?

Continuing to underestimate the danger. Safer is *27 . . .*
N – Q3.

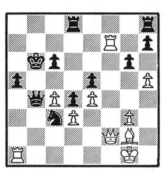

PETROSIAN

Position after 27 . . .
N – B6

FISCHER

28 R – KB1?   . . .

Why didn't I play *28* Q – B6! immediately? If then *28 . . .*
QR – KB1 (*28 . . .* KR – B1; *29* R – KB1!, R × R; *30* Q × R+!,
R – B2; *31* R – B7 wins); *29* Q × KP, R × R; *30* Q × R, Q – B4;
31 P – K5—it's difficult for Black in view of his exposed King and
White's passed KP.

Finally, after *28* Q – B6!, Q – B4; *29* Q – N7!, K – R3 (if *29
. . .* P – R5; *30* R – R7! or *29 . . .* R – R1; *30* R – N7+,
K – R3; *31* Q – QB7!, KR – QB1; *32* R – N5! wins. Or *29
. . .* QR – KN1; *30* R – N7+, K – R3; *31* Q – QB7, R – QB1;
32 R × P+!); *30* R – R7+!, Q × R; *31* R × P+, K × R; *32* Q × Q+,
K – N5; *33* Q – N6+, K – R6; *34* P – B5! and White's QBP is
dangerous.

28 . . .   P – R5

Still playing with reckless abandon! Safer is *28 . . .* Q – Q3
to prevent Q – B6.

29 Q – B6   Q – B4
30 R × P!   . . .

Now I decided to start playing for the win. On *30* Q – N7, QR – KN1!; *31* R – N7+, K – R3; *32* Q – QB7, R – QB1!; *33* Q – N7, QR – KN1! draws by a "perpetual check" on the Queen.

> *30* . . .   QR – KB1!

Forcing what looks like a favorable ending.

> *31* Q×NP   R×R+
> *32* B×R   R×R
> *33* Q×R   P – R6

Petrosian had been banking on the speed of this Pawn.

> *34* P – R6   P – R7
> *35* Q – N8   P – R8 = Q
> *36* P – R7   . . .

PETROSIAN

Position after 36 P – R7

FISCHER

> *36* . . .   Q – Q3?

In time-pressure, Petrosian overlooks *36* . . . N – K7+; *37* K – B2, N×P! and White has nothing better than to take a perpetual with *38* Q – N8+.

> *37* P – R8 = Q   Q – R2
> *38* P – N4   K – B4!

A good last-ditch try. Curiously, the King will be safer in White's territory where it obtains shelter from the cluster of Pawns.

> *39* Q – KB8?   . . .

Right is *39* Q – R2! immediately, preventing Black's King from reaching safety behind the lines. If then *39* . . . Q – B3; *40* P – N5. Or *39* . . . Q – R8 (*39* . . . Q – R7?; *40* Q×Q,

N×Q; *41* Q – QR8! wins a piece); *40* Q – N7 wins the KP. Finally on *39 . . .* Q/2 – K2; *40* Q – QR8 renews the attack.

39 . . .		Q/2 – K2

Forced, to defend against the threat of Q×P+.

Not *39 . . .* Q×Q; *40* Q×Q+, K – N3; *41* Q – N4+, K – R3 (if *41 . . .* K – B2; *42* Q – K7+); *42* Q – R3+, K – N2; *43* Q×Q+, K×Q; *44* P – N5 and queens.

40 Q – R8		. . .

I thought this was it! The two Queens are closing in for the kill.

40 . . .		K – N5!
41 Q – KR2		K – N6!

Slippery as an eel!

PETROSIAN

Position after 41 . . .
K – N6

FISCHER

Now White sealed. It's fantastically complicated!

The tournament bulletins suggest *42* P – B5, Q×P (if *42 . . .* Q – N3; *43* B – K2!, Q/3 – N4; *44* B – Q1+!); *43* Q – KN8+, K – R6; *44* Q – QB2, Q – N5; *45* Q – R8+, Q – R5 (not *45 . . .* N – R5?; *46* Q – B1+, K – R7; *47* Q – N8+, Q – N6; *48* Q – B2+! wins); *46* Q/2×Q+, N×Q; *47* Q×P "with good winning chances," but after *47 . . .* N – B6 it's likely Black can draw.

42 Q – QR1		. . .

After the game a kibitzer asked Petrosian if he thought *42* P – B5 would have won for White. Petrosian, who must have analyzed it for many hours (not knowing, of course, what my sealed move was), simply replied: "I don't know."

| 42 . . . | Q – R6 |

The only move to stop mate on QN2.

| 43 Q×Q+ | K×Q |
| 44 Q – R6 | . . . |

Now White has to try to make do with the KNP.

| 44 . . . | Q – KB2! |
| 45 K – N2 | . . . |

On *45* Q×P, N – Q8!

| 45 . . . | K – N6 |

Not *45* . . . N – Q8; *46* Q – B1+, N – N7 and the Knight is stranded out-of-play. The text renews the threat of . . . N – Q8.

| 46 Q – Q2 | Q – KR2! |
| 47 K – N3 | . . . |

A gross oversight, but probably best anyway! White can't win anymore. If *47* P – N5, Q – R5, etc.

| 47 . . . | Q×P! |

PETROSIAN

Position after 47 . . .
Q × P

FISCHER

| 48 Q – B2? | . . . |

Having overlooked Petrosian's last move, I was somewhat shaken! Not *48* P×Q?, N×P+; *49* K – R4, N×Q; *50* P – N5, N×B; *51* P – N6, P – Q6 wins. Also on *48* Q – Q1+ ? (*48* Q×N+ ?, P×Q; *49* P×Q, P – B7 wins), N×Q; *49* P×Q, N – K6; *50* B – K2, N×BP; *51* P – N5, N – Q3; *52* P – N6, N – K1 and Black again wins.

The right retort, however, is *48* P – N5! and it's still a hard fight.

48 . . .	Q – R8!

I offered a draw, afraid that he wouldn't accept. Black certainly has the edge now. If *49* P – N5, P – K5! Or if *49* B – N2, Q – R3. After having fought so hard for the draw, however, Petrosian was obviously unprepared to readjust his frame of mind and start playing for a win. So . . .

Drawn

17 Fischer - Tal [U.S.S.R.]

SICILIAN DEFENSE

A very near miss

This is one of the four games that Fischer lost to Tal who, in winning this tournament, earned the right to meet and trounce Botvinnik for the world championship.

In jest the whimsical Tal signed Fischer's name, in addition to his own, when asked for an autograph. "Why not?" he quipped; "I've beaten Bobby so often · · · that gives me the right to sign for him!"

A careful reading of Fischer's notes will reveal a clear echo of the strong emotions that engulfed him during this tense encounter. He misses a win in the opening and several draws along the way, demonstrating dramatically how a continuously advantageous position can abruptly be turned into defeat by seemingly insignificant miscalculations.

1	P – K4	P – QB4
2	N – KB3	P – Q3
3	P – Q4	P × P
4	N × P	N – KB3
5	N – QB3	P – QR3
6	B – QB4	. . .

We had some excellent results with this. See also games 55 and 58.

6	. . .	P – K3
7	B – N3	. . .

I had no better luck against Blackstone, in an exhibition game at Davis, California, 1964, with *7* O – O, B – K2; *8* B – N3, Q – B2; *9* P – B4, P – QN4; *10* P – B5, P – N5; *11* P × P!? (*11* QN – K2, P – K4; *12* N – KB3, B – N2 is bad for White), P × N; *12* P × P+, K – B1; *13* B – N5, N – N5! and Black should win.

7	. . .	P – QN4!

This reaction must be prompt!

In our first lap game here Tal played the weaker 7 . . . B – K2?; 8 P – B4, O – O (for 8 . . . P – QN4 see the note to Black's 8th move); 9 Q – B3, Q – B2 and now 10 P – B5! (instead of 10 O – O?, P – QN4; 11 P – B5, P – N5!; 12 N – R4, P – K4; 13 N – K2, B – N2 and Black stands better), P – K4 (not 10 . . . N – B3; 11 B – K3 with a bind); 11 N/4 – K2, P – QN4; 12 P – QR3, B – N2; 13 P – N4 with a strong attack.

8 P – B4!?   . . .

Against Olafsson, at Buenos Aires 1960, I continued 8 O – O, B – K2 (if 8 . . . P – N5; 9 N – R4, N × P; 10 R – K1, N – B3; 11 B – N5 with attack); 9 Q – B3!?, Q – B2 (not 9 . . . B – N2?; 10 B × P!); 10 Q – N3, P – N5; 11 QN – K2, P – N3; 12 P – QB3? (12 B – R6! is very strong), N × P; 13 Q – K3, N – KB3; 14 P × P, O – O = with a double-edged position.

R. Byrne-Evans, U.S. Championship 1967 went 8 Q – B3, but White got nothing after 8 . . . B – N2; 9 B – N5, P – N5; 10 N – R4, QN – Q2; 11 O – O, Q – R4; 12 B × N, N × B; 13 KR – K1, B – K2.

8 . . .   P – N5!

Indirectly undermining White's center.

9 N – R4   N × P

9 . . . B – N2 is also playable.

10 O – O   P – N3?

Correct is 10 . . . B – N2.

11 P – B5!   . . .

This riposte caught Tal completely unaware. Black's King, trapped in the center, will soon be subject to mayhem.

11 . . .   NP × P

Not 11 . . . KP × P; 12 B – Q5, R – R2; 13 N × P!, P × N; 14 Q – Q4.

12 N × BP!   . . .

Panov, with typical iron curtain "objectivity," commented in the Soviet tournament bulletins: "Almost all game Fischer played in Tal style. But all his trouble was in vain because Tal did not defend in Fischer style—instead he found the one and only saving counterchance!"

TAL

Position after 12 N × BP

FISCHER

12 . . .	R – N1

Woozy, Tal stumbles into a dubious defense. Better is *12 . . . P – Q4* (not *12 . . . P × N?; 13 Q – Q5, R – R2; 14 Q – Q4* spearing a Rook); *13 N – R6, B × N; 14 B × B*.

13 B – Q5!	. . .

A shot!

13 . . .	R – R2

"*13 . . . P × B; 14 Q × P, B × N; 15 R × B, R – R2; 16 Q × N+, R – K2; 17 Q × P, R – K7; 18 B – N5!, R × B; 19 R × R, Q × R; 20 Q × N+* wins." (PANOV.)

14 B × N?	. . .

Correct is *14 B – K3!, N – B4; 15 Q – R5!, R – N3* (if *15 . . . N × N; 16 B × R, P × B; 17 QR – K1+); 16 QR – K1!* and White's every piece is bearing down on Black's King (KEVITZ).

| 14 . . . | P × N |
15 B × P	. . .

Probably it's better to avoid exchanges with *15 B – Q5* or B – B3.

15 . . .	R – K2!

A unique way of shielding the K-file.

16 B × B	Q × B
17 B – B4?	. . .

The right move is simply *17* P – B3! (not *17* Q × P?, R × P+ ; *18* K × R, R – K7+ ; *19* K – B3, B × Q; *20* K × R, Q × P+ wins), and if . . . Q – B3; *18* R – B2.

17 . . .	Q – B3!
18 Q – B3	Q × N!

Such a surprise that I didn't dare believe my eyes! I had expected *18* . . . Q × Q; *19* R × Q, R – K7; *20* R – B2, R × R; *21* K × R and White has a slight edge after P – QR3 because of Black's disconnected Pawns.

19 B × P	Q – B3!

Tal finds an inspired defense.

20 B × N	Q – N3+

White remains a clear Pawn ahead after *20* . . . Q × Q; *21* R × Q, B – N2; *22* P – B3.

21 K – R1	Q × B

TAL

Position after 21 . . .
Q × B

FISCHER

The crowd was shouting and whistling with each move. Later I was informed that many sport fans were in the audience. Maybe some soccer match had been canceled. As a consequence chess was the main attraction that day in Belgrade.

22 Q – B6+	. . .

Many annotators believed that *22* QR – K1 was the winning move. Tal himself confessed he thought Black was lost after that. But *22* . . . K – Q1! holds in all lines (not *22* . . . R – N3?;

23 Q×P+, K – Q2;   *24* R – Q1+!, R – Q3;   *25* R×R+, K×R;
26 R – B6+! wins). I've studied this position for ages, it seems,
and the best I can find is *23* R – Q1+, K – B2! (*23* . . . K – B1?;
24 Q – B6+ wins); *24* Q – B4+ (if *24* R – Q4, Q – N2!), K – N2;
25 R – Q6, Q – B2; *26* Q×P+, K – B1; *27* R×RP, Q – N2!; *28*
Q×Q+, K×Q; *29* R/6 – KB6, R – N2=.

                    22 . . .   R – Q2
                    23 QR – K1+   . . .

Black holds after *23* QR – Q1, B – Q3; *24* R×P (if *24* R – B6,
R – N3; *25* R/1×B?, Q×R!), Q – B2, etc. And on *23* R×P,
Q – Q3.

                    23 . . .   B – K2

Finally Tal "develops" his Bishop. Not *23* . . . K – Q1; *24*
R×P!, B – K2; *25* R/7×B, R×R; *26* R – Q1+ wins.

                    24 R×P   K×R
                    25 Q – K6+   K – B1!

I thought he had to go to N2, whereupon *26* Q×R wins easily.

TAL

Position after 25 . . .
K – B1

FISCHER

                    26 Q×R   . . .

Not *26* R – B1+, K – N2; *27* R – B7+, K – R1 and if *28* Q×R,
R – Q1; *29* Q – N4, Q – K4 wins.

                    26 . . .   Q – Q3
                    27 Q – N7   R – N3

Within a handful of moves the game has changed its complexion.
Now it is White who must fight for a draw!

                    28 P – B3!   . . .

Black's extra piece means less with each Pawn that's exchanged.

28 . . .	P – QR4

On *28 . . . P×P; 29* Q – B8+, B – Q1; *30* Q×P=.

29 Q – B8+	. . .

On the wrong track. Right is *29* P×P!, Q×P (if *29 . . . P×P; 30* P – QR3!, P×P; *31* P×P, Q×P draws); *30* Q – B3+, K – N2; *31* Q – K2 draws, since Black can't possibly build up a winning K-side attack and his own King is too exposed.

29 . . .	K – N2
30 Q – B4	B – Q1
31 P×P	P×P

On *31 . . .* Q×P; *32* Q – K2 White should draw with best play.

32 P – KN3?	. . .

Creating losing chances. I don't see how Black can make any progress after *32* Q – K4. If *32 . . .* B – B2; *33* Q – K7+, K – N1; *34* Q – K8+, Q – B1; *35* Q – K4, etc.

32 . . .	Q – B3+
33 R – K4	Q×Q
34 R×Q	R – N3!

I overlooked this. Now Black has winning chances. I had planned on a draw after *34 . . .* B – K2?; *35* P – QR3! dissolving Black's QNP (*35 . . .* P – N6 is answered by *36* R – B7 followed by R – N7).

35 K – N2	K – B3
36 K – B3	K – K4
37 K – K3	. . .

37 P – QR3 is met, as always, by P – N6. Once White can eliminate Black's QNP it's a theoretical draw.

37 . . .	B – N4+
38 K – K2	K – Q4
39 K – Q3	B – B3

White might be able to draw this ending, but it's an ugly defensive chore.

40 R – B2?	. . .

Too passive. I wanted to avoid immobilizing my Q-side Pawns with *40* P – N3, but it's the best hope now. On *40* . . . B – K2; *41* R – Q4+ preserves drawing chances.

TAL

Position after 40 R–B2

FISCHER

40 . . .	B – K4
41 R – K2	R – KB3
42 R – QB2	R – B6+
43 K – K2	R – B2
44 K – Q3	B – Q5!

Little by little Tal inches his way in.

45 P – QR3	. . .

On *45* P – N3, R – B6+; *46* K – K2, R – B7+; *47* K – Q3, R × R; *48* K × R, K – K5 wins.

45 . . .	P – N6
46 R – B8	. . .

Equally hopeless is *46* R – K2 (or *46* R – Q2, R – B6+; *47* K – K2, R – B7+), R – B6+; *47* K – Q2, B × P, etc.

46 . . .	B × P
47 R – Q8+	K – B3
48 R – QN8	R – B6+
49 K – B4	R – B6+
50 K – N4	B – R8
51 P – QR4	P – N7!
White resigns	

If *52* K × R, P – N8 = Q+!

This discovered-check theme is strangely reminiscent of the finale of game 31.

I 8 Spassky *[U.S.S.R.]* - Fischer

MAR DEL PLATA 1960

KING'S GAMBIT

Old wine in a new bottle

Here is the second of the three losses contained in this volume. As in the previous example, Fischer misses a win by inches. Deviating from his cherished Sicilian, he enables Spassky to employ the King's Gambit—not quite believing he would. Spassky is one of the few Grandmasters who still does so in competition. Fischer promptly wins a Pawn and hangs on to it, but neglects to steer for a highly favorable ending (23 . . . Q – N6). Just four moves later, 27 R – K5! effects his undoing.

Undaunted by this early setback, Fischer scored 12½ out of his last 13, pulling neck and neck with Spassky for first.

1	P – K4	P – K4
2	P – KB4	P×P
3	N – KB3	P – KN4

This loss spurred me to look for a "refutation" of the King's Gambit, which I published in the *American Chess Quarterly*, Vol. 1 (1961), No. 1. The right move is *3 . . . P – Q3!*

4	P – KR4	. . .

The only realistic try for any advantage. There is no longer anything "romantic" about the Muzio Gambit, which has been analyzed to a draw after *4 B – B4, P – N5; 5 O – O* (if *5 N – K5, Q – R5+ ; 6 K – B1, N – QB3!), P×N; 6 Q×P, Q – B3,* etc.

4	. . .	P – N5
5	N – K5	N – KB3

On *5 . . . P – KR4; 6 B – B4, R – R2; 7 P – Q4, P – Q3; 8 N – Q3, P – B6; 9 P×P, B – K2; 10 B – K3, B×P+ ; 11 K – Q2,*

B – N4, *12* P – B4, B – R3; *13* N – B3, White has more than
enough compensation for the Pawn. This is vintage analysis.

6 P – Q4   . . .

On *6* B – B4, P – Q4; *7* P×P, B – N2 (the old *7* . . . B – Q3
is also adequate) is the modern panacea. And on *6* N×NP, N×P;
7 P – Q3, N – N6; *8* B×P, N×R; *9* Q – K2+ (*9* B – N5, B – K2;
10 Q – K2, P – KR4; *11* Q – K5, P – KB3!; *12* N×P+, K – B2
wins—Steinitz), Q – K2; *10* N – B6+, K – Q1; *11* B×P+, K×B;
12 N – Q5+, K – Q1; *13* N×Q, B×N and Black should win.
Morphy–Anderssen, Paris 1858.)

6 . . .	P – Q3
7 N – Q3	N×P
8 B×P	B – N2

FISCHER

Position after 8 . . .
B – N2

SPASSKY

9 N – B3?   . . .

After this White has no compensation for the Pawn. Better is
9 P – B3, Q – K2; *10* Q – K2, B – B4. At least White keeps a grip
on his KB4—for what that's worth.

9 . . .	N×N
10 P×N	P – QB4

Immediately nibbling at White's center. Keres gives *10* . . .
O – O first.

11 B – K2   . . .

On *11* Q – K2+, B – K3 (*12* P – Q5?, B×P+).

11 . . .	P×P
12 O – O	N – B3

It doesn't pay to be greedy with *12* . . . P – KR4. After *13* B – N5, P – B3; *14* B – B1 followed by N – B4 Black's K-side is all messed up.

13	B×NP	O – O
14	B×B	R×B
15	Q – N4	P – B4

Winning a second Pawn, but creating a K-side weakness. Simply *15* . . . K – R1 is stronger.

16	Q – N3	P×P
17	QR – K1	. . .

Black snatches the initiative after *17* B × P, R – B3; *18* B – B4, R – N3.

17 . . .		K – R1

Also good is *17* . . . Q – Q2; *18* B×P, KR – K1 and if *19* N – B5, Q – KB2 (KMOCH).

18	K – R1 ?	. . .

More accurate is *18* B×P, R – B3 (if *18* . . . R – KN1; *19* N – K5!); *19* B – K5, N×B; *20* N×N with a little play left for White.

18 . . .		R – KN1

On *18* . . . P – Q4; *19* N – B5 creates problems.

19	B×P	B – B1 !

The key! On *19* . . . B – Q5; *20* Q – R2, R – N5; *21* B – K5+! (to prevent Black from doubling Rooks on the KN-file), K – N1 (if *21* . . . B×B; *22* N×B, R×P?; *23* N – B7+); *22* B – N3 holds.

20	B – K5+	N×B
21	Q×N+	R – N2 !

Now White's KRP must fall.

22	R×P	. . .

What else? On *22* Q×KBP (not *22* R – B4?, B – Q3 or *22* Q – B4?, R – N5), Q×P+ ; *23* K – N1, Q – N5 forces a favorable exchange of Queens (if *24* Q – B2, B – Q3 produces a strong attack).

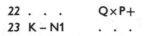

22 . . .	Q × P +
23 K – N1	. . .

FISCHER

Position after 23 K – N1

SPASSKY

23 . . .	Q – N5 ?

Drifting. Not realizing the danger, I thought Black could whip up an attack along the KN-file. But correct is *23* . . . Q – N6!; *24* Q × Q (if *24* Q – K2, B – Q3), R × Q (threatening . . . R × N followed by . . . P – B7) and White, a Pawn down, has a tough ending to hold—as Spassky pointed out in our post-mortem analysis.

24 R – B2	B – K2

Threatening . . . B – R5.

25 R – K4	Q – N4

I started to feel uncomfortable, but little did I imagine that Black's game would collapse in four short moves! I should have taken a draw by repetition with *25* . . . Q – Q8+ ; *26* R – K1, Q – N5; *27* R – K4, Q – Q8+, etc. And if *28* K – R2, R – B3; *29* Q – N8+, R – N1; *30* Q – K5+, R – N2.

26 Q – Q4!	. . .

This powerful centralization completely paralyzes Black.

26 . . .	R – KB1 ?

Overlooking White's real threat. I was worried about N – K5, not realizing it could be met successfully with . . . B – B4. The right defense is *26 . . . B – B1!*; *27* Q × RP (if *27* N – K5, B – B4; *28* N – B7+, K – N1; *29* N × Q, B × Q; *30* R × B, R × N), B – Q3=.

27 R – K5!   . . .

I had reckoned on *27* N – K5?, R × R; *28* Q × R, B – B4!; *29* Q × B, Q × P mate.

FISCHER

Position after 27 R – K5

SPASSKY

Incredibly, Black must lose a piece. While trying to figure out what was going on in Spassky's head, I blundered and lost the game!

27 . . .   **R – Q1**

Trying to squirm out! The Queen has no shelter. On *27 . . . Q – N3; 28* R × B wins. Or *27 . . . Q – R5; 28* R × R+. Or *27 . . . B – B3; 28* Q – Q6!

28 Q – K4   **Q – R5**

I knew I was losing a piece, but just couldn't believe it. I had to play one more move to see if it was really true!

29 R – B4   **Black resigns**

On *29 . . . Q – N6; 30* R × B is most efficient.

19 Gudmundsson [Iceland] - Fischer

REYKJAVIK 1960

GRUENFELD DEFENSE

A long voyage home

> Illustrating, rather subtly, how a weaker player may be lured
> to his own destruction, Fischer entices his opponent to abandon
> his passive though solid attempts to settle for a draw. Wrongly
> convinced that he holds an advantage, Gudmundsson,
> with 16 P – K4, gives Fischer the opportunity to launch a
> long, unclear sacrificial combination. Gudmundsson makes
> matters unexpectedly easy with 24 R – N1, but the analysis
> accompanying the text shows the sacrifice to be sound in all
> variations. Fischer's performance from here on is typical in its
> clarity and forcefulness.

1	P – Q4	N – KB3
2	N – KB3	. . .

Solid but passive.

2	. . .	P – Q4
3	P – K3	. . .

Voluntarily locking in the Bishop lacks energy and reduces White's options.

3	. . .	P – KN3
4	P – B4	. . .

4 P – B3 would lead to the Colle System.

4	. . .	B – N2
5	N – B3	O – O
6	Q – N3	. . .

After 6 B – K2, P – B4! it's difficult for White to equalize:
(a) 7 O – O?, BP × P; 8 KN × P, N – B3; 9 P × P, N × P; 10 N/3 × N,
Q × N; 11 B – B3, Q – B5; 12 N × N, P × N and Black stands better.

Aaron–Gligorich, Stockholm 1962. (b) 7 P × QP, N × P; 8 Q – N3, N × N; 9 P × N, Q – B2; 10 O – O, P – N3; 11 P – QR4, N – B3 again Black's better. Goglidze–Botvinnik, Moscow 1935. (c) 7 P × BP, Q – R4; 8 P × P (if 8 O – O, P × P; 9 B × P, Q × BP), N × P; 9 Q × N, B × N+; 10 B – Q2 (after 10 K – B1, B – N2; 11 B – Q2, Q – B2 Black regains his Pawn at will, with a strong attack), R – Q1!; 11 B × B, Q × B+; 12 P × Q, R × Q with the superior ending (if 13 R – Q1, R × P; 14 R – Q8+, K – N2; 15 O – O, N – B3; 16 R – K8, P – N3).

6 . . .		P – K3

Another good build-up is 6 . . . P – B3 followed by . . . P – K3, . . . P – N3, . . . B – N2, . . . QN – Q2, . . . P – QB4, etc.

7	B – K2	N – B3
8	Q – B2	. . .

Probably best (Black threatened . . . N – QR4 winning the two Bishops). As Evans pointed out in *Trophy Chess* (in an analogous position): "8 P × P, P × P permits Black to solve the problem of his QB. He has the semi-open K-file and good squares for his pieces It is now White who must fight for equality!"

8	. . .	P × P
9	B × P	P – K4!
10	P × P	. . .

Also good is 10 N × P (if 10 P – Q5?, N – QR4), N × N; 11 P × N, N – N5; 12 P – K6! (not 12 P – B4?, N × KP!; 13 P × N?, Q – R5+; 14 P – N3, Q × B, etc.), B × P; 13 B × B, P × B; 14 O – O=.

10 . . .		N – KN5

FISCHER

Position after 10 . . .
N – KN5

GUDMUNDSSON

                              11 O–O   . . .

Stronger is *11* P – K6!, B×P; *12* B×B, P×B; *13* O – O (*13* Q – K4?, QN – K4!; *14* N×N?, N×BP!; *15* Q – QB4, B×N; *16* Q×P+, R – B2; *17* Q×B, N – Q6+ wins), and Black seems to have nothing better than a draw by perpetual after *13* . . . R×N; *14* P×R, Q – R5; *15* P×N, Q×NP+; *16* K – R1, Q – B6+, etc.

11 . . .	QN×P
12 N×N	N×N
13 B – K2	P – QB3

The chances are now equal.

                              14 P – B4   . . .

Apparently stronger is *14* P – K4 but after Q – R5!; *15* P – KR3 (if *15* P – B4, N – N5), P – KN4!; *16* P – B4 (or *16* N – Q1, P – KB4; *17* P – B4, N – N3; *18* P×NP, P – B5!), P×P, *17* B×P (on *17* R×P, Q – N6), K – R1 gives Black good prospects along the ventilated KN file.

14 . . .	N – N5!
15 P – KR3	B – B4!

White was doubtlessly expecting *15* . . . N – B3; *16* P – K4 with an ideal center.

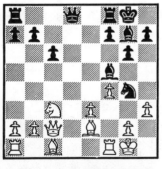

FISCHER

Position after 15 . . .
B – B4

GUDMUNDSSON

                              16 P – K4?   . . .

Provoking a powerful combination.

White should abandon his hopes in the center and settle for *16* Q – N3, N – B3; *17* Q×P, N – K5!; *18* Q×BP, R – B1; *19* Q – R6, N×N; *20* P×N, B×BP; *21* B – R3, B×R; *22* B×R,

B – Q5!; *23* P × B, Q × P+; *24* K – R1, K × B. Black is better, but White has excellent drawing chances.

16	. . .	Q – Q5+
17	K – R1	N – B7+
18	R × N	. . .

All forced. Not *18* K – R2, N × KP.

18	. . .	Q × R
19	P × B	B × N!

This clean-cut line reduces White's options. Inexact would be *19* . . . KR – K1; *20* N – K4!, Q – K8+; *21* K – R2, P × P (if *21* . . . B – Q5; *22* B – K3!, Q × R; *23* B × B); *22* N – N3 and if B – Q5?; *23* B – K3!

20	P × B	QR – K1
21	B – Q3	R – K8+
22	K – R2	Q – N8+
23	K – N3	KR – K1

Just as complicated is *23* . . . P × P; *24* B × P, KR – K1; *25* B × P+, K – N2; *26* Q – B5, etc.

FISCHER

Position after 23 . . .
KR – K1

GUDMUNDSSON

24 R – N1?   . . .

Also bad is *24* Q – B2, R/1 – K6+!; *25* B × R, R × B+; *26* Q × R, Q × Q+.

The toughest defense is *24* P × P!, RP × P and now:

A] *25* B × P?, R/8 – K7! (not *25* . . . R/1 – K7; *26* B × P+, K – R1; *27* Q – B5, R × P+; *28* K – R4, Q – B7+; *29* K – R5, Q – B6+; *30* K – R6! and White wins!); *26* B × P+, K – R1; *27* Q – B5, R × P+; *28* K – R4, Q – K8+; *29* K – R5, K – N2!

(threatening . . . R – R1+); *30* B×R, Q×B+; *31* K – R4, Q – Q1+; *32* Q – N5+, R×Q; *33* P×R, Q – Q8 with an easy win.

B] *25* R – N1, R/1 – K6+!; *26* B×R (if *26* K – N4, Q – R7; *27* B×R leads to the same), R×B+; *27* K – N4 (not *27* K – R4?, Q – R7; *28* Q – B2, R×P+!), Q – R7; *28* Q – B2 (if *28* B×P, Q – N6+; *29* K – R5, Q×BP!; *30* B – B5, R – N6!; *31* B – N4, K – N2; *32* Q – B1 [if *32* K – R4, R×B+; *33* P×R, Q – R7+ mates], R – K6 wins), R×B (if *28* . . . R×P!?; *29* B×P!, P×B; *30* R – KR1! holds); *29* R – N2! (*29* R×P loses to R×RP!; *30* R – N8+, K – R2; *31* P – B5, R – R3!), R×BP; *30* R – Q2 and White has drawing chances even though a Pawn behind.

24 . . .   P×P

Threatening either . . . K – R1 or . . . R/1 – K3 with devastating check to follow on the KN-file.

25 B – Q2   . . .

No better is *25* B×P, R/8 – K7; *26* B×P+, K – R1; *27* Q – B5, R×P+; *28* K – R4, R – N2 (among others) wins.

25 . . .   R×R
26 Q×R   Q×Q
27 B×Q   R – K7

This is what Gudmundsson overlooked. If now *28* B – B1, R – K8 picks off one of the Bishops. So . . .

White resigns

FISCHER

Final Position after 27 . . . R – K7

GUDMUNDSSON

20 Fischer - Euwe *[Holland]*

LEIPZIG OLYMPIC 1960

CARO-KANN DEFENSE

Theoretical scuffle

Former world champion, Dr. Max Euwe had for decades been considered one of the world's leading authorities on opening theory. His Chess Archives *ranks with* Modern Chess Openings *as an indispensable source of reference. It is no small wonder, then, when he selects a risky but playable variation. Fischer, however, just a little better versed in its intricacies, introduces a nuance on move 15 which ruffles his opponent no end.*

Fischer's method of dispatching his veteran adversary—on home grounds, as it were—is deceptively simple. After a mere eighteen moves the opening has become an ending and the duel is over. Euwe fights on, but to no avail.

1	P – K4	P – QB3
2	P – Q4	P – Q4
3	P×P	P×P
4	P – QB4	. . .

At that time I was convinced the Panov–Botvinnik attack was the sharpest.

4	. . .	N – KB3
5	N – QB3	N – B3

In our game at Buenos Aires 1960, Ivkov played *5 . . . P – K3; 6* N – B3, B – K2; *7* P – B5, O – O; *8* B – Q3, P – QN3; *9* P – QN4, P×P (better is *9 . . . P – QR4; 10* N – QR4, KN – Q2!); *10* NP×P, N – B3; *11* O – O, B – Q2; *12* P – KR3, N – K1; *13* B – KB4 with a bind.

6	N – B3	. . .

On Botvinnik's old *6* B – N5, P – K3! (*6* . . . P×P?; *7* P – Q5, N – K4; *8* Q – Q4 is strong); *7* P×P, P×P; *8* B×N, Q×B; *9* N×P, Q – Q1; *10* N – QB3 (if *10* B – B4, B – K3; *11* Q – K2?, P – QN4!), Q×P; *11* Q×Q, N×Q; *12* O – O – O, B – QB4; *13* N – R4, N – K3=.

| | 6 . . . | B – N5!? |

Risky but playable. Safer is *6* . . . P – K3.

7	P×P	KN×P
8	Q – N3	B×N
9	P×B	P – K3

On *9* . . . N/4 – N5!?; *10* B – K3, N×QP; *11* B×N, Q×B; *12* B – N5+, N – B3; *13* O – O White gets a strong attack. (Evans–Henin, Las Vegas Open 1965.)

10	Q×P	N×P
11	B – N5+	N×B
12	Q – B6+	K – K2
13	Q×QN	N×N

An alternative is *13* . . . Q – Q2; *14* N×N+, P ×N (*14* . . . Q×N; *15* Q×Q, P×Q; *16* O – O gives White good play against Black's isolated QP and QRP); *15* Q – N4+ (*15* Q – K2+, K – B3; *16* P – KR4 wins, according to Evans), K – K1; *16* Q – Q4 with a clear advantage.

| 14 | P×N | Q – Q2 |

After *14* . . . Q – Q4; *15* Q×Q, P×Q; *16* R – QN1 gives White a slight edge.

EUWE

Position after 14 . . . Q – Q2

FISCHER

15 R – QN1!   . . .

The innovation. Months before the game I had showed this line to Benko and he suggested this innocent-looking move. Upon looking deeper I found that, horrible as White's Pawn structure may be, Black can't exploit it because he'll be unable to develop his K-side normally. It's the little quirks like this that could make life difficult for a chess machine.

15 . . .   R – Q1?

Also difficult is *15* . . . Q × Q; *16* R × Q, K – Q3!; *17* R – N7, P – B3; *18* K – K2, K – B3; *19* R – B7, P – QR4; *20* B – K3 with an enduring pull.

16 B – K3   Q × Q
17 R × Q   R – Q2
18 K – K2   . . .

18 R – QR5 is unnecessary. White can win the QRP at his leisure.

18 . . .   P – B3
19 R – Q1!   . . .

To swap Black's only active piece.

19 . . .   R × R
20 K × R   K – Q2
21 R – N8!   . . .

21 B × P, B – Q3; *22* R – N7+, K – B3; *23* R × P, B × P would be hard to win. Now the threat is *22* B – B5.

EUWE

Position after 21 R – N8

FISCHER

21 . . .   K – B3
22 B × P   P – N4

Striving to untangle the K-side.

23	P – QR4	B – N2
24	R – N6+	K – Q4
25	R – N7	B – B1
26	R – N8	. . .

Still trying to decide how to squeeze the most out of it.

26	. . .	B – N2
27	R – N5+	K – B3
28	R – N6+	K – Q4
29	P – R5	P – B4
30	B – N8!	R – QB1
31	P – R6	R × P
32	R – N5+	. . .

EUWE

Position after 32 R – N5+

FISCHER

32	. . .	K – B5

After the game Euwe showed me a cute trap he might have played for—and almost fainted when I fell into it! The line arises after *32 . . . K – B3; 33 R – R5, B – Q5* and he asked, "What do you do now?" I looked a few seconds and played *34 B – K5?* whereupon he uncorked *R – B4!* which leads to a draw. Upon reconsideration, however, simply *34 K – K2* wins. It's these tidbits that you remember best.

33	R – N7	B – Q5
34	R – B7+	K – Q6
35	R × R+	K × R
36	B – K5	Black resigns

He can't stop the QRP.

2 I Letelier *[Chile]* - Fischer

LEIPZIG OLYMPIC 1960

KING'S INDIAN DEFENSE

A Queen for the King

Letelier transgresses opening principles by neglecting his development in order to win material. Pugnaciously, he mixes it up with the unorthodox 5 P – K5 and proceeds to snatch Pawns. But his judgment proves to be unwise.

Striking from behind the lines, Fischer causes the over-extended White center to crumble. Letelier, busily engaged on a material hunt, neglects to safeguard his rear, leaving his King marooned in the center. Fischer rapidly encircles the hapless monarch and, with a startling Queen sacrifice, induces abdication.

1	P – Q4	N – KB3
2	P – QB4	P – KN3
3	N – QB3	B – N2
4	P – K4	O – O
5	P – K5	. . .

Weak. Letelier snapped at the chance to take me "out of the book," but this premature advance leaves White with all the responsibility of holding his overextended center Pawns.

5	. . .	N – K1
6	P – B4	P – Q3

Weaker is *6* . . . P – QB4; *7* P × P, Q – R4; *8* B – K3, P – B3?; *9* N – B3, P × P; *10* P × P, N – QB3; *11* B – K2, N – B2; *12* O – O, N – K3; *13* N – Q5, Q – Q1; *14* Q – Q2, etc. (Koralev-Roshal, USSR 1962.)

7	B – K3	. . .

7 N – B3 is safer, though White can no longer lay claim to any kind of initiative. My game with Schoene in the US Junior Championship 1957 continued: *7. . .* P×P; *8* BP×P (better is QP×P), B – N5; *9* B – K2, P – QB4; *10* B – B4, P×P; *11* Q×P, N – QB3; *12* Q×Q, R×Q soon winning a Pawn.

7 . . .   P – QB4!

"Now the artificially constructed White center begins to crumble." (LOMBARDY.)

8 P×BP   N – QB3

"Black rapidly develops his pieces while White nurtures his own dreams with ill-gotten gains." (LOMBARDY.)

9 BP×P   . . .

White tries to compensate for his lack of development by continuing to snatch material. Instead he should be seeking to return the Pawn in the least damaging way (by keeping the lines closed). Better is *9* N – B3, B – N5; *10* B – K2.

9 . . .   P×P
10 N – K4   . . .

"More realistic would have been *10* N – B3." (LOMBARDY.) I intended *10 . . .* B – N5. After the text White no longer has time to castle.

10 . . .   B – B4!

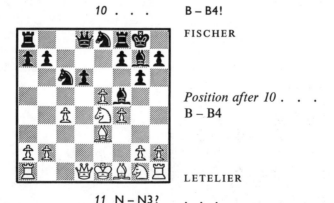

FISCHER

Position after 10 . . .
B – B4

LETELIER

11 N – N3?   . . .

A better chance is *11* N×P, N×N; *12* Q×N, Q×Q; *13* P×Q, B×P; *14* R – Q1, N – N5! (threatening . . . B – B7); *15* K – B2 (if *15* N – K2, B – B7; *16* R – Q2, N – Q6+), N×P; *16* N – K2 (if *16* R – Q2?, N – B6!), P – QR4. Black is better but White may have drawing resources.

11 . . .   B – K3

I also considered *11* . . . Q – B2; *12* N × B, P × B. White's center must collapse.

12 N – B3   . . .

By now White is more than willing to return the Pawn in order to catch up in development.

12 . . .   Q – B2

Also playable is *12* . . . P × P; *13* Q × Q, R × Q; *14* B – B5, P × P. But I wanted to fracture him in the middle game.

13 Q – N1   . . .

Continuing his "attack." On *13* B – K2, P × P; *14* B – B5, Q – R4+; *15* P – N4, N × P; *16* B × R, K × B!; *17* O – O, P × P; *18* N – K4, B – B4 is overwhelming. And on *13* Q – B2 (in order to prepare O – O – O), P × P; *14* P – B5, P × P; *15* N × BP, N – N5; *16* Q – N3 (if *16* Q – N1, B × N; *17* Q × B, N – Q3; *18* Q – N1, N × BP; *19* N – N5, P – B4; *20* N – K6, Q – B3; *21* B × N, Q × B; *22* N × R, R × N with a winning attack), B × N; *17* Q × N, N – B3! is strong. If *18* Q – B5, Q – N1 (threatening . . . N – N5).

13 . . .   P × P
14 P – KB5   P – K5!

"An unexpected shot that sends White spinning." (LOMBARDY.)

FISCHER

Position after 14 . . .
P – K5

LETELIER

15 P × B   . . .

On *15* Q × P, P × P!; *16* N × P? (if *16* Q – R4, B × NP), Q – R4+ wins a piece.

15	. . .	P × N
16	P × P	P – B4!

"The Pawn on K6 can be ignored in favor of the attack." (LOMBARDY.) The threat is . . . P – B5.

17	P – B4	N – B3
18	B – K2	KR – K1
19	K – B2	R × P

Finally Black regains the Pawn with interest.

20	R – K1	QR – K1
21	B – B3	. . .

"Anyone interested in sui-mate (helpmate) problems?" (LOM-BARDY.)

21	. . .	R × B!
22	R × R	R × R
23	K × R	Q × P+!

White resigns

FISCHER

Final Position after
23 . . . Q × P+

LETELIER

On *24* K × Q, B – R3 mate! Or *24* K – B2, N – N5+; *25* K – N2, N – K6+; *26* K – B2, N – Q5; *27* Q – R1, N – N5+; *28* K – B1, N × B with a winning attack.

22 Szabo [Hungary] - Fischer

LEIPZIG OLYMPIC 1960

KING'S INDIAN DEFENSE

Bad judgment

Once a contender for the title, Szabo's performances nowadays are spotty and unpredictable. Here, with breathtaking bluntness, he attempts to wipe Fischer from the board. In the process he leaves himself wide open on the dark squares. Fischer promptly invades on the Q-side, by means of a curious Queen maneuver, while Szabo, preoccupied with his own K-side attack, fails to realize the danger in time. 21 . . . R – K6! is the blow that ends all effective resistance. Rather than fight on against hopeless odds, Szabo resigns three moves later.

1	P – Q4	N – KB3
2	P – QB4	P – KN3
3	N – QB3	B – N2
4	P – K4	O – O
5	B – N5	. . .

For 5 P – K5 see game 21. For 5 N – B3 see games 7, 28 and 30.

5	. . .	P – Q3

After 5 . . . P – KR3; 6 B – K3! allows White to set up a Saemisch formation (6 . . . P – Q3; 7 P – B3) where the inevitable Q – Q2 will be more effective than usual.

6	Q – Q2	. . .

Better is simply 6 B – K2, P – B4; 7 P – Q5, P – K3; 8 N – B3, P – KR3; 9 B – R4, P×P; 10 BP×P, P – KN4; 11 B – N3, N – R4 (not 11 . . . P – N4?; 12 N – Q2!) with a double-edged struggle. Larsen–Fischer, Santa Monica 1966.

6	. . .	P – B4!
7	P – Q5	. . .

On *7* N – B3 (*7* P×P, P×P; *8* Q×Q, R×Q; *9* P – K5, N – N5; *10* P – B4, P – B3 is better for Black), P×P; *8* N×P, N – B3=.

7 . . .   P – K3
8 B – Q3   . . .

8 P×P, B×P; *9* N – B3, N – B3; *10* B – K2, B – N5!; *11* O – O, R – K1; *12* Q – B4, B×N; *13* B×B, N – Q5; *14* QR – Q1, R – K4 leads to equality. (Evans–Gligorich, Dallas 1957.)

8 . . .   P×P

FISHER

Position after 8 . . .
P×P

SZABO

White has no advantageous way to recapture.

9 N×P   . . .

A] *9* KP×P, QN – Q2;   *10* P – B4 (to stop . . . N – K4), P – KR3; *11* B – R4, R – K1+; *12* KN – K2, N – K5!; *13* B×Q, N×Q; *14* B – B7, B×N; *15* P×B, N – K5; *16* B×N, R×B; *17* B×P, N – N3; *18* K – B2, B – N5! with a promising ending.

B] *9* BP×P, P – QR3!; *10* P – B4 (if *10* P – QR4, Q – R4 threatening . . . P – N4), P – KR3; *11* B – R4, N×KP!; *12* B×Q, N×Q; *13* B – B7, B×N; *14* P×B, N – K5!; *15* B×N, R – K1, etc.

In this opening variation Black must play sharply. White has a space advantage, but he temporarily lags in development.

9 . . .   B – K3
10 N – K2   B×N

Releasing the tension and, by forcing White to recapture with a Pawn, eliminating the backward QP on an open file.

11 KP×B   . . .

On *11* BP × B, P – B5!; *12* B – B2, QN – Q2; *13* O – O, N – B4;
14 N – B3, P – N4!

11 . . .	QN – Q2
12 O – O	. . .

Not *12* P – B4, Q – K1!; *13* Q – B2? (to stop . . . N – K5),
N – N5! invading on the weak dark squares (notably K6).

12 . . .	N – K4

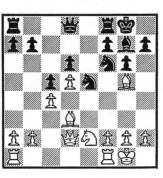

FISCHER

Position after 12 . . .
N – K4

SZABO

13 P – B4?	. . .

After *13* N – B3 the game is even.

This lemon, weakening White's K3 and K4, came as a pleasant
surprise. Szabo misjudges White's attacking prospects.

13 . . .	N × B
14 Q × N	P – KR3
15 B – R4	R – K1
16 QR – K1	. . .

16 N – B3 is the best of a bad choice, though Q – N3! (threatening . . . N – N5) creates problems. If *17* P – KR3, N – R4!
increases the pressure on White's game.

16 . . .	Q – N3!
17 B × N	. . .

On *13* P – QN3, N – K5! gives Black a nice bind.

17 . . .	B × B
18 P – B5	P – N4
19 P – QN3	Q – R4!

A nettlesome maneuver!

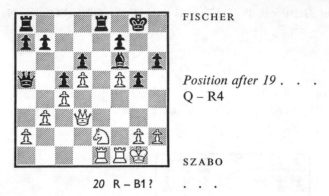

FISCHER

Position after 19 . . .
Q – R4

SZABO

         20   R – B1?   . . .

20 P – QR4 loses to B – Q5+; *21* K – R1 (not *21* N × B?, R × R), R – K6; *22* Q – Q1, QR – K1 and the pin on the K-file is decisive. The best defense is *20* Q – N1!

20 . . .	Q × P
21 R – QB2	R – K6!
22 Q × R	Q × R
23 K – R1	P – QR4
24 P – R4	P – R5
White resigns	

White's Pawns fall like ripe apples. I'll never forget the disgusted look on Szabo's face as he took his King and just sort of shoved it gently to the center of the board, indicating his intention to resign.

23 Fischer - Tal [U.S.S.R.]

LEIPZIG OLYMPIC 1960

FRENCH DEFENSE

No holds barred

Their first encounter after Tal became world champion proves
to be an old-fashioned slugfest. Typically aggressive, Fischer
rapidly achieves a winning bind, but unwisely permits Tal to
touch off "a dazzling array of fireworks" with 14 . . .
N × KP. The struggle seesaws for seven moves before settling in
a perpetual check.

The quality of this confrontation left little doubt that, in
time, Fischer would yet take Tal's measure. He did just that
less than a year later, after Tal had lost his return match
with Botvinnik (Game 32). Reading Tal's palm, Fischer
predicted: "The next world champion will be . . .
Bobby Fischer!"

1	P – K4	P – K3
2	P – Q4	P – Q4
3	N – QB3	B – N5
4	P – K5	P – QB4
5	P – QR3	B – R4

A dubious alternative to 5 . . . B × N+ (see game 24).

6	P – QN4!	. . .

Alekhine's recommendation.

6	. . .	P × QP

6 . . . P × NP; 7 N – N5 yields a potent attack.

7	Q – N4	N – K2

On 7 . . . K – B1; 8 P × B, P × N; 9 P – QR4! followed by
10 B – R3+ is strong. (LILIENTHAL and ZAGORYANSKY)

                    8 P×B   . . .

Also good is *8* N – N5.

                    8 . . .   P×N
                    9 Q×NP   R – N1
                    10 Q×P   QN – B3

On *10* . . . N – Q2; *11* N – B3, Q – B2; *12* B – QN5, P – R3;
13 B×N+, B×B; *14* O – O, P – Q5!? (*Archives*); *15* N×P, Q×
KP; *16* Q – Q3 is better for White.

                    11 N – B3   . . .

11 P – B4 bolsters the center but shuts in the QB and weakens
the dark squares.

                    11 . . .   Q – B2

On *11* . . . Q×P; *12* N – N5!, R – B1; *13* P – B4 (followed
by the advance of the KRP) ties Black up.

                    12 B – QN5!   . . .

Harmoniously pursuing development without losing time. Also
playable is *12* B – KB4, B – Q2; *13* B – K2, O – O – O; *14* Q – Q3,
Q×RP;   *15* O – O, R – N5;   *16* B – N3. (Unzicker–Duckstein,
Zurich 1959.)

                    12 . . .   B – Q2

Not *12* . . . R×P; *13* K – B1!, R – KN1; *14* R – KN1!, R×
R+; *15* K×R and Black's King remains hemmed in the center
while White merely marches his KRP to victory.

                    13 O – O   . . .

Unsound is *13* B×N?, B×B; *14* O – O, P – Q5!; *15* N – N5,
Q×KP; *16* Q×P+, K – Q2 with advantage.

                    13 . . .   O – O – O

After the game Petrosian suggested *13* . . . N×KP but *14*
N×N, Q×N; *15* B×B+, K×B; *16* Q – Q3! keeps White on top
(if *16* . . . Q – K5?; *17* Q×Q, P×Q; *18* P – B3! wins a Pawn).

                    14 B – N5?   . . .

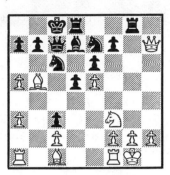

TAL

Position after 13 . . .
O – O – O

FISCHER

I simply underestimated the force of Tal's reply.

Correct is *14* B × N!, B × B   (if   *14 . . .* Q × B;   *15* B – N5,
P – Q5; *16* P – KR4! or *14 . . .* N × B; *15* R – K1 followed by
B – N5 and P – KR4 with a decisive bind); *15* Q × P, P – Q5 (unsound is *15 . . .* R × P+!?; *16* K × R, P – Q5; *17* K – N1,
R – N1+; *18* N – N5); *16* Q × P+, B – Q2 (*16 . . .* K – N1;
17 N – N5 is hopeless); *17* Q × N, R × P+; *18* K × R, B – R6+;
19 K × B, Q × Q; *20* B – N5 and White soon consolidates to
victory.

> *14 . . .*   N × KP!

Setting off a dazzling array of fireworks! I thought Tal was
merely trying to confuse the issue.

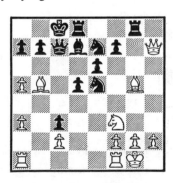

TAL

Position after 14 . . .
N × KP

FISCHER

> *15* N × N   . . .

Originally I'd intended *15* B × B+ but saw that after R × B; *16*
N × N (if *16* B × N, N × N+; *17* K – R1, Q × P+!), Q × N; *17*
B × N, R – R1! Black regains his piece with greater activity: e.g.,

18 QR – K1, R × Q; *19* R × Q, R × B and the compact center
Pawns far outweigh White's passed KRP.

Not playable is *15* B × N?, N × N+ ; *16* K – R1, R – R1!

> *15* . . .   B × B

Playing for a win. After *15* . . . Q × N; *16* B × N, R – R1; *17*
KR – K1 (*17* QR – K1? loses to Q – N1!), Q × R+ ; *18* R × Q,
R × Q; *19* B × R, K × B (weak is *19* . . . B × B; *20* B – B6!); *20*
B × B, K × B; *21* R – K3! bails White out.

> *16* N × P   . . .

White could still have kept some tension with *16* B × N, Q × B
(if *16* . . . Q × N?; *17* KR – K1); *17* KR – K1, etc.

> *16* . . .   B × R!

16 . . . QR – B1; *17* KR – N1, B – B3; *18* N – Q6+ !, Q × N;
19 Q × N is about equal.

> *17* N × R   R × B
> *18* N × KP   R × P+ !

TAL

Position after 18 . . .
R × P+

FISCHER

> *19* K – R1 !   . . .

The saving move. Not *19* K × B?, R × P!; *20* Q – B7 (if *20* N × Q,
R × Q wins a piece), R – R8+ ! produces a winning attack from
nowhere!

> *19* . . .   Q – K4

On *19* . . . Q – QB5; *20* Q × N, R – N1; *21* N – B4! holds
nicely (if *21* . . . Q × N?; *22* Q – K6+, K – B2; *23* Q × R).

20 R×B   Q×N

On *20 . . . R – N3; 21* Q×N, R×N; *22* Q – B8+, R – K1; *23* Q – B3 is in White's favor.

21 K×R   Q – N5+

Drawn

Black has a perpetual check.

TAL

Final Position after 21 . . . Q – N5+

FISCHER

24 Fischer - Darga *[W. Germany]*

WEST BERLIN 1960

FRENCH DEFENSE

Asking for trouble

The Winawer Variation has given Fischer consistent trouble. He has had the utmost difficulty cracking Black's tortoise-like shell; even his successes are unconvincing. Maintaining the same line of attack year after year has provided his opponents with ample opportunity to sharpen their defenses.

Darga's 12 . . . P – B3 obliges Fischer, in order to get something out of the opening, to speculate on a Pawn sacrifice (13 B – R3!?). Though Darga's reaction may not be ideal, he proceeds sensibly and equalizes. Underestimating Fischer's chances, however, he falls prey to a scintillating mid-game attack. And so, once again, by virtue of his native ability, Fischer avoids the retribution that is the usual price for failing to secure an advantage in the opening.

1	P – K4	P – K3
2	P – Q4	P – Q4
3	N – QB3	B – N5
4	P – K5	P – QB4
5	P – QR3	B × N+

For 5 . . . B – R4 see game 23.

6	P × B	N – K2
7	P – QR4	. . .

Smyslov's favorite, largely responsible for Botvinnik's giving up the Winawer Variation. Sharper is 7 Q – N4. I felt that Black's carapace could be cracked only by positional means, but my results have been somewhat disheartening.

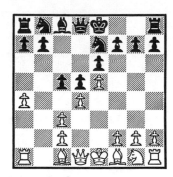

DARGA

Position after 7 P – QR4

FISCHER

7 . . .   Q – B2

More usual is *7 . . . QN – B3; 8 N – B3, Q – R4; 9 Q – Q2* (on *9 B – Q2, B – Q2; 10 B – K2, P – B5; 11 P – KR4!?, P – B3; 12 P – R5, P×P; 13 P – R6, P×RP; 14 N×P, N×N; 15 P×N, O – O – O; 16 R×P, N – N3* Black's better. Fischer–Padevsky, Varna 1962), *B – Q2; 10 B – Q3* and now Black has two main continuations:

A] *10 . . . P – B5; 11 B – K2, P – B3; 12 B – R3, O – O – O* (if *12 . . . N – N3; 13 O – O, O – O – O; 14 B – Q6* White keeps the edge. Fischer–Uhlmann, Buenos Aires 1960); *13 O – O, N – B4; 14 KR – K1, B – K1; 15 P – N4!?, N/4 – K2; 16 B – B1, B – Q2=.* (Fischer–Weinstein, US Championship 1960–1.)

B] *10 . . . P – B3!; 11 O – O, P×P; 12 N×P* (no better is *12 P×P* as Smyslov tried against Uhlmann at Havana, 1964), *N×N; 13 P×N, O – O; 14 P – QB4, Q×Q; 15 B×Q, B – B3=.* (Fischer–Uhlmann, Stockholm 1962.)

I may yet be forced to admit that the Winawer is sound. But I doubt it! The defense is anti-positional and weakens the K-side.

8 N – B3   P – QN3

The idea is to eliminate the bad Bishop with *. . . B – R3.* An alternative is *8 . . . B – Q2; 9 B – Q3, QN – B3.*

9 B – N5+!   B – Q2

More radical is *8 . . . K – B1!?; 9 B – Q3, B – R3.*

On *9 . . . KN – B3* (after *9 . . . QN – B3* Black can no longer enforce *. . . B – R3); 10 O – O, B – R3; 11 N – N5, P – R3; 12 N – R3* is in White's favor.

10 B – Q3   . . .

After *10* O – O, B × B; *11* P × B, P – QR4; *12* N – N5, P – R3;
13 N – R3, N – Q2; *14* N – B4, O – O! (Ivkov–R. Byrne, Sousse
1967) Black has no problems.

10 . . .   QN – B3

Black has gained a tempo, but whether his Pawn belongs on
QN3 is moot.

11 O – O   P – B5

Not *11 . . .* O – O?; *12* B × P+!, K × B; *13* N – N5+, etc.

12 B – K2   P – B3
13 B – R3!?   . . .

Keeping tension in the center at the cost of a Pawn. *13* R – K1
is solid but less aggressive. I tried this same Pawn sac against
Mednis in the 1962–3 US Championship with the slight but significant difference that Black's QNP was still on N2. The sac may well
have been unsound in that game.

13 . . .   P × P

Mednis declined and castled, but after *14* R – K1! got a cramped
game (*14 . . .* P × P is answered by *15* N × P! keeping the K-file
open).

14 P × P   . . .

White doesn't have anything to show after *14* N × P, N × N;
15 P × N, Q × P; *16* R – K1, Q × P; *17* B – R5+, P – N3; *18* B –
N4 (if *18* B × N, K × B; *19* Q × P?, Q × R! wins), Q – B3, etc.

14 . . .   N × P

After *14 . . .* O – O; *15* N – Q4! is followed by P – B4 and
White has not been inveigled into misplacing his Rook on K1.

15 R – K1   . . .

The threat is *16* N × N, Q × N; *17* B – R5+.

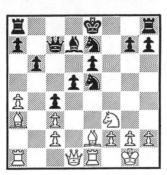

DARGA

Position after 15 R – K1

FISCHER

15 . . .   N/2 – B3

Black has a seeming multiplicity of defenses:

A] 15 . . . N/4 – B3; *16* N – N5!, O – O! (if *16* . . . P – KR3; *17* B – R5+, P – N3; *18* N × P, B × N; *19* R × B, P × B; *20* Q × P!, R – Q1; *21* Q × P+, K – Q2; *22* QR – K1 regains the piece); *17* B – KN4, Q – B5! (if *17* . . . P – K4; *18* B – K6+, K – R1; *19* B × P!); *18* B × P+! (if *18* N × KP, Q × BP+; *19* K – R1, R – B2!), B × B; *19* N × B, Q × BP+; *20* K – R1, R – B4!; *21* R – K2!, Q – R5; *22* N – Q4!, R – R4 (not *22* . . . N × N?; *23* B × N); *23* N – B3, Q – B3; *24* Q – K1, R – K1; *25* R – K6, Q – B2; *26* Q – K2!, R – R3; *27* R – K3 followed by R – K1 and Black's crushed.

B] *15* . . . N/4 – N3; *16* P – R4! (on *16* N – N5, O – O!; *17* B – KN4, Q – B5 holds), N – B3; *18* N – N5 and it's difficult for Black's King to escape the crisscross: if *17* . . . O – O – O?; *18* N – B7. Or *17* . . . P – KR3?; *18* N × P!, B × N; *19* B – KN4. Or on *17* . . . N – B5; *18* B – KN4 continues the pressure.

C] *15* . . . N/2 – N3; *16* N × N, N × N transposes to the game.

16 N × N   N × N
17 P – B4   N – B3

On *17* . . . N – B2 (*17* . . . N – N3?; *18* P – B5); *18* B – R5, P – N3; *19* P – B5!, O – O – O; *20* P × KP, B × KP; *21* R × B, P × B; *22* Q × RP White stands much better.

18 B – KN4   . . .

Better is the finesse *18* B – R5+!, P – N3 (*18* . . . K – Q1; *19* P – B5 is unhealthy); *19* B – KN4, O – O – O; *20* B × P, B × B;

21 R×B, R–Q2; *22* Q–B3, N–Q1; *23* R–KB6!, R–K1;
24 R–Q1, etc.

18	. . .	O–O–O
19	B×P	B×B
20	R×B	R–Q2
21	P–B5	. . .

To continue with P–B6 which gets a grip on the KB-file. On
21 Q–B3, N–Q1; *22* R–K5, Q–B3=.

21	. . .	N–Q1!

Driving the Rook from its command outpost on the sixth rank.

22	R–K3	Q–B5

Darga is defending with vigor!

23	R–B3	Q–K5
24	P–R5!	. . .

Commencing operations against the castled King while Black's
Queen is temporarily cut off from the Q-flank.

24	. . .	N–B3?

Correct was *24* . . . P–QN4 with an even game.

25	P×P	P×P
26	Q–N1!	K–B2

The opening of the QR-file is already decisive. On *26* . . .
K–N2; *27* B–B5 wins. Or *26* . . . R–N2; *27* P–B6, P×P;
28 R×P, P–Q5; *29* Q–N5, etc.

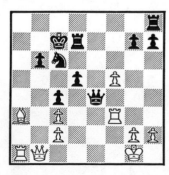

DARGA

Position after 26 . . .
K–B2

FISCHER

Problem: White to play and win.

27	B – B1 !	Q – K8+

There's no satisfactory defense to the threat of B – B4+. On 27 . . . N – K4; *28* B – B4, R – K1; *29* Q – N5 penetrates decisively.

28	R – B1	Q × P
29	B – B4+	K – N2
30	Q – N5!	Black resigns

25 Lombardy *[U.S.A.]* - Fischer

USA CHAMPIONSHIP 1960–1

SICILIAN DEFENSE

When the Maroczy didn't bind

> *Geza Maroczy left a strange legacy: the discovery that a certain type of Pawn formation imposes a near-decisive cramp on the opponent. In this game, after Lombardy's sixth move, he obtains, with Fischer's consent, the dread "Maroczy bind." From here on, given a few developing moves, White's game almost plays itself—unless Black takes early and energetic counter-measures. This is easier said than done.*
>
> *The method that Fischer chooses to free himself (9 . . . P – Q4) involves the sacrifice of a Pawn. Lombardy reacts sluggishly, overlooking a neat tactical point (17 . . . B – R5+) at the tail-end of a combination. Even so, he still has excellent drawing chances. But somewhat discouraged by the rapid turn of events, he indulges in a unique form of self-immolation. In short, Lombardy, not Maroczy, lost.*

1	P – K4	P – QB4
2	N – KB3	P – Q3
3	P – Q4	P × P
4	N × P	N – KB3
5	P – KB3	. . .

A passive, non-developing move which leads to nothing. White wants to gain control of Q5, establishing a Maroczy bind with P – QB4, N – B3, etc. But after going to all that trouble he can't prevent . . . P – Q4 after all. Correct is that tired old move—5 N – QB3.

5	. . .	N – B3

Sharper is 5 . . . P – K4!; *6* B – N5 + (*6* N – N5, P – QR3; 7 N/5 – B3, B – K3; *8* N – Q5, N × N; *9* P × N, B – B4=), QN – Q2; 7 N – B5, P – Q4!; *8* P × P, P – QR3; *9* B × N+, Q × B; *10* N –

K3, B – B4; *11* P – QB4, P – QN4=. (Cardoso–Fischer, 5th match
game 1957.)

            6 P – QB4   P – K3

6 . . . N×N; *7* Q×N, P – KN3 is a sound alternative.

            7 N – B3   B – K2

Premature is *7* . . . P – Q4?; *8* BP×P, P×P; *9* B – QN5 winning a Pawn.

            8 B – K3   . . .

8 N – B2, O – O; *9* N – K3, P – Q4!?; *10* BP×P, P×P; *11* P×
P? (better is KN×P), N – K4; *12* Q – N3, B – QB4; *13* B – Q2,
R – K1; *14* B – K2, N – N3; *15* N – B2, N – R5; *16* O – O – O,
N×NP with advantage. (Foguelman–Fischer, Mar del Plata 1960.)

            8 . . .   O – O
            9 N – B2   P – Q4!?

Reckoning that the loss of a Pawn is compensated for by
superior development. *9* . . . R – K1 is sound but passive.

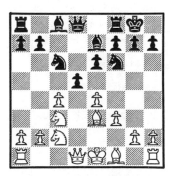

FISCHER

Position after 9 . . .
P – Q4

LOMBARDY

            10 BP×P   P×P
            11 N×P   . . .

Better is *11* P×P, N – QN5 (*11* . . . N – K4 doesn't work well
now because of *12* Q – Q4 followed by O – O – O); *12* B – QB4,
B – KB4; *13* N×N, B×N; *14* O – O, R – B1. Black regains the
Pawn, but with an inferior position.

            11 . . .   N×N
            12 Q×N   . . .

On *12* P × N, N – N5; *13* B – QB4, B – KB4; *14* N × N, B × N+;
15 K – B2, R – K1 with good play for the Pawn. (If *16* Q – N3,
B – R4 threatening . . . R × B.)

12 . . .		Q – B2!
13 Q – QN5?		. . .

Too intent on holding on to the Pawn. Correct is *13* B – K2,
B – R5+!; *14* P – N3, B – B3; *15* O – O, B × P; *16* QR – N1=.

13 . . .		B – Q2
14 R – B1		. . .

Again too optimistic. After *14* Q – K2, B – B3; *15* O – O – O
White can survive—temporarily anyway (if *15* . . . N – N5; *16*
R × B!).

FISCHER

Position after 14 R – B1

LOMBARDY

14 . . .		N – N5!

This unexpected "discovery" jolts White back to reality.

15 N × N		. . .

Loses the exchange, but avoids the worst. On *15* Q – K2, N × P
regains the Pawn with continuing pressure. And on *15* Q – B4,
Q – R4; *16* N × N, B × N+; *17* K – B2, QR – B1; *18* Q – Q5,
R × R; *19* B × R, B – K8+! White meets a devastating attack
wherever he turns: i.e., *20* K – K3 (if *20* K – N1?, Q – N3+),
Q – N3+; *21* K – B4 (not *21* Q – Q4?, B – B7+ or *21* K – K2,
Q – B7+; *22* K – Q1, B – K3), Q – B2+; *22* P – K5, Q × B+, etc.

15 . . .		Q × R+
16 B × Q		B × Q
17 N – Q5		. . .

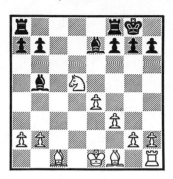

FISCHER

Position after 17 N – Q5

LOMBARDY

17 . . .	B – R5+!

The scorpion's sting at the tail-end of the combination.

18 P – N3	B × B
19 R × B	B – Q1

The smoke clears. Black is an exchange ahead for a Pawn. But there are still great technical difficulties. White's Knight is on a dominating outpost and his Pawn structure is solid.

20 B – Q2	R – B1
21 B – B3	P – B4!

Weaker would be *21 . . . R – K1* because of P – KN4 blocking the K-side.

22 P – K5	. . .

This advance is necessary, but it undermines the support of the Knight (which can now be driven away).

22 . . .	R – B4
23 N – N4	. . .

23 N – B4 (or N – K3) would cost a Pawn after B – R4.

23 . . .	B – R4
24 P – QR3	B × N
25 P × B	R – Q4
26 K – K2	K – B2
27 P – R4	K – K3
28 K – K3	R – B1
29 R – KN1	R – B5

Black has steadily improved his grip, but his winning chances are still problematic, hinging mainly on sacrificing on QN5 or K4 at the right moment.

30 R – K1 ?   . . .

A gross blunder. Correct is *30* R – QR1, P – QR3; *31* R – KN1.

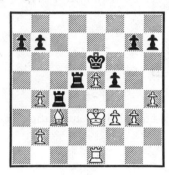

FISCHER

Position after 30 R – K1

LOMBARDY

30 . . .   R × B + !

Swapping everything leads to a won King and Pawn ending.

31	P × R	R × P +
32	K – Q2	R × R
33	K × R	K – Q4
34	K – Q2	K – B5
35	P – R5	P – QN3
36	K – B2	P – KN4
37	P – R6	P – B5
38	P – N4	P – R4
39	P × P	P × P
40	K – N2	P – R5
41	K – R3	K × P
42	K × P	K – Q5
43	K – N4	K – K6

White resigns

26 Fischer - Reshevsky [U.S.A.]

NEW YORK 1961 : 2nd Match Game

SICILIAN DEFENSE

Time will tell

The opening has always been regarded as the old warrior's weak point, and were it not for this handicap who knows how far Reshevsky might have gone toward the summit?

Whatever the case, being familiar with the latest wrinkles does have the merit of saving time on the clock and, hopefully, of catching an opponent off guard. Although Reshevsky is bested in the theoretical duel (after 13 B – B3) his practical cunning enables him to extricate himself—at a great cost of time. In the end it is the clock, as much as Fischer's persistence, that causes his downfall.

1 P – K4	P – QB4
2 N – KB3	N – QB3
3 P – Q4	P × P
4 N × P	P – KN3

Allowing White the chance to get a Maroczy bind (with 5 P – QB4). Apparently Reshevsky had booked up on this for the match. Black's idea is to dispense with an early . . . P – Q3 and possibly strive for a later . . . P – Q4 (thereby saving a tempo).

5 N – QB3	. . .

In match game 11 I got an edge with the more traditional 5 P – QB4, N – B3; 6 N – QB3, N × N; 7 Q × N, P – Q3; 8 B – K2, B – N2; 9 B – K3, O – O; 10 Q – Q2, etc.

5 . . .	B – N2
6 B – K3	N – B3
7 B – K2	. . .

In the 4th and 6th games of the match I continued with 7

B – QB4, O – O; *8* B – N3, N – KN5 (*8* . . . N – QR4? brought Reshevsky to grief against me in the US Championship 1958–9 after *9* P – K5, N – K1; *10* B×P+!, K×B; *11* N – K6!! winning Black's Queen); *9* Q×N, N×N and White got a clear advantage both with Q – R4 and Q – Q1, respectively.

7 . . .   O – O

On *7* . . . P – Q4?; *8* B – QN5 wins a Pawn.

8 P – B4   . . .

Despite his familiarity with the Dragon Variation, I felt Reshevsky really didn't know the latest wrinkles in Alekhine's Attack. The point of Black's "accelerated fianchetto" becomes apparent after the indifferent *8* O – O?, P – Q4!; *9* P×P, N – QN5=.

8 . . .   P – Q3

Now on *8* . . . P – Q4?; *9* P – K5, N – K5; *10* N×KN, P×N; *11* N×N, P×N; *12* Q×Q, R×Q; *13* B – B4 gives White a winning ending. (Olafsson–Larsen, Wageningen 1957.)

9 N – N3   . . .

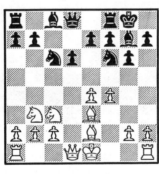

RESHEVSKY

Position after 9 N – N3

FISCHER

9 . . .   B – K3

I was right. This is the old (and second-rate) move. Correct is *9* . . . P – QR4!; *10* P – QR4, B – K3; *11* N – Q4? (after *11* P – N4, N – N5! Black's Knight can no longer be dislodged by P – QR3; the best White has is *11* O – O, R – B1=), Q – N3!; *12* N×B, Q×B; *13* N×R, N – KN5 with a strong attack. (Makievsky–Veresov, USSR 1954.)

10 P – N4   P – Q4
11 P – B5   B – B1

Lipnitzky recommends *11* . . . NP×P!? It's interesting.

12 P×QP   N – N5

RESHEVSKY

Position after 12 . . .
N – N5

FISCHER

13 B – B3!   . . .

The modern way—White maintains his center Pawn and sacs two Pawns on the K-side where Black must expose his King to get them.

13 P – Q6 has been known to be only a draw since the famous Alekhine–Botvinnik encounter, Nottingham 1936, which continued: *13* . . . Q×P! (if *13* . . . P×QP?; *14* P – N5); *14* B – B5, Q – B5; *15* R – KB1, Q×RP; *16* B×N, N×P!; *17* B×N, Q – N6+; *18* R – B2, Q – N8+ with a perpetual.

Another weak line is *13* P×P, RP×P; *14* B – B3, B×P!; *15* B×B, N×B; *16* Q×N, N×P+; *17* K – B2, N×R; *18* R×N, R – B1! with a good game. If *19* B – Q4?, R – B5. (PANOV)

13 . . .   P×P
14 P – QR3   P×P
15 B – N2!   . . .

On *15* P×N, P×B; *16* Q×P, B – N5 followed by . . . B – R4 – N3. White's whole idea is to keep Black's QB restricted to the Q-side.

15 . . .   N – R3
16 Q – Q3!   . . .

Ney's improvement over *16* Q – K2, B – B4! and the Bishop retreats to N3, when necessary, defending the K-side.

16 . . .   P – K3

The best choice in a difficult position. Up to here we had both played briskly, but now Reshevsky began to consume time on the clock. After *16 . . .* N – Q2; *17* O – O – O, N – K4; *18* Q – K2 Black's game is lifeless. White has P – R3 and B – Q4 in the offing.

17 O – O – O   . . .

Black gets the initiative after *17* P – Q6?, N – Q4!; *18* B × N, P × B; *19* Q × P, R – K1, etc.

17 . . .   N × P

The lesser evil. On *17 . . .* P × P; *18* P – R3, P – N6; *19* B – Q4 is strong.

18 P – R3!   P – N6
19 KR – N1   Q – Q3!

Reshevsky is putting up a first-rate defense.

20 B × N   P × B

RESHEVSKY

Position after 20 . . .
P × B

FISCHER

Despite his material deficit, it is obvious White has a strong attack. His problem is how to land a haymaker.

21 N × P?   . . .

This gives Black a little breathing space.

Nowadays I would have played *21* B – Q4! without giving it a second thought. After *21 . . .* B × B; *22* R × P+, B – N2 (*22 . . .* K – R1; *23* Q × B+, P – B3; *24* R – B3 leads to a bind); *23* QR – N1, Q – R3+; *24* K – N1, B – K3; *25* R × B+, Q × R; *26* R × Q+, K × R; *27* Q – N3+, K – R1 (if *27 . . .* K – B3; *28* Q – Q6, K – N2; *29* N × P wins); *28* Q – K5+, K – N1; *29* Q – N5+, K – R1; *30* Q – B6+, K – N1; *31* N – K2 with a winning bind.

21 . . .   K – R1
22 B – B4   . . .

22 B – Q4 is less convincing now after B×B (if *22* . . . P – B3?; *23* R×P, Q×N; *24* B×BP!); *23* Q×B+, P – B3 and White has no forced win.

22 . . .   Q – KN3
23 Q – Q2   . . .

Overlooking his reply. Vukovich suggests *23* Q – KB3 but B – B4!; *24* R×P, Q – QB3 holds.

23 . . .   B×P!

Reshevsky chopped it off fast—he doesn't wait to be asked twice.

24 R×P   B – N5

Black has succeeded in transferring this Bishop to the K-side and in sealing the N-file.

25 R – R1   . . .

So White begins operations on the R-file!

25 . . .   KR – K1
26 N – K3   . . .

RESHEVSKY

Position after 26 N – K3

FISCHER

26 . . .   Q – K5?

Anxious to simplify and ease the tension (in time-pressure), Reshevsky finally goes astray.

The tempting *26* . . . Q – KB3 is refuted by *27* N×B, Q×P+; *28* K – Q1, QR – Q1; *29* R – Q3, etc.

But simply *26* . . . P – B4! holds (if *27* Q – R2, K – N1).

27 Q – R2!   . . .

166 26/NEW YORK 1961

Now the roof caves in.

27 . . .   B – K3

The late Abe Turner suggested *27 . . . B – B4* but after *28 R × B!, K × R; 29 N × B+, Q × N; 30 N – Q4* wins.

28 R × B!   . . .

That does it! Once this Bishop is gone, White has a field day. "Why didn't White play *28 N – Q2 . . . ?* So far as I can see Black can then resign. Or am I missing something?" (A. R. B. Thomas in a letter to *Chess*) Right, Mr. Thomas!

          28 . . .   K × R
          29 Q – R6+   K – N1

On *26 . . . K – R1; 27 B – K5+* mates in two.

          30 R – N1+   Q – N3
          31 R × Q+   BP × R
          32 N – Q4   QR – Q1
          33 B – K5   R – Q2
          34 N × B   R × N
          35 N – N4   R – KB2
          36 Q – N5   R – B8+
          37 K – Q2   P – R4
          38 Q – Q8+   Black resigns

After *38 . . . R – B1; 39 N – R6+* taxes even Reshevsky's defensive ability.

27 Reshevsky *[U.S.A.]* - Fischer

NEW YORK 1961: 5th Match Game

SEMI-TARRASCH DEFENSE

Sheer pyrotechnics

Here, in probably the most exciting game of the match, Fischer, trying to win a Pawn, unwittingly triggers a series of "desperado" combinations which are brilliant and unorthodox. Pure tactics predominate for a period of ten moves (19 to 29). It is almost impossible to determine who is winning until Reshevsky emerges a clear exchange ahead. In the tricky ending that ensues Fischer obviously is fighting for a draw. But, once again, he has the clock as an ally.

In time-pressure, trying to preserve his slim advantage, Reshevsky plays an aggressive line in which Fischer finds a hole—enabling him to reverse their roles. Conscious of his newly acquired advantage, Fischer storms down the board with his K-side Pawns and overwhelms his opponent.

1	P – Q4	N – KB3	
2	P – QB4	P – K3	
3	N – QB3	P – Q4	
4	P×P	. . .	

This exchange variation, though insipid, has always been to Reshevsky's taste.

    4 . . .   N×P

4 . . . P×P leads to the kind of wood pushing that always bored me.

    5 N – B3   . . .

Prematurely forceful is *5 P – K4, N×N; 6 P×N, P – QB4; 7 N – B3, P×P; 8 P×P, B – N5+ =.*

5	. . .	P – QB4
6	P – K3	N – QB3
7	B – Q3	. . .

Botvinnik and Robert Byrne prefer 7 B – B4. A possible continuation might be 7 . . . P×P; *8* P×P, B – K2; *9* O – O, O – O; *10* R – K1, P – QR3= (weaker is *10* . . . P – QN3; *11* N×N, P×N; *12* B – QN5 Botvinnik–Alekhine, AVRO 1938).

7	. . .	B – K2

An alternative is 7 . . . P×P; *8* P×P, P – KN3; *9* P – KR4!? (*9* O – O, B – N2; *10* B – K4 is the positional approach), B – N2 (better is *9* . . . P – KR3); *10* P – R5, N/4 – N5; *11* B – KN5, N×B+; *12* Q×N, Q – R4; *13* K – B1, P – KR3?; *14* P×P!, P×B; *15* R×R+, B×R; *16* P×P+, K×P; *17* Q – R7+, B – N2; *18* P – Q5! White won shortly. (Balcerovsky–Dunkelblum, Varna 1962.)

8	O – O	O – O
9	P – QR3	P×P
10	P×P	. . .

FISCHER

Position after 10 P×P

RESHEVSKY

Fairly typical of the semi-Tarrasch formation: White has the freer game and attacking prospects, but the drawback of his isolated QP should not be minimized. Chances are even.

10	. . .	N – B3

Also playable is *10* . . . B – Q2; *11* Q – B2, P – KN3; *12* B – KR6, R – K1; *13* N – K4, QR – B1; *14* Q – K2, P – B4; *15* N – B3, B – B3. (R. Byrne–Bisguier, US Championship 1963–4.)

Another possibility is *10* . . . P – QN3!?; *11* N×N, Q×N; *12* Q – B2, B – N2!; *13* B×P+, K – R1; *14* B – K4, N×P; *15* B×Q, N×Q; *16* B×B, N×R; *17* B×R, R×B; *18* B – N5, P – B3 =.

11 B – B2   . . .

A more flexible plan is *11* B – K3 followed by Q – K2 and
QR – Q1.

11 . . .	P – QN3
12 Q – Q3	B – N2
13 B – N5	P – N3
14 KR – K1	R – K1
15 P – KR4	. . .

Evans criticized this "aggressive pass" and Barden extolled it. I
don't see how else White can make headway. He has to create
some K-side threats before Black consolidates and piles up on
his QP.

15 . . .	R – QB1
16 QR – B1	N – Q4
17 N – K4	P – B4!?

I knew this was an "ugly positional blunder." But I actually
thought Black would get the better of it after *18* N – B3, B × B; *19*
P × B, N × N; *20* P × N (not *20* Q × N?, N – K4), N – R4! (threatening . . . B × N and . . . Q × NP).

18 N – B3	B × B
19 N × B!	. . .

Crossing me up!

19 . . .	N – B5
20 Q – K3	. . .

Not *20* Q – N3?, N – R4; *21* Q – K3, N × P.

20 . . .	Q × P
21 N – N5!	. . .

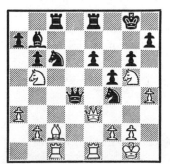

FISCHER

Position after 21 N – N5

RESHEVSKY

Marvelously alert! After the practically forced trade of Queens, White wins the exchange because of the imminent fork on Q6.

21 . . .   Q×Q

Best. After the game we analyzed *21 . . . Q – Q4; 22* Q×N, Q×N (if *22 . . . N – Q5?; 23* B – K4!, R×R; *24* Q×R!, P×B; *25* Q – B7); *23* N×KP, Q×P (if *23 . . . Q – Q4; 24* N – B7, R×R+; *25* R×R, Q – B2; *26* N –K6 keeps the advantage); *24* Q – R6! (RESHEVSKY) with an irresistible attack. On *24. . . N* – R4 (to stop B – N3; if *24 . . . R×N; 25* R×R, N – Q5; *26* R – K7 wins); *25* B×P!, P×B (if *25 . . . Q – B3; 26* N – N5! or *25. . . R×R; 26* R×R, P×B; *27* R – B7 wins); *26* R – N1, Q – R1 (if *26 . . . Q – B6; 27* R – K3); *27* Q – N5+, K – B2; *28* Q×P+, K – N1 (not *28 . . . Q – B3?; 29* Q×P+); *29* R – K3, R – B6; *30* N – N5!, R – KB1; *31* R – K8! forces mate.

22	P×Q	N×P!
23	K×N	N – Q5 dis.+
24	B – K4!	. . .

FISCHER

Position after 24 B – K4

RESHEVSKY

This game was played at the Beverly Hilton Hotel in Los Angeles, and I can still hear the audience gasping with each blow, thinking each of us had overlooked it in turn. "Fischer is winning!" "Reshevsky is winning!" The true state of affairs will crystallize in a matter of moves.

24	. . .	B×B+
25	N×B	N×N
26	N – B6+	. . .

So the fork, after all, takes place here instead of Q6!

26 . . .   K – B2
27 N×R   R×N
28 P – QR4!   . . .

Inaccurate is *28* KR – Q1, R – K2! and the Knight can climb back into the game via QB2 – Q4.

28 . . .   N – Q3
29 R – B7+   K – B3!

Black can't afford *29 . . . R – K2; 30* KR – QB1. The Rook is needed to mobilize the K-side Pawns.

30 KR – QB1!   . . .

Keeping control of the open file. On *30* R × P (either), R – QB1.

30 . . .   P – KR3
31 R×P   N – K5
32 R – R6   R – Q1!

32 . . . R – QN1; 33 R – B6 is hopeless.

FISCHER

Position after 32 . . .
R – Q1

RESHEVSKY

Now it's clear that Black's fighting for a draw.

33 R – B2   . . .

The only way to preserve winning chances. After *33* R × P, R – Q7+; *34* K – N1, P – N4; *35* P × P+ (on *35* R/1 – B6, P × P; *36* R × P+, K – N4; *37* R – N6+, K – R4; *38* R × P+, K – N5 Black has enough play on the K-side to hold the draw; but not *35* P – QR5?, P × P; *36* P – R6, P – R6; *37* P – R7, P – R7+; *38* K – R1, N – N6 mate), P × P; *36* R/1 – B6 (not *36* P – R5?, P – N5; *37* P – R6, N – N4; *38* P – R7, N – B6+; *39* K – B1, P – N6; *40*

P – R8 = Q, P – N7   mate!),   P – N5;   *37* R × P+, K – N4;   *38*
R – KR6, P – B5 keeps the balance.

33 . . .	R – Q6
34 R × P	. . .

After *34* K – B3, R – N6 Black is in great shape.

34 . . .	R × P
35 P – QR5	P – B5

FISCHER

Position after 35 . . .
P – B5

RESHEVSKY

36 R – B2?	. . .

Short of time, Reshevsky probably didn't see how Black's Rook
could get back in time to stop the QRP. But now it is doubtful
that White can even draw!

White should settle for *36* P – R6, P – B6+; *37* K – B1 (not *37*
K – R2?, R – K7+), R – Q6; *38* K – K1, R – K6+; *39* K – B1,
R – Q6 with a draw. If *40* K – N1, R – Q8+; *41* K – R2, P – B7;
42 R × BP+, N × R; *43* R – N3 (*43* P – R7, R – R8 wins), R – Q2;
44 R – B3+, K – N2; *45* R × N, R – R2=.

36 . . .	N × R
37 K × N	R – K4!
38 P – N4	R – K6!

This maneuver permits the Rook to get behind the passed Pawn.

39 P – R6	R – QR6

Now White is stymied. In order to mobilize his Q-side Pawns,
he must inch forward with P – N5, R – N7, P – R7, P – N6, etc.
But a half-dozen moves, in chess, can be a lifetime.

40 R – B6	. . .

The last move of the time-control, and it definitely loses. The best chance is *40* P – N5 with the possibility of R – N8 and P – N6 (giving up the RP) followed by P – N7, in some key variations.

40	. . .	P – N4
41	P×P+	P×P
42	P – N5	P – N5

The sealed move. Black's Pawns suddenly proliferate from nowhere!

FISCHER

Position after 42 . . .
P – N5

RESHEVSKY

43	R – B8	. . .

The line I had expected was *43* R – B1 (intending to bolster the Pawns from behind with R – QN1), P – N6+; *44* K – N1 (on *44* K – N2, R – R7+; *45* K – B3, K – B4 wins), R – R7!; *45* R – N1, P – B6; *46* P – N6, R – N7+; *47* K – B1, R – KR7!; *48* K – K1, R – R8+; *49* K – Q2, R×R; *50* P – R7, P – B7; *51* P – R8 = Q, P – B8 = Q and Black wins, since White has no perpetual check.

43	. . .	K – B4
44	P – N6	P – N6+
45	K – K1	. . .

He decides to let the Pawns through rather than get mated after *45* K – N2, R – R7+; *46* K – N1, P – B6, etc.

45	. . .	R – R8+
46	K – K2	P – N7
47	R – B8+	. . .

On *47* R – KN8, R×P; *48* P – N7 (if *48* R×P, R×P wins), R – N3 is decisive.

47	. . .	K – K5
48	R×P+	K×R

49	P – N7	P – N8 = Q

A hasty slip which, fortunately, still wins. As Isaac Kashdan pointed out after the game *50 . . . K – K5!* wins outright: e.g., *51* P – N8 = Q, R – R7+; *52* K – any, P – N8 = Q mate. "What will the Russians say when they see this match?" he inquired, with gentle irony.

FISCHER

Position after 49 . . . P –N8=Q

RESHEVSKY

50	P – N8 = Q+	K – B4
51	Q – B8+	K – K5
52	Q – R8+	. . .

No better is *52* Q – B3+, K – K4; *53* Q – B3+ (if *53* Q – R5+, K – Q3), Q – Q5; *54* Q – N3+, K – Q4; *55* Q – B3+, Q – K5+, etc.

52	. . .	K – Q5

Delicate footwork is required to escape the perpetual.

53	Q – Q8+	. . .

Better than *53* Q – R8+, K – B5; *54* Q – B8+, Q – B4; *55* Q × P+, K – N5; *56* Q – K4+, Q – B5+.

53	. . .	K – B5
54	Q – Q3+	K – B4
55	Q – B3+	K – Q3
56	Q – Q2+	K – K4
57	Q – N2+	K – B4
	White resigns	

He runs out of checks after *58* Q – N5+, K – B3; *59* Q – N2+, P – K4.

28 Reshevsky [U.S.A.] - Fischer

LOS ANGELES 1961: 11th Match Game

KING'S INDIAN DEFENSE

A peccable draw

What proved to be the last game of this ill-starred match is a good example of how Reshevsky, by virtue of pluck, stamina, and alertness, salvages a draw from a lost position. It exemplifies, too, the demoralizing effect that continuously strong resistance can have on even the most robust opponent.

Fischer rapidly wrests the initiative and wins the exchange as the result of a pretty combination (28 . . . Q×R). However, he has difficulty gaining the offensive because Reshevsky throws obstacle after obstacle in his path. Nevertheless, Fischer's material advantage begins to make itself felt. He misses clear wins (on moves 38 and 42), whereupon his game deteriorates sufficiently to permit his stubborn opponent to set up an adequate defense. Still, there are several surprises in store just at the very end.

1	P – QB4	N – KB3
2	P – Q4	P – KN3
3	N – QB3	B – N2
4	P – K4	O – O
5	B – K2	. . .

Inferior is *5* P – K5. See game 21.

5	. . .	P – Q3
6	N – B3	P – K4
7	O – O	. . .

For *7* P – Q5 see game 7.

7	. . .	N – B3
8	P – Q5	. . .

Match game 9 (Reshevsky as White) had continued: *8* B – K3, R – K1; *9* P×P (*9* P – Q5, N – Q5! equalizes fully), P×P; *10*

Q×Q, N×Q; *11* N – QN5, N – K3; *12* N – N5 ("full of sound and fury, signifying nothing"—Evans), R – K2=. See game 57 note to Black's move 13.

8	. . .	N – K2
9	N – K1	N – Q2
10	N – Q3	P – KB4
11	P×P	. . .

11 P – B3, P – B5 followed by P – KN4, etc., gives Black a strong K-side attack.

11	. . .	N×BP

11 . . . P×P keeping Black's Pawn front mobile is very strong.

12	P – B3	N – Q5

For *12* . . . N – B3 see game 30.

13	N – K4	P – N3

Hindering White's thematic break with P – QB5.

FISCHER

Position after 13 . . .
P – N3

RESHEVSKY

14	B – N5?	. . .

Apparently gaining a tempo, but only driving the Queen to a better square. *14* B – Q2 or R – K1 appear to be more accurate.

14	. . .	Q – K1
15	B – Q2	. . .

This Bishop must retreat eventually after . . . P – KR3. The idea is to prepare P – QN4 without having to fear the reply . . . P – QR4.

15	. . .	P – QR4

Gaining more time. White must now stop for P – QN3 (to enforce P – QN4). On the immediate *16* P – QR3, P – R5! fixes the Q-side.

16 R – K1   N × B+

Otherwise the Bishop retreats to KB1.

17 Q × N   P – R3
18 P – QN3   P – KN4
19 P – QR3   Q – N3

Now it's obvious that it was a mistake to force Black's Queen to K1—its presence on N3 lends momentum to the K-side initiative.

20 P – QN4   N – B3
21 P × P?   . . .

Correct is *21* N/3 – B2, but after N – R4 Black stands better.

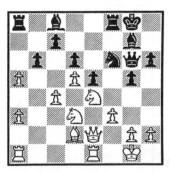

FISCHER

Position after 21 P × P

RESHEVSKY

Now Reshevsky is hoping to get some counterplay after *21 . . . .* P × P; *22* N/3 – B2, N – R4; *23* P – B5, etc. But—

21 . . .   P – N5!

—doesn't give him time to get it in.

22 N/3 – B2   . . .

Not *22* P × QNP?, P × BP; *23* Q × P, N × N; *24* Q × N, B – B4 wins a piece. On *22* N × N+, B × N; *23* P – B4, B – B4 White's in trouble.

22 . . .   P × BP
23 Q × P   N – R4

Increasing the pressure. On *23 . . . .* N × P; *24* Q – KN3 holds.

24 Q – K3	P × P

Finally!

25 QR – B1	. . .

Typically, Reshevsky wants to mobilize his Q-side without making any concessions or creating any K-side weaknesses. After *25* P – N3, N – B5; *26* K – R1, N – R6! it's just a matter of time before Black invades on the light squares.

25 . . .	B – B4
26 P – B5	. . .

Loses material, but probably the best chance. On *26* P – N3, R – B2 followed by QR – KB1, White is not long for this world.

26 . . .	N – B5
27 Q – KN3	. . .

Blunders the exchange. But no longer possible is *27* P – N3, N × P, etc.

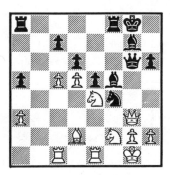

FISCHER

Position after 27 Q – KN3

RESHEVSKY

27 . . .	B × N!
28 R × B?	. . .

Flustered, White makes the task somewhat easier. Better is *28* N × B (not *28* B × N?, P × B), Q × Q; *29* P × Q, N – Q6; *30* P × P, P × P; *31* R – B6, N × R; *32* B × R with many more chances of holding the ending than in the actual game.

28 . . .	Q × R!
29 N × Q	N – K7+
30 K – R1	N × Q+
31 P × N	R – R3!
32 P × P	P × P
33 P – R4	. . .

"Black has won the exchange, but the technical difficulties confronting him are enormous. His Pawns are discombobulated, his Bishop is hemmed in and his Rooks are virtually immobilized. Still, one has the feeling Fischer should win this game." (EVANS.)

33	. . .	R – B2
34	P – N4	B – B1
35	K – R2	K – R2
36	R – B8	R – N3
37	R – R8	R – N6
38	B × QRP	. . .

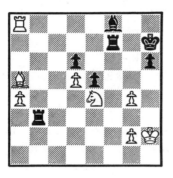

FISCHER

Position after 38 B × QRP

RESHEVSKY

38	. . .	R – B5?

The right concept is to destroy the blockade on K4 with *38* . . . R – K6!; *39* N – B3 (if *39* N – N3, R – Q6), P – K5; *40* R – K8, B – N2; *41* N × P, B – K4+, etc.

39	B – B7!	. . .

With his usual tenacity, Reshevsky finds the only move to keep the game alive. White is still quite lost, however.

39	. . .	R × N
40	R × B	R – Q6
41	R – B6	R × NP
42	R × P	R – N2?

Now the "technical difficulties" become more real than apparent. Correct is *42* . . . R – Q7!; *43* R – Q7+, K – N3; *44* B × P, R/5 × P+; *45* K – R3, R – N4 wins easily.

43	R – QB6!	. . .

Forced. *43* B – N6 loses to R – Q7. And *43* B – R5 loses to R/6 – KN6.

43 . . .   R × P

If *43* . . . R – Q7; *44* B × P, R/2 × P+; *45* K – R3, R – N4;
46 B – B4, R – Q6+; *47* K – R2 (if *47* K – R4?, R – Q5; *48*
R – B6, K – N2), R – R4+; *48* K – N2, R/6 × P; *49* R – B7+!,
K – N3; *50* R – B6+ draws.

44 R – B2!   . . .

Again I had overlooked White's reply.

44 . . .   P – K5

Discouraged, I gave it one last try.

45 P – R5   R – Q6

On *45* . . . P – K6; *46* B – B4, R – K2; *47* R – K2 draws.

46 B – B4   R – KB2
47 P – N3   P – K6
48 R – B1   . . .

Reshevsky, once more in severe time-pressure, overlooked that
48 K – N2 draws easily. For on *48* . . . R × B; *49* R – B7+! is
the saving clause.

48 . . .   R – K2
49 R – K1   R – R6
50 R – K2   K – N3
51 K – N2   . . .

Not *51* B – Q6?, R – Q2!; *52* B × R, R – Q7 wins.

51 . . .   R × P
52 R × P   . . .

52 B × KP draws easily. Black can't make anything out of the
pin on the K-file.

52 . . .   R – R7+
53 K – B3?   . . .

A comedy of errors. Correct is *53* K – R3! in order to keep
Black's King out of KN5 after the exchange of Rooks: e.g., *53*
. . . R × R; *54* B × R, P – R4; *55* B – B4, R – R8; *56* B – B7,
K – B4; *57* B – B4, R – QN8; *58* B – B7!, R – R8+; *59* K – N2,
R – QB8; *60* B – B4! (gaining a vital tempo by hitting the Rook),
R – any; *61* K – R3! maintaining the blockade.

FISCHER

Position after 53 K – B3

RESHEVSKY

53 . . .   R – QN2?

Returning the favor.

As Evans originally pointed out in *Chess Life*, "The best winning chance is *53 . . . R × R+; 54* B × R, P – R4 followed by K – B4."

Disgusted, I no longer thought there was a win. However, later I worked out a problem-like variation (after *54 . . . P – R4*):

A] *55* P – N4?, P – R5 wins.

B] *55* K – K4, K – B3!; *56* B – Q4+, K – K3; *57* K – B4, R – R5; *58* K – K3, K – B4 leads to variations similar to "D."

C] *55* K – B4, R – R4!; *56* B – Q2, R – B4+; *57* K – K4, K – B3 and Black's King will eventually penetrate to KN5. For example, *58* B – B4 (*58* K – K3?, K – N4), R – R4 followed by R – R5+ and K – B4.

D] *55* B – B4, K – B4; *56* B – Q6, R – QN7; *57* B – B4, R – N6+; *58* K – N2, K – N5; *59* B – Q6, R – N7+; *60* K – N1, K – R6; *61* B – K5, R – N5!; *62* B – B7 (not *62* B – B4?, P – R5), R – N5!; *63* K – B2, K – R7; *64* B – K5, K – R8; *65* K – B3, R – N1; *66* B – B4, R – KB1; *67* K – B2 (if *67* K – K3, K – N7), P – R5; *68* K – B3, P – R6; *69* K – B2, P – R7; *70* K – B1, R – QR1; *71* K – B2, R – R7+; *72* K – B1, R – R6!; *73* K – B2, R – B6+!!; *74* K × R, K – N8; *75* B – K3+, K – B8 and the Pawn queens.

54 R – K6+   K – B4
55 R – K5+   K – B3
56 R – Q5   R – N6+
57 K – N4

Drawn

29 Fischer - Geller [U.S.S.R.]

BLED 1961

RUY LOPEZ

Hoist with his own petard

As was his wont, Geller gambles with 7 . . . Q – B3 in an attempt to assume an early offense. To thwart this maneuver, part of a patently prepared variation, Fischer sacrifices a Pawn (9 P – Q4). Undaunted, Geller tries to continue his attack. But it backfires. With a series of rapier-like thrusts, Fischer demolishes Black in a mere twenty-two moves.

Subsequent attempts to improve on Geller's play have likewise failed. Thus, this fruitful encounter offers what has come to be accepted as the refutation of Black's ultra-aggressive system.

1	P – K4	P – K4
2	N – KB3	N – QB3
3	B – N5	P – QR3
4	B – R4	P – Q3
5	O – O	. . .

At that time this was considered inferior because it allows the pin which Black can initiate with his next move. 5 B × N+ or 5 P – B3 were more standard. The text is more non-committal. White can deploy his forces to greater effect after he gets a look at Black's reply.

5	. . .	B – N5

This aggressive sally weakens Black's Q-side.

6	P – KR3!	. . .

It's important to kick immediately, otherwise after . . . Q – B3 followed by . . . B × N White's Pawn formation could be smashed.

6 . . .   B – R4

As a result of this game 6 . . . P – KR4 became fashionable.
I had intended 7 P – Q4, P – QN4; 8 B – N3, N×P? (. . .
Q – B3 is better); 9 P×B, P×P; 10 N – N5. Unclear is 7 P – B4!?,
P – QN4 (if 7 . . . Q – B3; 8 Q – N3!, O – O – O; 9 B×N, P×B;
10 P×B, P×P; 11 N – R2, Q – R3; 12 Q – N3—but 11 . . .
P – Q4! is dangerous, Zhuravlev; 7 . . . B – Q2 avoids the piece
sac, but after 8 P – Q4 White has a superior variation of the Duras
Attack); 8 P×P, N – Q5; 9 P×P+, P – B3; 10 N×N!, B×Q; 11
B×P+, K – K2; 12 N – B5+, K – B3; 13 B×R, Q×B; 14 R×B,
Q×KP; 15 N – B3, Q – R1; 16 N – K3, Q×P; 17 P – Q4, K – N3;
18 P – QN4 and White's passed Q-side Pawns should win. (Grabczer-
ski-Brzuska, Warsaw 1961.)

7 P – B3   Q – B3?

Geller looked quite happy after his novelty, but sounder is 7
. . . N – B3; 8 P – Q4, N – Q2 bolstering the center.

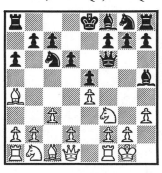

GELLER

Position after 7 . . .
Q – B3

FISCHER

8 P – KN4!   . . .

I realized the danger inherent in weakening my K-side, but felt
that I could capitalize on Black's lack of development (the traffic
jam on his K-side) before he could get to my King.

8 . . .   B – N3
9 P – Q4!   . . .

It's worth a Pawn to open up the game.

9 . . .   B×P

What else? The threat was 10 B – KN5 followed by P – Q5
winning a piece. He still looked happy.

10 QN – Q2   B – N3

No better is *10* . . . B × N; *11* N × B, P – K5; *12* R – K1,
P – Q4; *13* B – KN5, Q – Q3 (on *13* . . . Q – K3; *14* P – B4! is
the bone-crusher; or *13* . . . Q – N3; *14* Q – N3!, P – N4; *15*
Q × QP, P × B; *16* N – K5, Q – K3; *17* Q × Q+, P × Q; *18* N × N
wins); *14* P – B4!, P × P (if *14* . . . P – B3; *15* P × P, Q × P; *16*
B – N3); *15* P – Q5!, P – N4; *16* P × N, P × B; *17* R × P+, N – K2;
18 B × N, B × B; *19* Q – K2 wins.

An attempt to rehabilitate Geller's line was made in Smyslov–
Medina, Tel Aviv 1964, which continued: *10* . . . B – Q6; *11*
B × N+, P × B; *12* R – K1, O – O – O; but *13* R – K3! proved to
be very strong.

11 B × N+   . . .

Trading old advantages for new. Now Black's Q-side Pawns are
a shambles and his King can expect no shelter there.

11 . . .   P × B

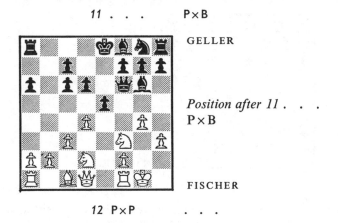

GELLER

Position after 11 . . .
P × B

FISCHER

12 P × P   . . .

A few weeks after the game it dawned on me that *12* Q – R4
would have been a tremendous shot. After *12* . . . N – K2
(apparently forced); *13* P × P, P × P; *14* R – K1, P – K5; *15* N × P,
Q × N; *16* Q × P+!, N × Q; *17* N – B6+, K – Q1; *18* R – K8 mate.
I was kicking myself for not having taken this course, but then I
found that after *12* Q – R4, K – Q2!; *13* P × P, P × P; *14* N – B4,
B – Q3 White has no immediate way to exploit the exposed King.

12 . . .   P × P
13 N × P!   B – Q3

On *13* . . . O – O – O; *14* Q – K2, K – N2; *15* N – N3 (intending N – R5+) is murderous.

     14 N×B!   . . .

A little surprise, permitting him to open his KR file. Of course not *14* N × QBP, P – KR4.

     14 . . .   **Q×N**

Geller took a half hour on this recapture and stopped looking happy. He rejected *14* . . . RP × N; *15* N – K4, Q – R5; *16* N × B+, P × N; *17* Q × P, Q × RP?; *18* R – K1+ and mates.

     15 R – K1+   **K – B1**

Another difficult decision. On *15*. . . N – K2; *16* N – B4, O – O – O; *17* Q – R4 White's attack comes first.

     16 N – B4   **P – KR4**

Still hoping to rise from the ashes and fan his attack.

     17 N×B   **P×N**

The best chance is *17* . . . Q × N.

     18 B – B4   **P – Q4?**

Loses outright. In the post-mortem Tal tried to hold the game with *18* . . . R – Q1; *19* Q – K2, P × P; but after *20* P × P Black is in virtual *zugzwang*. If *20* . . . Q – R2?; *21* B × P+ wins.

     19 Q – N3   **P×P**

Geller spent about forty minutes on this move. If *19* . . . N – K2; *20* R × N!, K × R; *21* Q – N7+ wins. Or *19* . . . N – B3; *20* Q – N7, R – K1; *21* R × R+, N × R; *22* R – K1, Q – B3; *23* Q – B8, etc.

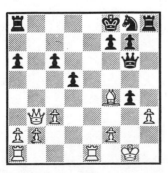

GELLER

Position after 19 . . .
P × P

FISCHER

                            20 Q – N7!   . . .

Stronger than *20* Q – N4+, N – K2; *21* Q × N+, K – N1; *22* P – KR4, etc.

                        20 . . .   P × P dis.+
                        21 B – N3   R – Q1
                        22 Q – N4+   Black resigns

He must now lose both a Knight *and* a Rook.

GELLER

Final Position after 22 Q – N4+

FISCHER

30 Gligorich [Yugoslavia] - Fischer

BLED 1961

KING'S INDIAN DEFENSE

A lyrical performance

This draw has the charm of perfection. Each move is interesting and, to this day, appears flawless.
With 17 . . . P – B4 Fischer launches an intricate double-Pawn sacrifice which involves exact timing. Gligorich rises to the occasion, returning material in an attempt to wrest the advantage. The economy and ingenuity displayed by both players produces a harmonious flow of movement, remarkable in its esthetic appeal. The effect is of a pas de deux *in which each partner contributes equally to the total symmetry.*

1	P – Q4	N – KB3
2	P – QB4	P – KN3
3	N – QB3	B – N2
4	P – K4	P – Q3
5	N – B3	O – O
6	B – K2	P – K4
7	O – O	N – B3
8	P – Q5	N – K2
9	N – K1	N – Q2
10	N – Q3	. . .

The older *10* P – B3, P – KB4; *11* B – K3, P – B5; *12* B – B2, P – KN4 has been abandoned. Black's K-side attack has practically been worked out to a forced mate!

10	. . .	P – KB4
11	P×P	. . .

Petrosian–Tal, in this same tournament, continued (with Black's N on K1): *11* P – B4, P×BP; *12* B×P, P×P; *13* N×P, N – B4; *14* B – N5, N – B3; *15* P – KN4, N – Q5; *16* N/3 – B2, Q – K2=.

11 . . .   N × BP

In this line White gets a grip on K4, Black on Q5. *11 . . .* P × P is more energetic.

12 P – B3   N – B3

For *12 . . .* N – Q5 see game number 28. Both moves give Black a nice game.

13 N – B2   N – Q5
14 N/2 – K4   N – R4

White has the P – QB5 lever; Black has the dynamic break with . . . P – KN4 – 5. Chances are roughly even.

15 B – N5   Q – Q2

Keeping an eye on the QP so that . . . P – B4 becomes possible.

16 P – KN3   P – KR3

In a later round Gligorich (as Black) played against Tal *16 . . .* P – B4? but after *17* N – N5!, N × N; *18* P × N White obtained a bind.

17 B – K3   P – B4!

I was informed that Gligorich thought I had blundered a Pawn, but it is a deliberate sac. On *17 . . .* N × B+; *18* Q × N, P – KN4; *19* P – B5 White has it all his own way.

18 B × N   . . .

Not *18* N – N5, N – B4; *19* B – Q2, P – R3, etc.

18 . . .   KP × B
19 N – QN5   P – R3

Not *19 . . .* B – K4?; *20* P – B4.

20 N/5 × P/6   . . .

Apparently Black has lost a Pawn without any visible compensation. His pieces, which are now so awkwardly placed, soon spring to life, however.

20 . . .   P – Q6!
21 Q × P   . . .

A double-edged game would result from *21* B × P, B – Q5 + ; *22* K – R1, N × P + ; *23* N × N, Q × N; *24* Q – B2, B – R6.

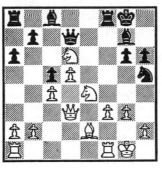

FISCHER

Position after 21 Q × P

GLIGORICH

21 . . .   B – Q5+

The combination requires intricate footwork. A mistake would be 21 . . . B × P; *22* N × B, B × R; *23* N – N6 and it's all over (*23* . . . B – Q5+ ?; *24* Q × B).

          22 K – N2   . . .

After *22* K – R1, N × P + ; *23* N × N, Q × N White is weak on all the squares and his K-side looks like Swiss cheese. Chances would be even.

          22 . . .   N × P!

This is the resource it was necessary to visualize as far back as move *17*.

FISCHER

Position after 22 . . . N × P

GLIGORICH

          23 N × B!   . . .

Best. Not *24* P × N? (or K × N), Q – R6 mate. On *24* N × N, Q × N again is good.

```
23 . . .         N × R
24 N – N6!       Q – QB2!
```

Blow for blow! The threat of mate on KR7 keeps the exchange.

```
25 R × N         Q × N
26 P – N4!       . . .
```

The saving clause.

```
26 . . .         Q × P
```

I saw the draw coming but felt the position was too precarious
to play for a win. On *26 . . . P × P; 27 P – B5!, B × P; 28 N × B,
Q × N; 29 Q × P+, K – R1; 30 Q × P+, K – N1; 31 K – R1* wins.
The only other try is *26 . . . R – B2; 27 P × P, B × P; 28
R – QN1* followed by P – Q6 with tons of play.

```
27 R – QN1       Q – R4
28 N × P         . . .
```

On *28 R × P, R – B2.*

```
28 . . .         Q × N
29 Q × P+        B – N2
30 R × P         Q – Q5
```

The only move. Gligorich was so sure I'd "find" it that he wrote
it down on his scoresheet while I was taking a minute to look for
something better.

```
31 B – Q3        R – B5
```

FISCHER

*Position after 31 . . .
R – B5*

GLIGORICH

```
32 Q – K6+       K – R1
33 Q – N6
```

Drawn

3 I Fischer - Petrosian [U.S.S.R.]

BLED 1961

CARO-KANN DEFENSE

The sincerest form of flattery

This is Fischer's only win against Petrosian and it is achieved through an unconscious mimicry of the latter's style. Right up to the endgame Fischer seems content to return the ball without trying to force the issue. Each attempt to seize the initiative is meticulously rebuffed. Move by move, they seem to be drifting toward a draw. Petrosian offers one at move 27, but Fischer declines. Perhaps out of irritation, Petrosian immediately commits his first and only error. And Fischer, reverting to his normal style of play, takes full advantage of it.

1	P – K4	P – QB3
2	P – Q4	. . .

For 2 N – QB3 see game 16.

2	. . .	P – Q4
3	N – QB3	. . .

For 3 P × P see game 20.

3	. . .	P × P
4	N × P	N – Q2

For 4 . . . B – B4 see game 49.

5	N – KB3	. . .

5 Q – K2, QN – B3 (weaker is 5 . . . KN – B3; 6 N – Q6 mate) gives White nothing. I tried 5 B – QB4 against Portisch at Stockholm 1962, which continued: 5 . . . KN – B3; 6 N – N5, N – Q4 (the idea is to omit the usual . . . P – K3 until after the QB has been developed); 7 KN – B3, P – KR3; 8 N – K4, QN – N3; 9 B – N3 (better is 9 B – Q3, N – N5; 10 O – O, N × B; 11 Q × N, P – K3; 12 N – K5! with pressure), B – B4; 10 N – N3, B – R2; 11 O – O, P – K3=.

```
        5 . . .              KN – B3
        6 N x N+             . . .
```

The Knight is not particularly well-placed after *6* N – N3.

```
        6 . . .              N x N
        7 B – QB4            B – B4
        8 Q – K2             P – K3
        9 B – KN5            B – N5!
```

This super-refinement reduces all of White's attacking prospects. Petrosian has a knack of snuffing out such dreams twenty moves before they even enter his opponent's head! After *9* . . . B – K2; *10* O – O – O, P – KR3; *11* B – R4, N – K5!?; *12* P – KN4, B – R2; *13* B – KN3, N x B; *14* BP x N, Q – B2; *15* N – K5, B – Q3; *16* P – KR4 keeps the initiative. (Tal–Fuster, Portoroz 1958.)

```
        10 O – O – O          B – K2
        11 P – KR3            . . .
```

It might have been better to prevent further simplifications with *11* K – N1, N – Q4; *12* B – B1!, O – O (not *12* . . . B x N; *13* Q x B, B – N4; *14* Q – N3!); *13* B – Q3, etc.

```
        11 . . .              B x N
        12 Q x B             N – Q4!
```

Forces an exchange of Bishops. If *13* B – Q2, B – N4, etc.

```
        13 B x B             Q x B
        14 K – N1            R – Q1
```

I had expected . . . O – O – O.

```
        15 Q – K4            P – QN4!
```

PETROSIAN

Position after 15 . . .
P – QN4

FISCHER

Now it's apparent why Black didn't castle long. He wants to

drum up counterplay on the Q-side, which he couldn't do if his King lived there.

16	B – Q3	P – QR4
17	P – QB3	. . .

The threat was . . . P – R5 – 6. Weaker is *17* P – QR3, P – N5. Already White has been thrown on a mild defensive.

17	. . .	Q – Q3

17 . . . P – R5 would be met by *18* P – R3.

18	P – KN3	. . .

I thought he wanted to exchange Queens.

18	. . .	P – N5!
19	P – QB4	. . .

Practically forced—but now the QP is weak.

19	. . .	N – B3
20	Q – K5	. . .

After *20* Q – K2, O – O (if *20* . . . Q × QP; *21* B × P); *21* B – B2, P – B4 White could easily end up with the bad Bishop.

20	. . .	P – B4

20 . . . Q × Q; *21* P × Q, N – Q2; *22* P – B4, N – B4 produces a drawn ending. And not *20* . . . Q × P; *21* Q × P.

21	Q – N5	. . .

This looked like a shot—

21	. . .	P – R3!

—but instead it's a shock.

PETROSIAN

Position after 21 . . .
P – R3

FISCHER

22 Q × BP   . . .

Now I saw that *22* Q × NP, K – K2!; *23* P × P, Q – B3! (not
23 . . . Q × BP; *24* KR – K1, QR – KN1; *25* R × P+!, K × R;
26 R – K1+ should win); *24* B – N6 (forced), QR – KB1; *25*
B × P, Q – K5+!; *26* K – R1, R – R2! and Black wins.

22 . . .   Q × Q
23 P × Q   K – K2

23 . . . R – QB1 immediately is also good.

24 P – B6   R – Q3
25 KR – K1   R × P
26 R – K5   R – R1
27 B – K4   . . .

After *27* R – QN5, R – R2 followed by . . . N – Q2 – B4
Black's solid as a rock. Right after I made this move, Petrosian
offered a draw. I was ready to accept, but Tal happened to be
standing there at that instant, hovering anxiously, since a drawn
result would practically clinch first place for him. So I refused—
not because I thought White has anything in the position, but
because I didn't want to give Tal the satisfaction!

27 . . .   R – Q3?

Serendipity. Simply *27* . . . N × B leads to a dead draw.

PETROSIAN

Position after 27 . . .
R – Q3

FISCHER

28 B × R   . . .

This obvious capture shattered Petrosian, who apparently had
been engrossed in analyzing the intricacies of *28* R × R, K × R; *29*
R × P+, P × R; *30* B × R, K – B4; *31* P – N3, N – Q2; *32* K – B2,
K – Q5 with an absolute bind on the dark squares.

28 . . .	R × R+
29 K – B2	R – B8

There's no turning back. If *29* . . . R – Q1; *30* R × P wins.

30 R × P	R × P+
31 K – N3	R – R7
32 P – B5	K – Q1

On *32* . . . R × P; *33* R – R7+, K – Q1; *34* R × P, R × P+;
35 K × P the Q-side Pawns hurtle toward a touchdown. The Bishop,
since it can control both wings at once, is vastly superior to the
Knight.

33 R – N5!	. . .

Not *33* R – R7, N – Q2!; *34* P – B6, N – N3 holds.

33 . . .	R × P

Now *33* . . . N – Q2 is refuted by *34* P – B6.

34 R – N8+	K – B2

Or *34* . . . K – K2; *35* K × P (not *35* P – B6?, N – Q4), R × P;
36 P – R4 wins.

35 R – N7+	K – B3

I suspect Petrosian saw White's reply, but wanted to be put
out of his misery. *35* . . . K – B1; *36* R × P, R × P+; *37* K × P
is futile.

36 K – B4!	Black resigns

There's no defense to the discovered checkmate.

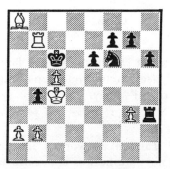

PETROSIAN

Final Position after 36
K – B4

FISCHER

32 Fischer - Tal [U.S.S.R.]

BLED 1961

SICILIAN DEFENSE

The moral victor

After an early lapse by Tal on move 6, Fischer relentlessly presses home his advantage. He misses several opportunities to shorten Tal's resistance, but the outcome is never really in doubt.

"Finally, he has not escaped me!" exulted Fischer.

"It is difficult to play against Einstein's theory," sighed Tal, who went on to capture first prize.

But it was Fischer, finishing a strong second, who had the consolation of scoring 3½ out of 4 against the Russian contingent, and of being the only player (in a field of twenty) to emerge undefeated.

1	P – K4	P – QB4
2	N – KB3	N – QB3
3	P – Q4	P × P
4	N × P	P – K3
5	N – QB3	. . .

No doubt Tal expected 5 N – N5 which I had played exclusively at Buenos Aires 1960. I still think that might be best (see game 54).

5	. . .	Q – B2
6	P – KN3	. . .

A perfectly legitimate treatment which Botvinnik labeled a "very cunning and well-masked idea." Actually no trap is intended. It becomes one only by virtue of Tal's reply.

6	. . .	N – B3 ?

Probably the losing move! Tal looked worried immediately after having made it, but I'm not sure he was convinced he had

really been careless. Correct is 6 . . . P – QR3; 7 B – N2,
N – B3; 8 O – O, etc.

7 N/4 – N5!   . . .

Curiously enough, Bisguier, who was present at Bled and wit-
nessed this game, forgot this move when he reached the identical
position against Benko at San Antonio, 1962!

7 . . .   Q – N1

On 7 . . . Q – R4; 8 B – Q2, Q – Q1; 9 B – B4, P – K4; 10
B – N5 is strong.

8 B – KB4   N – K4

Tal took a long time on this risky reply. The alternative 8 . . .
P – K4; 9 B – N5, P – QR3; 10 B × N (not 10 N – R3, P – N4;
11 B × N, P – N5!), P × N (not 10 . . . P × B; 11 N – R3, P – N4;
12 N – Q5); 11 B – N5 gives a clear advantage.

9 B – K2!   . . .

Perhaps Tal underestimated this simple move. It prepares
Q – Q4 and keeps an eye on the QN5 square.

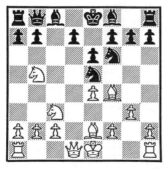

TAL

Position after 9 B – K2

FISCHER

On 9 . . . P – QR3; 10 Q – Q4, P – Q3; 11 R – Q1, P × N;
12 B × N wins at least a Pawn. Or 9 . . . P – Q3; 10 Q – Q4,
N – B3; 11 N × P+ (Tal pointed out 11 Q × QP!, B × Q; 12 B × B),
K – Q2; 12 B – QN5, B × N; 13 O – O – O, etc.

In the tournament book Tal suggested the rather startling
9 . . . N – N1 to avoid material loss. After 10 Q – Q4, P – B3;
11 O – O – O (if 11 B × N, P × B; 12 Q – B4, K – Q1! holds),
P – QR3; 12 N – Q6+, B × N; 13 Q × B, Q × Q; 14 R × Q leads to
a promising endgame.

9	. . .	B – B4
10	B×N!	Q×B
11	P – B4	Q – N1
12	P – K5	P – QR3

Tal didn't give this a second thought. On *12* . . . N – N1; *13* N – K4, B – K2; *14* Q – Q2 followed by N/5 – Q6+ and O – O – O is crushing.

13	P×N	P×N
14	P×P	. . .

Keres thought *14* N – K4, B – B1; *15* Q – Q4 was stronger. But I wanted the Pawn. With only two draws against Tal, out of six times at bat, I was in no mood to speculate!

14	. . .	R – N1
15	N – K4	B – K2
16	Q – Q4	R – R5

A desperate attempt to complicate. *16* . . . Q – B2 (BOTVINNIK) held out more chance for survival.

17	N – B6+	B×N

17 . . . K – Q1? loses to *18* Q – N6+.

18	Q×B	Q – B2
19	O – O – O!	. . .

19 B – R5 is answered by P – Q4. And *19* B×P?, Q – R4+ wins a piece.

19	. . .	R×RP
20	K – N1	. . .

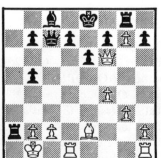

TAL

Position after 20 K – N1

FISCHER

20	. . .	R – R3

Not *20 . . . R – R4*; since *21* B – R5, P – Q4 (if *21 . . .*
P – Q3; *22* R × P!); *22* R × P!, P × R; *23* R – K1+ wins outright.
Also bad is *20 . . .* Q – R4; *21* P – N3! and the threat of
B – R5 is decisive.

21 B × P . . .

I was so intent on snatching material and not botching this one
that I missed *21* B – R5, P – Q3 (or *21 . . .* P – Q4; *22* R × P!);
22 KR – K1, Q – K2; *23* Q – R6, K – Q2; *24* Q × P with a quick
win in view.

21 . . . R – N3
22 B – Q3 P – K4

The best chance. On *22 . . .* Q – Q1; *23* Q – R6, P – B4; *24*
Q – R5+, K – K2; *25* P – KN4 cracks Black open.

23 P × P! . . .

Black was hoping for *23* Q × KP+, Q × Q; *24* P × Q, R × P with
some drawing prospects, even though a Pawn behind. In top-
flight chess, you have to drive your advantage home unmercifully.

23 . . . R × Q
24 P × R . . .

TAL

Position after 24 P × R

FISCHER

The threat is simply B × P.

24 . . . Q – B4

The only move. On *24 . . .* Q – N3; *25* KR – B1 wins easily.

25 B × P Q – KN4
26 B × R Q × BP
27 KR – B1 Q × P
28 B × P+ K – Q1

Black has succeeded in staving off immediate defeat, but the endgame is hopeless.

| | 29 | B – K6 | Q – R3 |

On *29 . . . K – B2; 30 B – B5* maintains the pressure.

30	B × P	B × B
31	R – B7	Q × P
32	R/1 × B+	K – K1
33	R/Q7 – K7+	K – Q1
34	R – Q7+	K – B1
35	R – B7+	K – Q1
36	R/KB7 – Q7+	K – K1
37	R – Q1	. . .

White has been gaining time on the clock.

| 37 | . . . | P – N4 |
| 38 | R – QN7 | Q – R4 |

38 . . . Q × P; 39 R × P is equally convincing.

| 39 | P – KN4 | Q – R6 |

Or *39 . . . Q × P; 40 R – R1, Q – Q5; 41 R – R8+ !, Q × R; 42 R – N8+* wins.

40	P – N5	Q – B6
41	R – K1+	K – B1
42	R × P	K – N2
43	R – N6	Q – KN6
44	R – Q1	Q – B2
45	R/1 – Q6	. . .

Threatening *46 R – N6+, K – R2; 47 R – R6+, K – N2; 48 R/N6 – N6+, K – B1; 49 R – R8+, K – B2; 50 R – R7+* winning the Queen.

| 45 | . . . | Q – B1 |

45 . . . Q – B4; 46 R – N7+, K – any; 47 R – Q8 mate.

| 46 | P – N3 | K – R2 |
| 47 | R – R6 | Black resigns |

Black must submit to the loss of his Queen or get mated. There is no defense against *48 R – R7+, K – N1; 49 R/6 – Q7*, etc.

33 Fischer - Trifunovich *[Yugoslavia]*

BLED 1961

RUY LOPEZ

The drawing master

Trifunovich has earned the reputation of being a very hard man to beat, and the other Grandmasters have acquired a healthy respect for his technical skill. At Bled, for example, he lost only this one game.

Trifunovich's experiment with a dubious line in the opening meets with an abrupt and effective antidote (13 N×P), saddling him with an isolated KP for the duration of the mid-game. He decides, perhaps unwisely, to sacrifice it at an appropriate moment to gain some counterplay. Although he succeeds in outplaying Fischer in the endgame, he cannot overcome his material deficit. What ultimately defeats him is force majeure.

1 P – K4	P – K4
2 N – KB3	N – QB3
3 B – N5	P – QR3
4 B – R4	N – B3
5 O – O	N × P
6 P – Q4	P – QN4
7 B – N3	P × P?

Considered to be weak—and it is. But Trifunovich must have had some equalizing idea in mind, since he rarely chooses a genuinely risky line. The tried and tested *6 . . . P – Q4* must be played.

8 R – K1 . . .

A reader of Tal's Latvian chess magazine (*Shakhmaty*) suggested *8 N×P*, but . . . N – K2! seems to hold: *e.g.*, 9 R – K1 (if 9 B×P+, K×B; *10* Q – B3+, K – N1; *11* Q × N, P – Q4 is adequate), P – Q4; *10* N – B6!, N×N; *11* B×P, B – N2!; *12* B×N, B – K2; *13* B×N+, B×B; *14* Q – K2, K – B1, etc.

	8 . . .	P – Q4
	9 N – B3!	. . .

9 N × P?, N × N; *10* Q × N, B – K3 (threatening P – QB4) is better for Black.

	9 . . .	B – K3

On *9* . . . P × N; *10* B × P, B – N2; *11* B × N (not *11* R × N+?, N – K2!), B – K2 (*11* . . . Q × Q? loses to *12* B × N+ +); *12* Q – K2 prevents Black from castling.

	10 N × N	P × N
	11 R × P	B – K2
	12 B × B	P × B

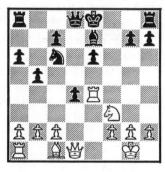

TRIFUNOVICH

Position after 12 . . .
P × B

FISCHER

	13 N × P!	. . .

An improvement over the "book" line. Trifunovich probably expected the usual *13* R × KP, but after Q – Q4!; *14* Q – K2, O – O; *15* R × B, N × R; *16* Q × N, QR – K1; *17* Q × P, R – B2; *18* Q – N3, R × N!; *19* P × R, R – K8+; *20* K – N2, Q – B5; *21* K – R3, Q – K3+; *22* Q – N4, Q – QB3 and shortly drawn. (Dolodonov–Kicin, corres., USSR 1965.)

	13 . . .	O – O

He thought quite a while on this. Weak is *13* . . . P – K4?; *14* Q – R5+, P – N3; *15* N × N, etc. On *13* . . . Q – Q4; *14* Q – N4, O – O – O; *15* B – K3 Black's KP is untenable. Finally the "simplifying combination" *13* . . . N × N; *14* R × N, Q × R?; *15* Q × Q, R – Q1 falls short after *16* Q – KN4.

	14 Q – N4	N × N
	15 R × N	Q – B1
	16 R – K4	R – B3

White has a strategically won game, but the technical problems are considerable. Moreover a tempting trap now stared me in the face.

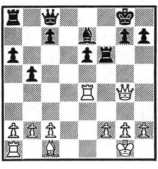

TRIFUNOVICH

Position after 16 . . .
R – B3

FISCHER

| 17 B – K3 | . . . |

Keres suggests *17* B – B4 in the tournament book, but B – Q3 is an adequate reply.

I was considering the blunder *17* B – N5?, R – N3; *18* P – KR4, P – R3; *19* Q – R5, but Trifunovich seemed too quiet all of a sudden, and I suspected he had tuned in on my brain waves. At the last minute I saw *19 . . .* Q – K1! wins; for if *20* B × B, R × P+!; *21* K × R, Q × Q.

17 . . .	Q – Q2
18 R – Q1	Q – B3
19 B – Q4	R – N3
20 Q – K2	R – Q1
21 P – KN3	Q – Q4

Threatening . . . P – B4.

| 22 R – K1! | P – B4 |

Black's welcome to *22 . . .* Q × P; *23* P – N3, Q – R4 (otherwise R – R1); *24* R × P with a crushing attack.

23 B – B3	R – Q3
24 B – K5	R – Q1
25 B – B4!	. . .

Preventing . . . Q – Q7.

| 25 . . . | P – B5 |

Again *25 . . .* Q × P is met by *26* P – N3 followed by R × P. Black decides to sacrifice his KP in order to get some activity.

After *25* . . . K – B2; *26* P – N3 (threatening P – QR4 at the right moment) leaves Black with little to do but sit back and wonder where White will penetrate next.

26	R × KP	R × R
27	Q × R+	Q × Q
28	R × Q	B – B3
29	R × P	R – Q8+
30	K – N2	. . .

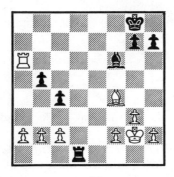

TRIFUNOVICH

Position after 30 K – N2

FISCHER

30 . . .   B × P

After the game Gligorich suggested that *30* . . . R – N8! offered drawing chances. It makes things harder, but White should win after *31* P – QR4! (not *31* P – N3, R – N7), R × P (if *31* . . . P – N5; *32* R – B6, R × P; *33* R × P, B – B6; *34* B – Q6!); *32* P × P, R × NP; *33* R – B6, P – B6; *34* R – K6, K – B2; *35* R – K2 and eventually White's King marches to Q3 and, after trading Bishops, captures the weak QBP.

31	R – QN6	R – QR8
32	R × P	R × P
33	R – QB5	R – R5

On *33* . . . P – B6; *34* B – K5, B – R8; *35* R – B7, R × P; *36* R × P+, K – B1; *37* R – B7 leads to an easy win. Black's QBP isn't going anywhere.

34	B – K5	B × B
35	R × B	R – R7

On *35* . . . R – R6; *36* R – K3!, R – R7; *37* R – QB3 wins.

36	R – K2	K – B2
37	K – B3	K – B3

38	K – K4	P – N4
39	K – Q4	K – B4
40	P – B3	. . .

While not bad in itself, the text indicates a wrong frame of mind. White should be looking for the quickest win, not ways to prolong Black's agony.

Simply *40* K × P, K – N5; *41* K – N3 is easy.

40	. . .	P – B6!
41	R – B2?	. . .

The simplest path is *41* K × P, R – R6+; *42* K – Q4, R × P; *43* P – B4, etc. (KERES) Curiously now, I never do win his QBP!

41	. . .	R – R6
42	K – B4	P – R4
43	K – N4	R – R1
44	P – B4	. . .

On *44* K × P, P – R5 offers a few little problems.

44	. . .	K – K5!

I hadn't seen this defense. Now Black saves his QBP and the win takes twenty moves longer than it should have.

45	P × P	K – K6
46	R – N2	. . .

If the Rook leaves the second rank, then . . . K – Q7.

46	. . .	K – Q5

On *46* . . . R – QB1; *47* P – R4, K – B6; *48* R – N1, K – B7; *49* R – Q1, K × P; *50* R – Q4 followed by R – QB4 does the trick.

TRIFUNOVICH

Position after 46 . . .
K – Q5

FISCHER

47	R – K2	R – N1+
48	K – R4	R – N1
49	P – R4	R – KB1
50	R – K7	R – B6
51	R – Q7+	K – B5
52	R – B7+	K – Q5
53	R – Q7+	. . .

Repeating moves to gain time on the clock.

53	. . .	K – B5
54	R – B7+	K – Q5
55	K – N3	R × P
56	R – Q7+	K – K5
57	R – KR7	K – Q5
58	R × P	R – N8
59	R – R8	R – N8+
60	K – R4	R – R8+

There is no time for *60* . . . R – N7 because of *61* P – N6.

61	K – N5	R – N8+
62	K – B6	R – N8
63	R – Q8+	K – B5
64	R – K8	. . .

Threatening R – K4 mate!

| 64 | . . . | K – N5 |
| 65 | K – Q5 | R – Q8+ |

On *65* . . . K – R6; *66* R – QN8 wins.

66	K – K6	R – K8+
67	K – B7	R – B8+
68	K – N6	R – B7
69	P – R5	. . .

Now the RP becomes the dangerous candidate.

69	. . .	R × P
70	P – R6	R – KR7
71	P – R7	P – B7
72	R – QB8	K – N6
73	K – N7	Black resigns

34 Bertok *[Yugoslavia]* - Fischer

STOCKHOLM 1962

QUEEN'S GAMBIT DECLINED

Hanging pawns unhung

*Classical theory expounds the danger of "hanging Pawns,"
but Fischer demonstrates here, in a revolutionary manner, that
they are just as often an asset as a liability.
Bertok's errors seem insignificant, yet he drifts into a
passive position. On the verge of exploiting Black's loose
center, he always lacks just the one tempo needed to do so.
Meanwhile, using the open QN-file as a base of operations,
Fischer manages to force White into a defensive posture. In the
midst of this Q-side tension, the winning move (21 . . .
P – N4) comes unexpectedly on the opposite wing.*

1	P – Q4	P – Q4
2	P – QB4	P – K3
3	N – QB3	B – K2

A refinement attributed to Petrosian, but actually played by Charousek in the 'nineties—and probably dating back even farther.

4	N – B3	. . .

White, having no other good waiting move, is obliged to develop, thus restricting his option of playing this Knight to K2.

4 P×P, P×P; *5* B – B4, P – QB3; *6* P – K3, B – KB4; *7* P – KN4 (R. Byrne's *7* KN – K2! is best), B – K3 (*7* . . . B – N3! is better); *8* P – KR3 was played frequently in the 1963 title match between Botvinnik and Petrosian. White is slightly better.

4	. . .	N – KB3
5	B – N5	. . .

Back to the main line. The shadow boxing is over.

5	. . .	O – O
6	P – K3	P – KR3

Petrosian usually omits this move (see note to Black's 8th).

7	B – R4	P – QN3

Tartakover's Defense.

8	P × P	. . .

The best procedure, opening the QB-file and preparing R – QB1
with pressure on Black's QBP. An alternative is *8* B – Q3, B – N2;
9 O – O, QN – Q2; *10* R – B1, P – B4; *11* Q – K2, P × BP; *12*
B × P, N – K5=. (Petrosian–Fischer, Candidates' 1959.)

8	. . .	N × P

Inferior here is *8* . . . P × P; *9* B – Q3, O – O; *10* N – K5!
followed by P – B4 with a Pillsbury attacking formation: White has
P – KN4 – 5 in the air—this line is playable for Black only with
his Pawn on KR2 (instead of KR3).

9	B × B	Q × B
10	N × N	P × N

The text is drawish, but I had already clinched first prize.

FISCHER

Position after 10 . . .
P × N

BERTOK

11	B – K2	. . .

Sharper is *11* R – QB1, B – K3!; *12* Q – R4, P – QB4; *13* Q – R3,
R – B1; *14* B – K2 and now K – B1 levels while *14* . . . Q – N2!
is the prescription for maintaining tension. If *15* P × P, P × P; *16*
O – O (*16* R × P?, R × R; *17* Q × R, Q × P is bad for White),
Q – N3 is double-edged.

11	. . .	B – K3!

The right post. At QN2 this Bishop would block the QN-file and obstruct later operations there.

12 O – O   P – QB4
13 P×P?   . . .

Producing hanging center Pawns which, in this case, exert a tremendously cramping influence on White's future development. Better is *13* N – K5, N – Q2 (not *13* . . . P – B5?; *14* P – QN3, P – QN4; *15* P – QR4) with equality.

13 . . .   P×P
14 Q – R4   Q – N2!
15 Q – R3   N – Q2
16 N – K1   . . .

What else is there? Black's center is well-protected, and he is ready to assume the Q-side initiative with . . . P – QR4 and Q–N5.

16 . . .   P – QR4
17 N – Q3   P – B5
18 N – B4   KR – N1

FISCHER

Position after 18 . . . KR – N1

BERTOK

19 QR – N1?   . . .

White's game is already difficult, e.g., *19* B – B3, N – B3; *20* KR – Q1, Q×P; *21* Q×Q, R×Q; *22* N×P, N×N; *23* B×N, B×B; *24* R×B, P – B6!; *25* R/5 – Q1 (if *25* R – QB5, P – B7; *26* R – QB1, R – Q1 wins), P – B7; *26* R/Q1 – QB1, QR – N1; *27* K – B1, R – N8; *28* K – K2, R×QR; *29* R×R, R – N8 wins.

Best is *19* N×B, P×N; *20* B – N4, R – R3!; *21* P – QN3! (if *21* Q – K7?, N – B1; or *21* QR – N1, Q – N5; *22* Q – B3, Q×Q; *23* P×Q, R/3 – N3), P×P; *22* P×P, Q×P; *23* Q – K7, N – B1;

24 R – R3 with good drawing chances (if *24* . . . Q – N5; *25* Q × Q, R × Q; *26* B – K2, R – R2; *27* KR – R1, P – R5; *28* B – Q1, etc.).

	19 . . .	B – B4!
	20 QR – Q1	N – B3
	21 R – Q2	. . .

The following variation gives some insight into the nature of White's problem: *21* B – B3, Q × P; *22* Q × Q, R × Q; *23* N × P, N × N; *24* B × N (if *24* R × N, B – K3; *25* R – QB5, R – QB1!; *26* R × RP, P – B6; *27* R – QB1, P – B7; *28* B – K4, R – N8!; *29* R × R, P × R = Q+; *30* B × Q, R – B8 mate), R – QB1; *25* P – K4, B – K3!; *26* B × B, P × B; *27* P – QR4, P – B6; *28* R – QB1, P – B7 and White, completely tied up, must lose material.

	21 . . .	P – N4!

FISCHER

Position after 21 . . .
P – N4

BERTOK

Practically forcing the win of a piece.

	22 N × P	. . .

To break the hammer-lock. On *22* N – R5, N – K5; *23* R – B2, Q – N5 is crushing.

	22 . . .	N × N
	23 B × P	. . .

Not *23* B – B3?, B – Q6.

	23 . . .	B – K3

Black has some temporary discomfort but it's only a matter of time before he consolidates and wins with his extra piece.

	24 KR – Q1	. . .

Blundering a Pawn. The lesser evil is *24* B × N, B × B; *25* P – B3, but White is still lost if Black exercises a modicum of caution.

24 . . .		N × P!

Threatening mate.

25	Q × N	B × B
26	P – KR4	R – K1
27	Q – KN3	Q – K2
28	P – N3	B – K3
29	P – B4	P – N5

Sealing the N-file and neutralizing all threats.

30	P – R5	Q – B4+
31	R – B2	B – B4
White resigns		

FISCHER

Final Position after 31 . . .
B – B4

BERTOK

35 Fischer - Julio Bolbochan [Argentina]

STOCKHOLM 1962

SICILIAN DEFENSE

A brilliant cadenza

*Called upon to face his favorite defense, Fischer quickly
obtains the advantage against Black's rather passive
opening strategy. Bolbochan, burdened with a bad Bishop
against a good Knight, defends with extreme care but is
gradually forced to retreat behind his lines. Disdaining several
opportunities to enter a favorable ending, Fischer presses
for a quick decision in the mid-game. His judgment is rewarded
when the pressure which he painstakingly has accumulated
erupts in a violent attack, beginning with 34 P×P. Fischer's
invasion on the weakened squares is a model of accuracy. It
culminates in a keen combination which, appropiately, earned
a tie for the first brilliancy prize.*

1	P – K4	P – QB4
2	N – KB3	P – Q3
3	P – Q4	P×P
4	N×P	N – KB3
5	N – QB3	P – QR3
6	P – KR3	. . .

Black's loss of time with . . . P – QR3 may possibly justify
this loss of time. The variation is specifically directed against the
characteristic. . . P – K4 of the Najdorf System. Thus if *6* . . .
P – K4; *7* KN – K2, B – K2 (or *7* . . . B – K3; *8* P – KN4,
P – Q4; *9* P×P, N×QP; *10* B – N2 with a comfortable edge);
8 P – KN4, O – O; *9* N – N3!, P – KN3; *10* P – N5, N – K1; *11*
P – KR4 with a powerful attack: e.g., *11* . . . P – B3?; *12*
B – B4+, K – N2; *13* P – R5, P×NP; *14* P×P, P×P; *15* N – R5+!

6 . . .   N – B3

For 6 . . . P – KN3 see game 43. For 6 . . . P – QN4 see game 41.

7	P – KN4	N × N
8	Q × N	P – K4
9	Q – Q3	B – K2

More accurate is 9 . . . B – K3 immediately.

10 P – N5!   . . .

Weak is 10 P – N3 as played in Gereben–Geller, Budapest 1952.

10 . . .   N – Q2

Now the Knight interferes with the normal development of the QB. But on 10 . . . N – R4; 11 P – KR4 followed by an eventual B – K2 will cause trouble.

11 B – K3   . . .

Sharper is 11 P – KR4, N – B4; 12 Q – B3.

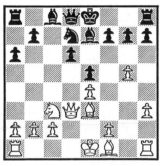

BOLBOCHAN

Position after 11 B – K3

FISCHER

11 . . .   N – B4?

The best chance is 11 . . . B × P; 12 B × B, Q × B; 13 Q × P, Q – K2; 14 Q × Q+, K × Q; 15 N – Q5+, K – B1; 16 O – O – O, P – KN3 (котоv) holding White to a minimal endgame edge.

12	Q – Q2	B – K3
13	O – O – O	O – O
14	P – B3	R – B1
15	K – N1	. . .

Amateurs are often puzzled by this apparent loss of time. Actually it is a handy defensive move, getting out of the pin on the

QB-file which could become annoying after . . . P – QN4 – 5. One never knows when lightning will strike!

15 . . .	N – Q2

The Knight has no future on QB4, so Bolbochan tries to bring it into play via QN3.

16 P – KR4	P – N4
17 B – R3	B × B

After *17* . . . N – N3; *18* B × N, Q × B; *19* N – Q5, Q – Q1 (not *19* . . . B × N?; *20* B × R); *20* N × B+, Q × N; *21* Q × P, etc.

On *17* . . . R – K1; *18* N – Q5, B – B1; *19* P – R5 with a tremendous bind. Black has to reckon with the possible breakthrough on KN6.

18 R × B	N – N3
19 B × N	Q × B
20 N – Q5	. . .

White has a strategically won game; his Knight cannot be dislodged.

20 . . .	Q – Q1
21 P – KB4	. . .

Threatening P – B5. An example of some of the nonsense that has been written about my games, both by admirers and detractors, is the following (by Lublinsky) in the 1962 Russian *Yearbook:* "Brilliant intuition! Fischer refuses to enter into the Rook and Pawn endgame and plays to continue his attack." But White can't! Not *21* N × B+?, Q × N; *22* Q × P??, KR – Q1 and Black wins.

21 . . .	P × P
22 Q × P	Q – Q2
23 Q – B5	QR – Q1

Insufficient is *23* . . . KR – Q1? (or *23* . . . Q × Q?; *24* N × B+); *24* Q × Q, R × Q; *25* N – N6.

24 R – R3!	. . .

Shows how ideal the position is—White can afford the luxury of probing weaknesses on both wings.

24 . . .   Q – R2

BOLBOCHAN

Position after 24 . . .
Q – R2

FISCHER

25 R – QB3   . . .

Tempting is *25* N – B6+!?, B×N (if *25* . . .P×N?; *26*
P×P, K – R1; *27* Q – N5, R – KN1; *28* P×B!); *26* P×B, P – N3;
27 Q – N5, K – R1 and White has no forced win in sight.
Objectively best is *25* N×B+, Q×N; *26* R×RP, KR – K1; *27*
P – R4! But I was hoping to win in the middle game. Ironically, I
wouldn't have been awarded the brilliancy prize had I chosen the
best line here. They don't give medals for endgame technique!

25 . . .   P – N3!

On *25* . . . Q – Q2?; *26* R – B7 wins. Or *25* . . . R – Q2?;
26 N – B6+!, B×N (*26* . . . P×N; *27* P×P, K – R1; *28* P×B
wins); *27* P×B, P – N3; *28* Q – N5, K – R1; *29* Q – R6, R – KN1;
30 R – B8! forces mate.

26	Q – N4	Q – Q2
27	Q – B3	Q – K3

Not *27* . . . R – B1?; *28* R×R, R×R; *29* N – N6.

28	R – B7	QR – K1

On *28* . . . R – Q2; *29* N – B4 wins. And after *28* . . .
KR – K1; *29* R – KB1 Black hardly has any moves. *29* . . .
R – QB1 is answered by *30* R – R7, R – R1; *31* R×R, R×R; *32*
N – B7.

29	N – B4	Q – K4
30	R – Q5	Q – R1
31	P – R3	. . .

BOLBOCHAN

Position after 31 P – R3

FISCHER

|31 . . .|P – R3|

A bid for freedom—otherwise R – R7 mops up the Q-side Pawns.
On *31* . . . P – B3; *32* Q – QN3!, R – B2; *33* R × QP, P × P;
34 P × P, Q – K4; *35* R – KB6!, R – KB1; *36* R × R, R × R; *37*
R – B8+, B – B1; *38* N – K6 wins.

|*32* P × P|Q × P|

On *32* . . . B × P?; *33* N × P!, P × N; *34* Q – QN3 is decisive
(*34* . . . R – B2; *35* R – KB5).

|*33* P – R5|B – N4|

After *33* . . . P – N4; *34* N – K2 followed by N – Q4 (or
N3) – B5 maintains a winning bind. Black also has to contend with
the threat of R – R7.

|*34* P × P!|P × P|

On *34* . . . B × N; *35* P × P+, R × P; *36* R × R, K × R; *37*
R – R5! wins.

BOLBOCHAN

Position after 34 . . .
P × P

FISCHER

35 Q – QN3! . . .

The *coup de grâce.*

35 . . . R x N

On 35 . . . K – R1 (or 35 . . . B x N; 36 R – R5+); 36 N x P+, Q x N; 37 R x B, R – B8+ (if 37 . . . Q x R; 38 Q – R3+ forces mate); 38 K – R2, Q x R; 39 Q – R3+, K – N1; 40 Q x R leads to a win.

36 R – K5+	K – B1
37 R x R+	Black resigns

After 37 . . . K x R; 38 Q – K6+, K – B1; 39 Q – B8+ mates.

36 Fischer - Korchnoi *[U.S.S.R.]*

STOCKHOLM 1962

RUY LOPEZ

Gaston and Alphonse

"I like to coax my opponents into attacking, to let them taste the joy of the initiative, so that they may get carried away, become careless, and sacrifice material," wrote Korchnoi, whose comments are interwoven in the notes.

Fischer needs no coaxing. He improves on a well-known Capablanca line (with 15 P – Q5). Still, the advantage he derives, if any, is microscopic. Korchnoi seems to labor under the delusion that he has the worst of it, though Fischer keeps asserting that White has nothing. Nevertheless, he over-reaches himself, giving Korchnoi a chance to assume the initiative. But Black falters and then cracks under the pressure of the clock.

1	P – K4	P – K4
2	N – KB3	N – QB3
3	B – N5	P – QR3
4	B – R4	N – B3
5	O – O	B – K2
6	R – K1	P – QN4
7	B – N3	O – O
8	P – B3	P – Q3
9	P – Q4	. . .

An old try, championed by Yates and Alekhine, but discarded in the course of progress. It is still theoretically crucial—on its success (or failure) hinges the necessity of White's losing a tempo here with the customary 9 P – KR3.

9	. . .	B – N5
10	B – K3	P × P

Gligorich's *10 . . . P – Q4* is probably best. On the old *10 . . . N × KP!?; 11 B – Q5, Q – Q2; 12 B × KN, P – Q4; 13 B × P+!, K × B; 14 P × P*, White, according to Robert Byrne, can keep his extra Pawn and weather the attack.

11 P × P   N – QR4

11 . . . P – Q4; 12 P – K5, N – K5; 13 QN – Q2, N × N; 14 Q × N, B × N; 15 P × B, B – N5; 16 Q – B2, B × R; 17 Q × N, B – N5; 18 B × P is known to favor White.

12 B – B2   . . .

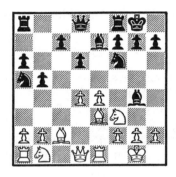

KORCHNOI

Position after 12 B – B2

FISCHER

12 . . .   N – B5

12 . . . P – B4 may be better; *13 QN – Q2, P × P; 14 B × P, N – B3; 15 B – K3, P – Q4; 16 P × P, N – N5=.* (Yates–Bogol-yubow, New York 1924.) Hence *13 P × P, P × P; 14 QN – Q2* seems the only try for an advantage.

13 B – B1   P – B4
14 P – QN3   . . .

Interesting is *14 QN – Q2, N × N; 15 Q × N, B × N; 16 P × B.* (Geller–Panno, Amsterdam 1956.)

14 . . .   N – QR4

Korchnoi is of a mind that the retreat *14 . . . N – N3* com-pletely equalizes. But White can keep a pull after *15 QN – Q2, P × P* (maybe better is *15 . . . KN – Q2; 16 P – KR3, B – R4; 17 P – KN4, B – N3; 18 P – Q5, B – B3; 19 R – N1, P – KR4!* Pietzsch–Szabo, 1962); *16 P – KR3, B – R4; 17 P – KN4!, B – N3; 18 N × P.* (Pietzsch–Matanovich, Havana, 1962.)

15 P – Q5!   . . .

"A strong continuation which improves on *15* B – N2, N – B3!;
16 P – Q5, N – N5 (Capablanca–Bogolyubow, London 1922); when
Black gains the advantage of the pair of Bishops." (KORCHNOI.)

15 . . .   N – Q2

On *15* . . . N × KP; *16* R × N, B × N; *17* Q × B, B – B3; *18*
N – B3, P – N5; *19* B – N2, P × N; *20* B × P, B × B; *21* Q × B White
has a big advantage.

16 QN – Q2   B – B3

Aiming to strike on the dark squares before White can mobilize
a K-side initiative.

17 R – N1   P – B5

Korchnoi considers this overambitious, believing that it creates
too many Pawn weaknesses. He thinks Black ought to play *17*
. . . N – K4; *18* P – KR3, N × N+; *19* N × N, B × N; *20* Q × B,
P – N5; but after *21* B – B4, R – K1 (too passive is *21* . . .
N – N2; *22* B – Q3, etc.); *22* Q – N3, B – K4; *23* B × B, R × B (if
23 . . . P × B; *24* B – Q3); *24* P – B4, R – K2; *25* QR – Q1
(threatening P – K5) maintains the pressure.

18 P – KR3   . . .

"White does not fall for *18* P – N4?, P – B6!; *19* P × N, P × N;
20 B × P, N – K4 when the ensuing break-up of the Pawn protection of White's King more than compensates for his extra doubled
Pawn." (KORCHNOI.)

18 . . .   B × N

"Giving White the two Bishops, but if *18* . . . B – R4; *19*
P – QN4! is now strong: *19* . . . P – B6; *20* P × N, P × N; *21*
B × P, N – K4; *22* P – N4." (KORCHNOI.)
In this line simply *19* . . . N – N2 followed by . . . P – R4
yields good counterplay. On *18* . . . B – R4 I intended *19*
P – KN4! (deadening Black's Bishop is worth this weakness).
B – N3; *20* N – B1 – N3, etc.

19 N × B   P × P

On *19* . . . R – K1; *20* P – QN4, N – N2; *21* N – Q4 is strong.
And *19* . . . P – B6?; *20* P – R3! leaves the BP artificially

isolated: White can encircle it by B – K3 – Q4, R – K3, etc. Black's Knight on QR4 is stranded; should it retreat to QN2, then P – QN4 smothers its future.

20	P×P	Q – B2
21	B – K3	. . .

"Up to here, White has played in excellent style, but this inaccurate move considerably improves the Black position. White ought to play *21* B – Q2 or, still better, *21* R – K2! protecting the KB and preparing the powerful maneuver N – Q4." (KORCHNOI.)

The truth is, White just doesn't have that much. After *21* B – Q2 or R – K2 Black can still reply with . . . B – B6.

21	. . .	B – B6!
22	R – K2	P – N5

"Now Black has sufficient play on the black squares." (KORCHNOI.)

23	N – Q4	. . .

KORCHNOI

Position after 23 N – Q4

FISCHER

23	. . .	KR – K1

"Worried by his loose Pawn front and his scattered minor pieces, Black decides that he ought to get another piece into play rather than spend a move protecting his King's side. However, Fischer soon demonstrates that the White Knight obtains splendid prospects on the King's side, hence *23* . . . P – N3 is much better." (KORCHNOI.)

On *23* . . . P – N3; *24* B – Q3, N – B4; *25* R – B2, N/R4–N2; *26* N – K2, B – N2 the Bishop dances away and White has nothing.

24	N – B5	N – N2
25	B – Q4	P – N3

The threat was N × P.

          26 N – R6+   K – B1
          27 R – B1!   . . .

"This powerful move is a reminder to Black that he has problems on the QB-file as well as in the neighborhood of his King." (KORCHNOI.)

          27 . . .   QR – B1

"In the event of White's exchanging Bishops, Black wants to be ready to recapture with a piece (Queen or Rook) rather than be left with a Pawn on QB6 which will most likely be fatally weak." (KORCHNOI.)
   Not 27 . . . B × B; 28 Q × B, P – B3; 29 Q × NP.

          28 B – Q3   . . .

"This inaccuracy grants Black a fresh chance of recovery. A very strong continuation here was 28 R – K3! with the threat of 29 B × B, P × B; 30 Q – Q4!, P – B3; 31 B – N1, when the QBP would fall." (KORCHNOI.)

          28 . . .   Q – R4

On 28 . . . Q – Q1; 29 R/2 – B2 maintains the pin.

          29 R/2 – B2   N – K4
          30 B – B1   N – B4

"Sacrificing a Pawn for the moment; but the Black pieces obtain. excellent activity." (KORCHNOI.)

          31 B × B   P × B
          32 R × P   K – N2
          33 N – N4   N × N
          34 Q × N   R – QN1

Breaking the pin and threatening the KP and/or the NP. Not 34 . . . R × P??; 35 Q × R/8.

          35 R – B3   . . .

"White's best chance is to revive his attack on the King's wing." (KORCHNOI.)

          35 . . .   N × KP
          36 Q – B4   P – B4

"*36 . . .* R – N2 may be safer here." (KORCHNOI.)
The text weakens the K-side, but White can't exploit it.

37	R – K3	R – K4
38	R – B6	QR – K1!?

"Short of time, I overlooked White's next move completely.
Even so, the text is not bad, but for practical purposes Black ought
to choose the simple *38 . . .* P – N4 maintaining a good position
without risk." (KORCHNOI.)
    After *38 . . .* P – N4; *39* Q – B3, QR – K1; *40* R × RP, Q × P;
41 P – QN4 the chances are approximately equal.

                    39 R × QP!   . . .

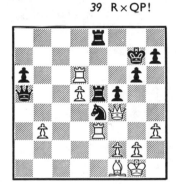

KORCHNOI

Position after 39 R × QP

FISCHER

        39 . . .   Q – R8?

"A bad error, after which Black is two Pawns behind with no
compensation. Correct and necessary is *39 . . .* P – N4!; *40*
R – Q7+, K – N3; *41* Q – B3, Q – N3! with the threat *42 . . .*
N × P! For instance:
    "A] *42* B – Q3?, N × P; *43* R × R, N × B dis. ch.
    "B] *42* P – N4?, N × P; *43* R × R, N × NP dis. ch.
    "C] *42* R × N! (best), R × R; *43* P – N4, R – KB5; *44* P × P+,
K – R3; *45* Q – N3, R – K4 with at least a draw.
    "Instead, Black panics at the unexpected turn of events, and
Fischer efficiently finishes the game in a few moves." (KORCHNOI.)
    Incidentally, Korchnoi neglects to add that after *41 . . .*
Q – N3! Black has the additional threat of . . . N – B3 (as well
as . . . N × P) trapping the Rook. He also neglects to analyze
the right defense: *42* Q – K2!, N × P (What else? If *42 . . .*
P – B5; *43* R × N, R × R; *44* Q – B2, K – R3; *45* R – QB7! wins);
43 R × R!, N – K5+ (it's fascinating that Black has no better

discovery; if *43 . . . N – N5+* ; *44* R – K3!, R × R; *45* Q × P, Q × Q; *46* B × Q, N – B3!; *47* R – Q8, R × NP=. But not *43 . . . N × P++?* ; *44* K – R2, Q – N8+ ; *45* K – N3!, P – B5+ ; *46* K – B3!, R × R; *47* Q × P+! wins); *44* K – R2, R × R; *45* Q × P, Q × Q; *46* B × Q, N – B3 regaining the QP with a draw in view.

40	R × RP	Q – Q5
41	R – Q3	Q – N7
42	P – Q6	P – N4
43	Q – K3	P – B5
44	Q – R7+	Black resigns

Black must lose a Rook after *44 . . . K – B1; 45* P – Q7, R – Q1; *46* Q – N6, K – K2; *47* Q × R+, K × Q; *48* R – R8+ followed by P – Q8 = Q+.

KORCHNOI

Final Position after 44 Q – R7+

FISCHER

37 Keres [U.S.S.R.] - Fischer

CURAÇAO 1962

SICILIAN DEFENSE

Only a draw

This contest brings to mind Emanuel Lasker's axiom: "When evenly matched opponents play 'correctly,' the games seldom have any content and frequently end in draws." Here a little incorrect play provokes a series of brilliant moves leading to a most unusual draw.

Employing a slow, closed system against the Sicilian, Keres is strategically outplayed. By adjournment, however, he manages to achieve equality. Fischer refuses a draw, and the struggle flares anew. Working with a Rook against two minor pieces, he makes steady inroads. Each serpentine twist in the endgame, including the double error on move 56, is a joy, a revelation, and a study in itself. Keres' saving resources smack of sheer wizardry.

1	P – K4	P – QB4
2	N – K2	P – Q3
3	P – KN3	P – KN3

Sharper is 3 . . . P – Q4! 4 B – N2, P×P; 5 B×P (on Lombardy's 5 N – QB3, N – KB3 equalizes—but not 5 . . . P – B4; 6 P – Q3, P×P; 7 P×P, N – KB3; 8 O – O and White's attack is worth more than a Pawn), N – KB3; 6 B – N2, N – B3; 7 O – O, P – K3=.

4	B – N2	B – N2
5	O – O	. . .

Harmless. Correct is 5 P – QB3, N – QB3; 6 P – Q4 with a powerful center. If Black goes Pawn hunting now he gets shattered: 6 . . . P×P; 7 P×P, Q – N3?; 8 QN – B3, N×P?; 9 N – Q5, Q – B4; 10 N×N, B×N; 11 B – K3!, B×B; 12 P×B, Q – R4+; 13 P – N4, Q – Q1; 14 R – QB1, R – N1; 15 O – O, B – Q2; 16 Q – Q4, P – B3; 17 N – B7+, K – B2; 18 P – K5! with a strong

attack. (Samarian–Wesen, corres. 1958.) The sober *6* . . . P – K4;
7 P × BP, P × P; *8* Q × Q+, N × Q; *9* N – R3 allows White only a
slightly better ending.

> *5* . . .   N – QB3
> *6* P – QB3   P – K4!
> *7* P – Q3   . . .

Now White has to regroup in order to get in P – Q4.

> *7* . . .   KN – K2
> *8* P – QR3   . . .

A lemon, but already White must fight for equality. On *8* B – K3,
O – O; *9* P – Q4, KP × P; *10* P × P, P × P (also good is *10* . . .
P – Q4; *11* QN – B3, B – N5!); *11* N × P, N – K4 Black captures
the initiative. (Pachman–Tal, Amsterdam 1964.)

> *8* . . .   O – O

Deciding to ignore the Q-side. Keres hoped for *8* . . . P – QR4;
9 P – QR4! and White has tricked Black into weakening his QN4
square.

> *9* P – QN4   . . .

Probably played against Keres' better judgment, but I guess he
wanted to justify his last move. One lemon leads to another.

> *9* . . .   P – N3
> *10* P – KB4   P × P!

Abandoning the center to play against White's shaky Pawn
structure.

> *11* P × KBP   . . .

Not *11* N × P? (if *11* B × P, P – Q4), P × P; *12* RP × P, N × P!

> *11* . . .   P – Q4!

Wrong is *11* . . . P × P; *12* RP × P, N × P?; *13* P – B5!,
N/2 – B3; *14* P – Q4, N – R3; *15* P – K5, etc.

> *12* P – K5   . . .

Poker-faced, as always, Keres made this move as though it were
the most natural one on the board. But it was the last thing he
wanted to do, since it exposes the poverty of White's strategy.

FISCHER

Position after 12 P – K5

KERES

12 . . .   B – N5

Not bad, but *12 . . . N – B4 à la* Nimzovitch is even better. After *13* N – N3, N/3 – K2 maintains a solid blockade, and Black can break with . . . P – B3 at his leisure.

13 P – R3   B × N

Even stronger is *13 . . . B – K3; 14* N – N3, Q – Q2; *15* K – R2, P – B3. The absence of Black's QB makes it difficult to exploit the white square weaknesses.

14 Q × B   P – B3
15 P – N5   . . .

The only way to keep the center from crumbling. After *15* P – K6, P – B4 the advanced KP becomes a target.

15 . . .   N – R4
16 N – Q2   . . .

Better is *16* R – R2. If then *16 . . . P × P; 17* P × P, R × R+; *18* Q × R, B × P; *19* B – N5! is strong.

16 . . .   P × P
17 P × P   R × R+
18 N × R   . . .

Any recapture proves to be awkward. Also *18* B × R, Q – B2!; *19* N – B3 (not *19* P – Q4, P × P; *20* P × P, Q – B6), N – N6 is similar to the game.

18 . . .   N – N6
19 R – N1   N × B
20 R × N   Q – B2!
21 R – K1   . . .

Still impossible is *21* P – Q4?, P × P and White can't recapture because of the pin. Despite the drawing tendency of the opposite colored Bishops, White has a difficult game: he's weak on all the squares and his King is somewhat exposed.

21 . . .		R – Q1
22 N – R2		. . .

Black gets an iron grip after *22* P – Q4, P × P; *23* P × P, N – B4 followed by . . . B – R3, etc.

22 . . .		P – Q5
23 P × P		P × P
24 N – B3?		. . .

A terrible boner, just when White could equalize with *24* N – N4!, R – KB1; *25* R – KB1.

24 . . .		B – R3!

Keres probably underestimated the strength of this reply.

25 Q – R2+		K – R1
26 Q – K6		. . .

FISCHER

Position after 26 Q – K6

KERES

26 . . .		N – Q4?

Tempting but wrong. Correct is *26* . . . N – B4!; *27* Q – B6+ (if *27* N – R2?, B – K6+ wins), B – N2; *28* Q – K6, R – KB1 followed by . . . B – R3 again, and it's just a matter of time before Black invades on the weak dark squares. For example, *29* N – N5 (not *29* N – R2, Q – B6!), B – R3; *30* N – K4, B – K6+; *31* K – R1, B – B5; *32* N – B6, Q – B6; *33* R – Q1, Q – B7, etc.

27 N – R2!		. . .

The saving clause. Not *27* N × P?, Q – B4.

| | 27 . . . | N – K6 |

After 27 . . . N – B5?;   28 Q – B6+, K – N1;   29 N – N4
White wins!

| | 28 B – B6! | . . . |

Now the Queen is hemmed in and Black has nothing. The
Knight on K6 must coordinate with the heavy artillery to be really
meaningful.

| | 28 . . . | R – KB1 |
| | 29 N – B3 | B – B5 |

On 29 . . . Q – Q1; 30 Q – Q6 holds. The chances are now
even.

30	N×P	B×P
31	N – B3	B – Q5!
32	R×N	. . .

Not 32 N × B??, Q – N6+.

| | 32 . . . | B×R+ |

On 32 . . . Q – B5; 33 K – B2! holds.

33	Q×B	Q – N6+
34	K – B1	Q×P+
35	K – K1	Q – B4
36	P – Q4	K – N2

36 . . . P – KR4?; 37 Q – R6+, K – N1; 38 B – Q5+, Q×B;
39 Q×P+ draws.

| | 37 K – B2! | . . . |

The right plan—the King must stay on the K-side to blockade
Black's Pawns. Eventually Black, to make progress, must advance;
but in so doing he will expose his King to a perpetual check.
    Wrong is 37 Q – K5+, Q×Q; 38 P×Q, R – B5 (intending
R – QR5). White's KP can always be stopped by the King.

	37 . . .	P – KR4
	38 K – N3	Q – N5+
	39 K – R2	R – B5

On 39 . . . Q – B5+; 40 Q×Q, R×Q; 41 K – N3 holds. And
not 39 . . . P – R5?; 40 Q – K7+, R – B2; 41 Q×R+!

40 Q – K7+   K – R3

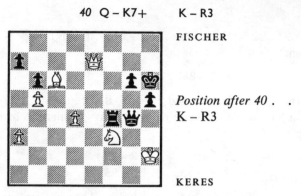

FISCHER

Position after 40 . . .
K – R3

KERES

    The game was adjourned and Keres sealed his move. Upon resuming the next day, he offered me a draw, which I rejected. I knew Black no longer had a winning advantage, but felt no harm could come from continuing since there was little danger of losing. Besides, winning this game would still have put me in contention for first place even as late as round 14, the halfway mark.

    41 Q – K2   Q – B4
    42 Q – K3   P – N4
    43 K – N2   R – N5+
    44 K – B2   R – B5
    45 K – N2   Q – B7+

    Beginning a series of exploratory checks to see if White goes to the wrong square. For instance, *46* K – N3?, R – N5+ ; *47* K – R3, Q – N7 mate. Hope springs eternal!

    46 K – R1   Q – N8+
    47 K – R2   Q – R7+
    48 K – R3   Q – B2
    49 K – R2   Q – B3
    50 K – N2   K – N2

    Getting out of the potential pin. Not *50* . . . P – N5?; *51* K – N3. Black must strive to advance the Pawns so that they retain maximum mobility.

    51 K – N3   P – R5+
    52 K – N2   . . .

52 K – R2? loses to P – N5.

    52 . . .   R – N5+

52 . . . P – N5 is refuted by *53* N×P!

53	K – R1	R – N6
54	Q – K4	P – N5
55	N – R2	Q – N4
56	N – B1 ?	. . .

A blunder on the last move of the second time-control. Perhaps Keres has allowed me to get a little too much out of the position, but he can still hold a draw with *56* Q – K5+!, Q×Q; *57* P×Q (threatening B – Q7), R×P; *58* N×P, etc.

FISCHER

Position after 56 N – B1

KERES

56 . . .   R – R6+?

I had a feeling this might be a mistake, but time was short and I had to make a move—any move. "Patzer sees a check, gives a check." But now the game can no longer be won.

Correct is *56 . . .* R×P!; *57* P – Q5, P – N6; *58* P – Q6 (if *58* B – Q7, R – R8; *59* K – N2, R – R7+; *60* K – N1, Q – B3; *61* B – B5, R – KB7), R – R8; *59* Q – K7+ (if *59* K – N1, Q – B4+ wins), Q×Q; *60* P×Q, P – R6!; *61* P – K8 = N+, K – B1 wins.

57	K – N1	R×P
58	P – Q5	P – N6
59	B – Q7!	R – R8

No longer gains a tempo, as in the last note.

60 B – B5!   . . .

The idea is to advance the Pawn to Q6 without allowing . . . Q – B4+. I must confess that I still expected to win. But now Keres really starts to find moves!

60 . . .		Q – B3
61	Q – KB4	R – K8

62	P – Q6	R – K4
63	Q – N4+ !	. . .

Not *63* P – Q7?, R × B; *64* Q × R, Q × Q; *65* P – Q8 = Q, Q – B7+ and mate next.

63	. . .	K – B1
64	P – Q7	R – Q4

Now *64* . . . R × B; *65* P – Q8 = Q + !, Q × Q; *66* Q × R+ draws.

FISCHER

Position after 64 . . .
R – Q4

KERES

65	K – N2!	R × QP!

On *65* . . . Q – N7+ ; *66* K – R3, Q – KB7; *67* B – K4!, Q × N+ ; *68* B – N2, Q – B7; *69* Q – N4+ ! holds.

66	B × R!	. . .

I thought this was a mistake at the time, but that he was lost anyway. Keres, however, has seen just one move further—

66	. . .	Q – B7+
67	K – R3	Q × N+
68	K × P	P – N7
69	Q – N4+	K – B2!
70	Q – N3+	K – N2
71	Q – N3+	K – R2!

Haven—at last. Now I was sure I had him. Surely he would go in for *72* B – B5+, Q × B; *73* Q × P, Q – B5+!; *74* Q – N4 (on *74* K – R3, Q – R3+! wins), Q × Q+ ; *75* K × Q, K – N3! gaining the opposition and winning White's last Pawn by force.

72	Q – K5!!	. . .

What's this? He makes no attempt to stop me from queening!?
Gradually my excitement subsided. The more I studied the situa-
tion, the more I realized Black had no win.

FISCHER

Position after 72 Q – K5

KERES

72 . . .   Q – R8+

The main line also draws—by a miracle: *72 . . .* Q – B7+ ;
73 K – R3, P – N8 = Q (making a Knight with check also doesn't
win); *74* B – B5+, K – R3 (*74. . .* Q×B+; *75* Q×Q+, Q –
N3; *76* Q×Q+, K×Q; *77* K – N4! is similar to the final note);
75 Q – B6+, K – R4; *76* B – N6+!, Q×B; *77* Q – N5+!!, K×Q;
Stalemate!

73 B – R3   Q×B+

73. . . P – N8 = Q; *74* Q – R5+, K – N2; *75* Q – N6+!
forces stalemate or a perpetual.

74 K×Q   P – N8 = Q
75 Q – K7+   K – R1
76 Q – B8+   K – R2
77 Q – B7+
           Drawn

A last try might have been *77. . .* Q – N2; *78* Q×Q+!,
K×Q; *79* K – N3! holding the "distant opposition": e.g., *79*
. . . K – B3; *80* K – B4, K – K3; *81* K – K4, K – Q3; *82* K –
Q 4, K – B2; *83* K – Q5, K – N2; *84* K – B4, K – B2; *85* K – Q5,
K – Q2; *86* K – K5 and Black can't penetrate.

38 Fischer - Keres [U.S.S.R.]

CURAÇAO 1962

RUY LOPEZ

Detective story

Occasionally one comes across a miraculous victory in which, despite intensive post-mortems, there seems to be no losing move or pattern, no blunder on the part of the vanquished. But how can that be possible? A loser must make a mistake somewhere, however infinitesimal, however it may evade detection. Is it Keres' opening novelty which leads him to disaster? Could his defense have been improved afterward? If so: where? Whatever the answer, the reader is invited to share the magnifying glass with Fischer and hunt for that elusive error.

1	P – K4	P – K4
2	N – KB3	N – QB3
3	B – N5	P – QR3
4	B – R4	N – B3
5	O – O	B – K2
6	R – K1	P – QN4
7	B – N3	P – Q3
8	P – B3	O – O
9	P – KR3	. . .

For 9 P – Q4 see game 36.

9	. . .	N – QR4
10	B – B2	P – B4
11	P – Q4	N – Q2

"Now it is not easy to find a satisfactory continuation for White." (KERES.)

Keres' novelty, introduced on this occasion, has since become quite fashionable. I was—and still am—unimpressed. Black loses

time redeveloping his Knight to QN3, but the K-side is weakened
by its absence and it's questionable whether the Knight is not
better where it stands originally.

KERES

Position after 11 . . .
N – Q2

FISCHER

12 P×BP!   . . .

12 QN – Q2 was all the rage, but BP×P; *13* P×P, N – QB3 may
equalize. But not *12* P×KP, N×P! with complete freedom.

"In spite of having won this game, it is probable that Fischer
is not very convinced of the correctness of this continuation, because
in a later game he closed the center with *12* P – Q5." (KERES.)

According to that logic, Keres must not be convinced of the
correctness of *11* . . . N – Q2 since he later varied with the
old *11* . . . Q – B2 (against Gligorich at Hastings 1965).

12 . . .   P×P
13 QN – Q2   Q – B2?

This is supposed to lead to trouble. If such a natural developing
move is bad, then what kind of a position is this for Black? At the
time Boleslavsky in his notes gave "*13* . . . P – B3!=" and this
cryptic evaluation apparently cowed the chess world into abandoning *12* P×BP—until very recently. After *13* . . . P – B3; *14*
N – R4, N – N3; *15* N – B5, R – B2 (Fischer-Ivkov, Havana 1965);
16 Q – N4! (instead of my *16* N×B+ ?), K – R1; *17* P – KR4!
threatening P – R5 followed by N – B3 – R4 is in White's favor:
e.g., *17* . . . P – N3; *18* N – R6, R – N2; *19* Q – B3, etc.

14 N – B1   N – N3
15 N – K3   R – Q1
16 Q – K2   B – K3
17 N – Q5!   . . .

The idea is to open lines and take advantage of Black's weakened K-side.

$$17 \ . \ . \ . \quad N \times N$$

On *17* . . . B×N; *18* P×B, P – B3; *19* P – KR4! is strong. Now if *19* . . . N×P (*19* . . . N/4 – B5; *20* P – R5, N – Q3; *21* Q – Q3!, P – K5; *22* R×P!, N×R; *23* Q×N wins); *20* P – R5 (threatening Q – K4) is powerful.

18 P×N	B×QP
19 N×P	. . .

KERES

Position after 19 N × P

FISCHER

Since his early attacking days, Keres has switched to positional–defensive chess. But this type of position is too much even for him.

$$19 \ . \ . \ . \quad R - R2$$

To defend the second rank. What else can Black do? White threatens to build up with B – B4 and QR – Q1, and already sacrificial themes are in the air.

On *19* . . . B – Q3; *20* Q – Q3!, B×N; *21* Q×P+, K – B1; *22* P – KB4 wins. Or *19* . . . B – K3; *20* N×P! Or *19* . . . B – B1; *20* Q – R5, P – N3 (if *20* . . . P – R3; *21* N – N4); *21* Q – R4, B – N2 (if *21* . . . B – K2; *22* Q – N3 threatening N×NP); *22* N – N4. Finally *19* . . . P – B3 (*19* . . . R – K1?; *20* Q – Q3); *20* Q – R5!, P×N; *21* B×P+, K – B1; *22* R×P, B – B2; *23* R – B5, B – B3; *24* R×B!, P×R; *25* B – R6+, K – K2; *26* R – K1+, B – K3 (if *26* . . . K – Q3; *27* B – B4+, K – B3; *28* B – K4+ wins); *27* B – B5, R – Q3; *28* B – B4 wins.

$$20 \ B - B4 \qquad Q - N3$$

The threat was N – N6. On *20* . . . Q – B1; *21* QR – Q1 quietly continues the build-up.

21 QR – Q1! . . .

Threatening *22* R × B, R × R; *23* Q – K4. Instead of seeking a "violent solution," my instinct told me to strengthen the position.

21 . . . P – N3

Eliminating stock combinations against KR7, but creating new weaknesses on the dark squares. What's better? On *21 . . .* B × RP; *22* R × R+, Q × R (if *22 . . .* B × R; *23* N – B4!, Q – K3; *24* Q – Q1, R – Q2; *25* N – Q2); *23* P – QN4!, P × P; *24* P × P, B × P (the Knight can't move because of N – B6); *25* Q – K4!, B × R; *26* Q × P+, K – B1; *27* Q – R8+, K – K2; *28* B – N5+, P – B3; *29* N – N6+, K – Q2; *30* B – B5+, K – B2; *31* B – B4+ wins the Queen.

22 N – N4 . . .

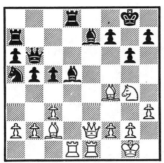

KERES

Position after 22 N – N4

FISCHER

22 . . . N – B5

An attempt to bring this Knight toward the embattled sector. After *22 . . .* B × RP; *23* R × R+, Q × R; *24* B – R6! White has just too many threats. For example, *24 . . .* P – B4 (not *24 . . .* P – B3; *25* P – QN3! or *24 . . .* B – B1; *25* Q – K8, R – R1; *26* N – B6+, K – R1; *27* B × B wins); *25* Q – K5!, B – Q3 (if *25 . . .* B – B1; *26* Q – K8, Q × Q; *27* R × Q, R – KB2; *28* N – K5, R – B3; *29* N – Q7); *26* R – Q1!, N – B5 (if *26 . . .* P × N; *27* R × B, R – Q2; *28* Q – N7+!! wins); *27* Q – K6+, K – R1 (if *27 . . .* R – B2; *28* P – QN3, P × N; *29* P × N, Q – R5; *30* R × B, Q × B; *31* R – Q8+, K – N2; *32* Q – K5+); *28* P – QN3!, P × N; *29* P × N, R – Q2; *30* B – N5! wins.

23 B – R6 . . .

Some recommended the more direct *23* N – R6+, K – N2; *24*

R × B, R × R; *25* N × P. I thought this might win at the time, but it looked speculative—and *25 . . . Q – KB3!* refutes. Since Black is tied up in knots, I felt sure of a patient strategical victory.

23 . . . B – K3

23 . . . N × P loses to *24 R × B!, R × R; 25 B – K4, R – Q1; 26 Q × N, P – B4; 27 P – QB4!* (threatening *Q – N7* mate).

24 B – N3! . . .

Pinning the Knight and piling on the pressure.

24 . . . Q – N1

To prevent White's Queen, in some variations, from penetrating to K5.

25 R × R+ B × R

Not *24 . . . Q × R?; 25 B × N, B × B* (if *25 . . . P × B; 26 Q – K5); 26 N – B6+!, K – R1; 27 Q – K5,* etc.

26 B × N P × B
27 Q × P! . . .

Cashing in! "Converting a spatial advantage into a material one." (See Evans' *New Ideas in Chess*.)

KERES

Position after 27 Q × P

FISCHER

27 . . . Q – Q3

Not *27 . . . Q × P; 28 R × B!* Or *27 . . . B × Q??; 28 R – K8* mate.

28 Q – R4 Q – K2
29 N – B6+ K – R1

30	N – Q5	Q – Q2
31	Q – K4!	. . .

Back to the old stand, angling for K5 again.

| 31 | . . . | Q – Q3 |

31 . . . B × N?; 32 Q – K8+ mates. The weakness of Black's first rank has consistently proved to be his undoing throughout the mid-game.

| 32 | N – B4 | . . . |

32 P – QB4 is also good.

| 32 | . . . | R – K2 |

Token resistance.

| 33 | B – N5 | . . . |

33 B – B8! wins outright.

| 33 | . . . | R – K1 |
| 34 | B × B | R × B |

On *34 . . . Q × B; 35 Q – K5+, P – B3* (not *35 . . . K – N1; 36 N – Q5!*); *36 Q × P, B × QRP; 37 R × R+, Q × R; 38 P – B4* is the easiest path to victory.

| 35 | N × B | Q × N |

On *35 . . . R – K1; 36 Q – K5+* is decisive.

36	Q × Q	P × Q
37	R × P	R – Q8+
38	K – R2	R – Q7
39	R – N6	R × BP
40	R – N7!	R – B3
41	K – N3	Black resigns

Not only is Black a Pawn behind, but his King on the first rank is cut off as well. A likely winning line is *41 . . . K – N1; 42 P – N4, P × P; 43 P × P, R – Q3; 44 P – QR4, R – Q6+; 45 K – R2, R – R6; 46 P – R5, R – R5* (if *46 . . . K – R1; 47 K – N1, R – R7; 48 K – B1, K – N1; 49 K – K1, R × P; 50 P – N5, P × P; 51 P – R6, R – QR7; 52 P – R7*); *47 K – N3* and the King invades!

39 Botvinnik *[U.S.S.R.]* - Fischer

VARNA OLYMPIC 1962

GRUENFELD DEFENSE

The confrontation

This dramatic meeting between the generations took place on board 1 after it was rumored that Botvinnik would be given a "rest day" against the American team. But it was fated that Fischer, at last, albeit with Black, would have a crack at the world champion.

Walking into a prepared variation, Fischer promptly refutes it. "The reader can guess that my equanimity was wrecked," confesses Botvinnik, whose notes are incorporated here. Nervously, he proceeds to run his still tenable position downhill. But Fischer, instead of nursing his winning advantage, simplifies too quickly and reaches an adjournment where victory is problematical. After a sleepless night of analysis, Botvinnik finds a stunning defense. Fischer engages in a seemingly harmless transposition of moves (51 . . . P – QN4), and falls into a pit—throwing away the win he maintains was still there.

1	P – QB4	P – KN3
2	P – Q4	. . .

If White so desires, he can prevent the Gruenfeld by *2* N – QB3, N – KB3; *3* P – K4.

2	. . .	N – KB3
3	N – QB3	P – Q4

The spur of the moment. I could see by the glint in his eye that he had come well armed for my King's Indian.

4	N – B3	. . .

The sharpest try is *4* P×P, N×P; *5* P – K4.

4	. . .	B – N2
5	Q – N3	. . .

The main line, but I don't believe this early development of the Queen can give White anything.

5	. . .	P×P

A solid alternative is *5* . . . P – B3.

6	Q×BP	O – O
7	P – K4	B – N5

Also interesting is Donald Byrne's provocative *7* . . . N – B3.

8	B – K3	. . .

On *8* N – K5, B – K3; *9* P – Q5, B – B1 followed by . . . P – K3 equalizes.

8	. . .	KN – Q2

Smyslov's Variation.

FISCHER

Position after 8 . . .
KN – Q2

BOTVINNIK

So far theory has found no way to derive any clear advantage for White.

A] *9* O – O – O, N – QB3; *10* B – K2, N – N3; *11* Q – B5, Q – Q3; *12* P – KR3, B×N; *13* P×B, P – B4! (*13* . . . KR – Q1?; *14* P – K5! [Reshevsky–Evans, Las Vegas 1965], practically forces a won endgame for White, since if *14* . . . Q – Q2?; *15* P – Q5!, N×KP; *16* P – B4); *14* P – Q5 (if *14* P – K5, Q×Q; *15* P×Q, P – B5! is adequate), N – K4; *15* P – B4 (if *15* N – N5?, Q – KB3;

16 B – Q4, P × P; *17* P × P, Q – B5+, etc.), N/4 – Q2 with a nice game.

B] *9* R – Q1, N – QB3; *10* Q – N3, P – K4!; *11* P × P, B × N; *12* P × B, QN × P; *13* B – R3, N × P+; *14* K – K2!, N/6 – K4; *15* B × N, N × B; *16* Q – N5, P – QB3; *17* Q × NP, R – N1; *18* Q × N, R × P+; *19* K – B1, Q × Q (Simagin's *19* . . . Q – B3 has also been analyzed to a draw; *20* R × Q, B × N=. Evans–Fischer, US Championship 1962-3.)

$$\text{9 B – K2} \qquad \text{N – QB3}$$

Botvinnik thinks *9* . . . N – N3 first is more accurate.

$$\text{10 R – Q1} \qquad \text{N – N3}$$

10 . . . B × N followed by . . . P – K4 also gives Black active play.

$$\text{11 Q – B5} \qquad \text{Q – Q3!}$$
$$\text{12 P – KR3} \qquad \text{. . .}$$

12 Q × Q is answered by BP × Q! improving Black's Pawn structure and neutralizing White's center.

$$\text{12 . . .} \qquad \text{B × N}$$
$$\text{13 P × B} \qquad \text{KR – Q1}$$

Wrong is *13* . . . Q × Q; *14* P × Q, B × N+; *15* P × B, N – R5; *16* K – Q2! Botvinnik is of the opinion that *13* . . . P – K3 (FURMAN) gives Black an equal game. But I feel it is not in the hypermodern spirit, which is precisely to tempt White into advancing his center Pawns in the hope they will become overextended.

$$\text{14 P – Q5} \qquad \text{. . .}$$

Opening the diagonal for Black's KB can't be right, but White is still striving for an opening advantage. On *14* P – K5, Q × Q; *15* P × Q, R × R+; *16* K × R, N – Q2; *17* P – B4, P – KN4!; *18* P × P, B × P=. Or *14* Q × Q (if *14* N – N5, Q × Q; *15* P × Q, N – R5!), BP × Q=.

$$\text{14 . . .} \qquad \text{N – K4}$$
$$\text{15 N – N5} \qquad \text{. . .}$$

"At once *15* P – B4 is not good because of *15* . . . N/4 – B5; *16* B × N, Q × Q; *17* B × Q, N × B; *18* P – K5, N × NP; *19* R – Q4,

P – KB3! and White's central position breaks up." (BOTVINNIK.)

On *15* P – B4 also playable is simply N/4 – Q2; *16* Q – N5 (*16* Q×Q, BP×Q gives Black a comfortable ending), P – K4!; *17* P – B5 (*17* P×P *e.p.*, B×N+!; *18* P×B, Q×KP) with equal chances.

15 . . .   Q – KB3!

Weak is *15 . . .* Q×Q; *16* B×Q, P – QB3; *17* N – B7 (not *17* N×P?, N – R5), QR – N1; *18* B×P, R – Q2; *19* P – Q6, N – B1; *20* N – K8! (not *20* P – B4, N×B; *21* P×N/5, B×P; *22* P×N, R×P), N×B; *21* N×B, K×N; *22* P – B4!

16 P – B4   N/4 – Q2
17 P – K5   . . .

On *17* Q×BP?, Q×NP White can't castle and . . . Q – N5+ is threatened.

FISCHER

Position after 17 P – K5

BOTVINNIK

"When I was preparing to meet Smyslov, I, of course, made a thorough analysis of the Smyslov System in general and of the position on the diagram in particular! Here I reckoned that whether the black Queen went to KR5 or KB4, it would be in danger; for example, *17 . . .* Q – B4; *18* Q – N4, P – QR4; *19* Q – Q4, threatening B – N4 or *17 . . .* Q – R5; *18* Q – B2, P – N4; *19* R – Q4!

"Alas, my opponent found a third continuation!" (BOTVINNIK.)

17 . . .   Q×BP!

"A very unpleasant surprise—now White really had to start playing. Up to here I had only had to remember my analysis, though that was not so easy. I had a recollection of the Black Queen being trapped somewhere on the K-side; and following this track I managed to recall the whole variation. At last everything was in order—on the board was the familiar position; then suddenly it was obvious that in my analysis I had missed what Fischer had found with the greatest of ease at the board. The reader can guess that my equanimity was wrecked.

"However, if you assess *17 . . .* Q × BP from an objective point of view, then although it is the best way out for Black, as you will see from what comes later, his position is still difficult." (BOTVINNIK.)

When I made this move, I felt sure he had overlooked it.

18 B × Q   . . .

Black's last is tactically justified after *18* Q × N, Q – K5!; *19* P – B3, Q – R5+!; *20* B – B2, Q – N5+ followed by . . . RP × Q! (toward the center).

18 . . .   N × Q
19 N × BP   QR – B1
20 P – Q6   P × P
21 P × P   . . .

Not *21* R × P?, N/4 – Q2.

21 . . .   B × P

"So Black has won a Pawn; but the Knight on QB7 and the Pawn on Q6 confine his Rooks—and also, White has two Bishops. The first thing White must do is complete his development." (BOTVINNIK.)

22 O – O   N/3 – Q2

"A bad mistake; evidently, Black overestimated his possibilities. Of course, he had to prepare the move . . . B – K4; the only way this could be done was by *22 . . .* N/4 – Q2 and after *23* B – B3, B – K4; *24* B × B, N × B; *25* B × P, R – N1 White has no more than a minimal advantage.

"Now White has the two important squares Q5 and QB4 at his disposal and his spatial advantage becomes crushing." (BOTVINNIK.)

Needless to add, I couldn't disagree more. Why should Black return the Pawn?

23 R – Q5 . . .

Archives recommends *23* N – Q5, but after K – N2 the burden of proof rests with White—he's a Pawn down.

23 . . . P – N3

FISCHER

Position after 23 . . . P – N3

BOTVINNIK

24 B – B3? . . .

"Feeble play. Actually, White had played quite consistently so far and here he could have deployed his force with maximum efficiency by *24* B – B4! with the threat of R – K1 – K7.

"The Bishop is out of it on KB3 and merely becomes an object of attack. Black now frees himself, and a Pawn down White is in a critical position." (BOTVINNIK.)

After *24* B – B4! it is true that White has a bind, but with N – K3 Black can practically force a draw, if he wants it, after *25* B – R2, N – Q5 (threatening . . . N – KB3); *26* R – N1, B – B6; *27* R – QB1, B – N7, etc.

24 . . . N – K3!

"Apparently, this forces the exchange of the Knight on QB7, for *25* B – R2, N – Q5; *26* B – N2, N – KB3 is very bad for White. In fact, even here *26* R x N! (pointed out by Geller), B x R; *27* R – K1 gave White a real chance to get out of all his troubles. A second error running makes his position hopeless." (BOTVINNIK.)

The reader is invited to judge for himself whether, in Geller's line, White has any real compensation for the exchange and a Pawn. Here *27* . . . B – B4 followed by . . . N – KB3 or . . . N – KB1 should extricate Black.

25 N x N? . . .

This really took me aback. After *25* B – K3 at least White's still in the game.

                25 . . .   P×N
                26 R – Q3   . . .

On *26* R/5 – Q1? (or *26* R – Q2?, B – B8; *27* R – Q4, P – K4), R – B1!; *27* B – N4, R×B; *28* B×P+, R – B2 wins.

                26 . . .   N – B4
                27 R – K3   . . .

Bad is *27* R – Q2, R – B1; *28* P – Q7, QR – Q1.

                27 . . .   P – K4

"The simplest. If *27* . . . B – Q5; *28* R – R3, P – K4; *29* B – N5, R×P; *30* B – K7, R – Q2; *31* B – N4, Black lost the exchange." (BOTVINNIK.)

                28 B×P   . . .

Just leads to a dead lost ending. I expected *28* R×P!? (hopeless though it is) to try and keep a little "dynamic imbalance."

                28 . . .   B×B
                29 R×B   R×P
                30 R – K7   R – Q2
                31 R×R   . . .

On *31* KR – K1, R/1 – B2! flushes White off the 7th rank.

                31 . . .   N×R
                32 B – N4   . . .

"A pointless move, since White cannot go into the lost Rook and Pawn ending; he should have played at once *32* R – K1, K – B1; *33* R – K3 (or *33* B – Q5)—Black would still have had technical difficulties." (BOTVINNIK.)

                32 . . .   R – B2
                33 R – K1   K – B2
                34 K – N2   . . .

"And now *34* B – K6+ was preferable, as the Bishop is poorly posted at KN4." (BOTVINNIK.)

34 . . .	N – B4
35 R – K3	R – K2
36 R – B3+	. . .

"White's best practical chance consisted in an exchange of Rooks and a position with his King on Q4 (or K3), his Bishop on QB2 and his KBP at B4. But all that is impossible—*36* K – B3, P – KR4! and White loses his Bishop." (BOTVINNIK.)

36 . . .	K – N2
37 R – B3	R – K5
38 B – Q1	R – Q5

"Before this I considered the game completely hopeless for me, but the text move gave me new heart: why had my opponent allowed my Bishop to get to a good post (and the only good one!) at QB2? Surely, by *38* . . . R – K8! (*39* B – B2, R – QB8) White's defenses could have been completely disorganized." (BOTVINNIK.)

After *38* . . . R – K8 simply *39* B – B3 is more logical.

39 B – B2	K – B3
40 K – B3	K – N4

"In general terms, Q3 is the best square for the King; for then the Knight would not need to defend the QNP and Black would win by advancing his Q-side Pawns. But this maneuver is also not bad." (BOTVINNIK.)

41 K – N3   . . .

FISCHER

Position after 41 K – N3

BOTVINNIK

41 . . .   N – K5+

"Could have led to an immediate draw—and just at the very

moment when Black was nearing his goal. You see, White was already in *zugzwang*: against a King move Black plays . . . K – R5 and . . . N – K3 – B5 (×P); if B – N1, the reply . . . R – Q8 wins; and if the White Rook moves from its place, then . . . R – QB5 is decisive. So after, for instance, *41* . . . R – N5; *42* P – R3, R – Q5; *43* P – B3, P – QR4 White would have had no satisfactory reply.

"It is psychologically understandable why Black decided on the Rook and Pawn ending—earlier (see White's 23rd move) White had avoided it. But there is a difference between these two endings —the Black King is in a bad position on KN4." (BOTVINNIK.)

Although I agree that Black can win by keeping the minor pieces and gradually improving his position, the text should also produce the same result, if only by a hair's breadth.

42	B×N	R×B
43	R – R3	. . .

"Natural and bad. White is now in danger of defeat again. *43* R – B7!! was essential, and White gets a draw as in the game. The fact that his Pawn is on QR2 and not QR4 has no significance." (BOTVINNIK.)

After *43* R – B7, R – QR5; *44* R×KRP, R – R6+!; *45* P – B3 (if *45* K – N2, R×QRP; *46* R – QN7, R – R8; *47* K – B3, K – B4; *48* R – B7+, K – K4; *49* R – KN7, P – QN4 gains a tempo over the game because White's Pawn is on R3 instead of R4), R×P; *46* P – R4+ leads to the same ending as the game, except White has already played P – B3 which Botvinnik, for some reason, carefully avoided. So the difference may be significant.

43	. . .	R – K2

"Perhaps *43* . . . P – QR4!; *44* R – N3, R – N5 was better; Black obtained either a won Rook and Pawn ending or—after *45* R×R, P×R; *46* P – B4+, K – B4; *47* K – B3, K – K3; *48* K – K4 (*48* K – N4, P – R3), K – Q3; *49* K – Q4, P – QN4; *50* K – Q3, K – Q4—a probably won Pawn ending." (BOTVINNIK.)

44	R – KB3	R – QB2

"His last chance consisted in improving the position of his King by the maneuver . . . K – R3 – N2." (BOTVINNIK.)

45	P – R4	. . .

FISCHER

Position after 45 P – R4

BOTVINNIK

"Here Black sealed a move. White's threat is to exchange a pair of Pawns on the Q-side by P – QR5 (for example, *45 . . . R – B5; 46 P – R5, P × P* [or *46 . . . P – N4; 47 R – B7*]; *47 R – B7, P – QR3; 48 P – R4+, K – R3; 49 R – Q7*), after which the weakness of Black's KRP together with the unfortunate position of his King would guarantee the draw.

"The most subtle move was *45 . . . K – R3*, although even then Black gets nowhere after *46 R – Q3!, R – B4; 47 P – R4, R – QR4; 48 R – Q4.*

"What happened in the game is also most probably a draw." (BOTVINNIK.)

The game was officially "drawn" at breakfast. The Russian team had a table near the American team. Someone inquired of Botvinnik what he thought of the adjourned position. Hardly looking up from his plate, the world champion shrugged, *"Nichia"* (draw). The word quickly spread, and I overheard someone at the English table saying: "The Russians said Fischer could have won before adjournment . . ."

45 . . .	R – B4
46 R – B7	R – R4
47 R × KRP!	. . .

"A very fine idea, found during overnight analysis by Geller. Because of his bad King position Black finds it difficult to mobilize his connected passed Pawns." (BOTVINNIK.)

This was the first defense I had considered! Passive play is hopeless: e.g., *47 R – B4, R – KB4; 48 R – B4, R – B2* followed by *. . . K – B4* and Black brings his King to the Q-side.

47 . . .	R × P
48 P – R4+!	. . .

I had analyzed mainly *48* P – B4+ but Botvinnik's line is best and also contains a sly trap.

                48 . . .   K – B4

"Or *48* . . . K – B3; *49* R – QN7!, R – R4; *50* K – N4, P – QN4; *51* P – B4, P – R3; *52* R – N6+, K – B2; *53* R – N7+ and White is quite safe." (BOTVINNIK.)

                49 R – B7+   K – K4
                50 R – KN7   . . .

"The weakness of the KNP and QRP gives White sufficient counterplay." (BOTVINNIK.)

                50 . . .   R – R8
                51 K – B3   . . .

FISCHER

Position after 51 K – B3

BOTVINNIK

                51 . . .   P – QN4?

Originally Botvinnik wrote in *Chess Life*: "This is a mistake in analysis. But even after *51* . . . K – Q4!; *52* R × NP, P – N4; *53* K – K2, K – B5; *54* P – R5, P – N5; *55* R – N4+, K – N4 (if *55* . . . K – B6 or *55* . . . K – N6; then *56* R – R4 followed by P – R6 – R7 is very strong); *56* K – Q3 the White King reaches the Q-side and it is easy to credit the draw."

Later, in the 1962 Russian yearbook, he analyzed the entire ending more exhaustively and came to the conclusion, after considerable soul-searching, that it was drawn even against the best line: *51* . . . K – Q5! The bracketed comments are mine. "*52* R × NP, P – N4; *53* P – R5, P – N5; *54* K – N2, P – N6; *55* P –R6, P – N7; *56* P – R7, R – R8!; *57* K × R, P – N8 = Q+; *58* K – R2, Q – N1+; *59* K – N1, Q – KR1 [*59* . . . Q – K4! seems to do the trick; if *60* R – N8, Q – K8+; *61* K – R2, Q × P+; *62* K – R3,

Q – B6+! forces the win of the RP; or if *60* K – B1, Q – R7; *61* R – N7, P – R4; *62* R – R7, K – Q6!]; *60* R – N4+, K – B6; *61* R – KR4, P – R4; *62* K – N2, K – N6; *63* R – R3+, K – B7; *64* R – R4, P – R5; *65* R×P, Q – N2+! (if *65* . . . Q×P; *66* R – KN4 – N3, and the Rook holds the third rank, shuttling to K3, if necessary, keeping Black's King out—with a draw); *66* K – B1, Q×P wins, since White can't get his Rook back to the third rank: e.g., *67* R – R2+, K – N6 [*68* R – R5 seems to hold here] or *67* R – R3, Q – R8+; *68* K – K2, Q – Q8+; *69* K – K3, Q – B8+ wins the Rook. Or *67* R – KN4, Q – R8+; *68* R – N1 (if *68* K – K2, Q – Q8+ wins the Rook), Q – R6+; *69* R – N2 (if *69* K – K1, Q – B6 forces mate), K – Q7; *70* K – N1, K – K8 wins (*71* R – N3, Q – B8+).

"Was it really true that the adjourned position was lost? Was I mistaken?" (BOTVINNIK.)

Botvinnik then went on to give a corrected analysis which, as we shall see, also falls short. *51* . . . K – Q5!; *52* R×P, P – N4; *53* P – R5, P – N5; *54* P – R6! (instead of his previous K – N2), P – N6 (if *54* . . . R – R8; *55* K – N2!, R – R4; *56* R – R6, P – N6; *57* R×P, R×P; *58* R – QN7, K – B5; *59* K – B3 leads to a theoretical draw); *55* R – N4+ (if *55* P – R7, R – R8; *56* R – N7, P – R4 wins), K – B4! (not *55* . . . K – B6?; *56* R – KR4 and White queens with check; or *55* . . . K – Q6?; *56* R – QN4, K – B7; *57* R – B4+ draws); *56* R – N5+, K – B3! [Here I break camp with Botvinnik, only to meet at the next diagram. He gives *56* . . . K – N5 overlooking that White can obtain an immediate draw with *57* R – N7!, P – N7 (*57* . . . P – R4? loses to *58* K – N2!); *58* P – R7, R – R8!; *59* R×P, K – N6; *60* R – N7+, K – B7; *61* R – B7+, K – Q7; *62* R – QN7, etc.]; *57* R – N6+, K – N2!; *58* R – N7+ (if *58* R – N4, P – R4 wins), K – R3! (the idea is to keep the King off the N-file so that White's Rook can't check from behind); *59* R – N6+ (if *59* K – N2, P – N7; *60* P – R7, P – N8 = Q; *61* P – R8 = Q, Q – K5+! and White is bombarded with checks which lead to probable mate, certainly win of material), K – R4! (not *59* . . . K – N4?; *60* R – N7, P – R4?; *61* K – N2! wins); *60* R – N5+ (if *60* R – N7?, P – N7; *61* R×P+, K – N3 wins), K – R5! (finally Black has crawled up along the R-file); *61* R – N4+ (*61* R – N7, P – R4; *62* R – N7, R – R8 is easy; or *61* R – R5, P – N7; *62* P – R7, P – N8 = Q; *63* P – R8 = Q, Q – Q6+; *64* K – B4, R – K8! is the pause that refreshes—White is checkless—if *65* R – K5, Q – Q5+; *66* K – B5, Q×P+; *67* K –

K6, Q – N3+ is decisive), K – R6; *62* R – R4, P – N7; *63* P – R7,
P – N8 = Q; *64* P – R8 = Q.

FISCHER

Possible position after
64 P – R8 = Q
(analysis)

BOTVINNIK

Botvinnik also reached this position in his analysis independently,
and concluded that it was a draw. However, it is precisely here, in
this barren wilderness, that Black can wend his way to a win.
Correct is *64* . . . Q – N6+!; *65* K – K2 (if *65* K – B4,
Q – B2+ or *65* K – N2, Q – Q4+; *66* P – B3, Q – Q7+), Q –
Q8+; *66* K – K3, R – N8!!; *67* Q – B8+ (not *67* Q – B3+?,
R – N6; or *67* R – R3, K – R7!; *68* Q – N8+, Q – N6+ wins),
K – R7 and White's King will be without shelter from the coming
avalanche of checks.

Now to return to the dreary (for me) game.

         52 P – R5!   . . .

"Now Black is left with two RP's and the draw becomes a
question of theory." (BOTVINNIK.)

The move I overlooked. *52* R × P, K – Q5 transposes into the
note to Black's 51st.

         52 . . .   R – R6+
         53 K – N2   P × P

Botvinnik visibly relaxed. I had played right into his hands.

54	R – N5+	K – Q3
55	R × NP	P – R5
56	P – B4	K – B3
57	R – N8!	P – R6+
58	K – R2	P – R4
59	P – B5	K – B2
60	R – N5	K – Q3

FISCHER

Position after 60 . . .
K – Q3

BOTVINNIK

"Generally speaking, this ending would be drawn even without the KBP—any textbook on the end-game will tell you this." (BOTVINNIK.)

61	P – B6	K – K3
62	R – N6+	K – B2
63	R – R6	K – N3
64	R – B6	P – R5
65	R – R6	K – B2
66	R – B6	R – Q6
67	R – R6	P – R6
68	K – N1	

Drawn

" 'Too many mistakes?' the reader may justly ask. Yes, there were rather a lot!" (BOTVINNIK.)

FISCHER

Final Position after 68
K – N1

BOTVINNIK

40 Fischer - Najdorf *[Argentina]*

VARNA OLYMPIC 1962

SICILIAN DEFENSE

The Najdorf Variation

The durable Najdorf Variation remains Fischer's favorite, and he constantly experiments when confronted with it. Here, against the originator of the defense, he employs an unorthodox continuation. Najdorf counters sharply, launching an early struggle.

In order to preserve the initiative, Fischer gambits a Pawn with 7 N – Q5. Najdorf unwisely declines, only to accept three moves later under more unfavorable circumstances. He loses his way in the complications, allowing a devastating sacrifice which pins his King in the center. Although Najdorf defends with precision, it is too late to compensate for his earlier dilatory tactics. He finds himself ensnarled in a mating net after twenty-four moves. Rather than prolong his agony, the grand old master tenders his resignation.

1	P – K4	P – QB4
2	N – KB3	P – Q3
3	P – Q4	P × P
4	N × P	N – KB3
5	N – QB3	P – QR3
6	P – KR3	. . .

For 6 B – N5 see games 9 and 15. For 6 B – K2 see games 4 and 42. For 6 B – QB4 see games 17, 55, 58.

6	. . .	P – QN4!?

The sharpest reply. For 6 . . . P – KN3 see game 43. For 6 . . . N – B3 see game 35.

7	N – Q5!?	. . .

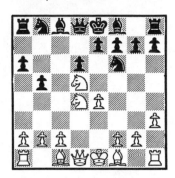

NAJDORF

Position after 7 N – Q5

FISCHER

The idea is to exploit the hole on QB6. Najdorf apparently underestimated the strength of this "eccentric" move which appears to violate principle by moving the same piece twice.

A good alternative was 7 P – QR4.

7 . . .   B – N2?

Black's subsequent troubles can be traced to this. No better is 7. . . QN – Q2??; *8* N – B6 winning the Queen. And on 7. . . KN – Q2; *8* B – N5!, P – R3?; *9* N – K6!

On 7. . . P – K3; *8* N x N+, Q x N; *9* P – QB4, P – N5 Black's Queen is misplaced and his Q-side has been weakened.

Unclear are the complications stemming from 7. . . N x P!; *8* Q – B3, N – B4 and White is confronted with 2 main lines: (a) *9* N – B6+?, NP x N; *10* Q x R, B – N2; *11* Q – R7, Q – B2 (or *11* . . . P – K4; *12* P – QN4, P x N; *13* P x N, Q – K2+; *14* B – K2, N – B3; *15* Q – N6, P x P; *16* O – O! is good for White); *12* P – QN4, KN – Q2 and Black has excellent play for the Exchange. (b) *9* P – QN4!, P – K3 (not *9* . . . N – N2?; *10* Q – B3! but interesting is *9* . . . KN – Q2; *10* Q – B3!, R – R2; *11* B – N5!? or even *11* B x P); *10* P x N (if *10* N – B6+, Q x N; *11* Q x R, Q x N; *12* Q x N, Q x R; *13* Q x B+, K – K2), P x N; *11* Q x P, R – R2=.

8 N x N+   NP x N
9 P – QB4!   . . .

White must play sharply, else his advantage evaporates. After the tame 9 B – Q3, N – Q2 is tenable.

9 . . .   P x P

Had Najdorf correctly evaluated the results of this decision, he would have chosen 9 . . . P – N5. The 1962 Russian Yearbook gives 9 . . . B×P; *10* P×P, B – KN2; *11* Q – N4, B – N3; *12* N – B5 with advantage. But *12* . . . O – O is unclear.

10 B×P   B×P

On *10* . . . Q – R4+ ; *11* B – Q2, Q – K4; *12* Q – N3!, Q× P+ ; *13* K – Q1 White has a very strong attack.

11 O – O   P – Q4
12 R – K1!   . . .

NAJDORF

Position after 12 R – K1

FISCHER

12 . . .   P – K4

A] *12* . . . R – N1; *13* R×B!, P×R; *14* Q – R5, R – N2 (if *14* . . . R – N3; *15* Q×P, R – N2; *16* Q×P, R – QR2; *17* N – B5 or B – B4); *15* N – B5, etc.

B] *12* . . . P – K3; *13* Q – R5, B – N3; *14* Q×QP, Q×Q; *15* B×Q, R – R2; *16* B – KB4, R – Q2; *17* N×P, P×N; *18* B×P, N – B3; *19* QR – B1, etc.

C] *12* . . . P – KR4; *13* R×B!, P×R; *14* Q – N3!, Q×N; *15* B – K3 with a winning attack.

D] *12* . . . N – Q2; *13* N – B6, Q – B2; *14* B×QP, etc.

E] *12* . . . B×P; *13* K×B, P×B; *14* Q – B3, N – Q2; *15* N – B5, R – N1+ (if *16* . . . P – K3; *17* R×P+!, P×R; *17* Q – R5 mate); *16* K – R1, P – K4 (if *16* . . . P – K3; *17* Q – B6 threatening R×P+); *17* B – K3 with a winning bind despite the two-Pawn deficit.

F] Relatively best is *12* . . . P×B; *13* R×B, Q – Q4; *14* Q – B3, P – K3.

13 Q – R4+!   . . .

Inferior is *13* R × B, P × R; *14* Q – R4+, Q – Q2; *15* B – QN5, P × B; *16* Q × R, P × N; *17* Q × N+, K – K2, etc.

13 . . .   N – Q2

On *13* . . . Q – Q2; *14* B – QN5!, P × B; *15* Q × R, B – Q3; *16* R × B!, P × R; *17* Q × KP followed by N – B5 with a powerful bind.

NAJDORF

Position after 13 . . .
N – Q2

FISCHER

14   R × B!   P × R

14 . . . P × B; *15* N – B5 leads to the same type of position as the game, except Black is without any material compensation.

15   N – B5!   . . .

Perhaps Black had hoped for *15* Q – N3, Q – N3; *16* B × P+, K – Q1 with some chances for survival.

15 . . .   B – B4
16   N – N7+!   K – K2

On *16* . . . K – B1; *17* B – R6, K – N1; *18* Q – N3 is murder.

17   N – B5+   K – K1

Back where we started—but Black has lost the right to castle.

18   B – K3   . . .

Tal suggested *18* B – R6, but after R – R2; *19* R – Q1, Q – N3 Black is still alive. The text robs Black of any possible counterplay.

18 . . .   B × B
19   P × B   . . .

The exchange of Bishops has failed to ease Black's defensive task. The threat of N – Q6+ is now in the offing.

        19 . . .   Q – N3
        20 R – Q1   . . .

Again after *20* B×P+, K – Q1!; *21* R – Q1, Q – N4 White has no immediate forced win.

        20 . . .   R – R2
        21 R – Q6!   . . .

The crusher! Either *21* B×P+, K – Q1 or *21* N – Q6+, K – K2 allow resistance.

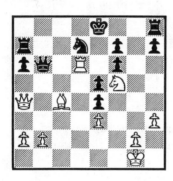

NAJDORF

Position after 21 R – Q6

FISCHER

        21 . . .   Q – Q1

Best under the circumstances. On *21* . . . Q – B2; *22* R×BP wins. And on *21* . . . Q×P; *22* B×P+! (finally!), K×B (if *22* . . . K – Q1; *23* Q – R5+, K – B1 [*23* . . . R – B2; *24* B – K6 wins]; *24* N – K7+, K – N1; *25* N – B6+, K – R1; *26* N×R); *23* R×N+, R×R; *24* Q×R+, K – N3; *25* Q – N7+, K×N; *26* Q – N4 mate.

        22 Q – N3   Q – B2

On *22* . . . R – B1; *23* N – N7+, K – K2; *24* Q – R3! is very decisive.

        23 B×P+   K – Q1

On *23* . . . K – B1; *24* B – R5 and mates.

        24 B – K6   . . .

NAJDORF

Position after 24 B – K6

FISCHER

24 . . .   Black resigns

Najdorf has no taste for prolonging the torture. If, for example,
24 . . . R – N2; *25* Q – R4, Q – B1; *26* Q – R5+, K – K1; *27*
Q × RP, K – Q1; *28* B × N, R × B; *29* R × R+, Q × R (*29 . . .*
K × R; *30* Q – Q6+, K – K1; *31* Q – K7 mate); *30* Q × P+, K –
B2; *31* Q × P+, K – N3; *32* Q × R with a winning endgame.

41 Fischer - Robatsch *[Austria]*

VARNA OLYMPIC 1962

CENTER COUNTER DEFENSE

A bright cameo

Facing one of Robatsch's pet lines, Fischer proceeds to institute such a crisp attack that one is reminded of Morphy in his heyday. Noteworthy are White's 5th and 6th, practically refuting the whole variation.

Seeking safety for his King, Robatsch makes the mistake of castling too early. Fischer, already castled on the opposite wing, incurs no risk advancing his K-side Pawns, using them as battering rams to pry open the KN-file. Robatsch is unable to effect a closure and Fischer rushes into the breach— compelling resignation in only twenty moves.

1	P – K4	P – Q4
2	P×P	Q×P

This old move is considered weak but Black has a new twist in mind. The modern way is *2 . . . N – KB3*. Then White has the choice of either *3* P – QB4 or *3* B – N5+ to hold the Pawn, or simply *3* P – Q4.   Against Bergrasser at Monaco 1967, I chose *3* B – N5+, B – Q2; *4* B – B4, B – N5; *5* P – KB3, B – B4 (safer is . . . B – B1); *6* P – KN4!, B – B1; *7* N – B3, QN – Q2; *8* P – N5, N – N3; *9* B – N5+, N/B3 – Q2; *10* P – B4, N×P; *11* N×N, P – QB3; *12* B – B4, P×N; *13* B×P and White's extra Pawn should prevail.

3	N – QB3	Q – Q1

A hypermodern approach, championed by Bronstein. The idea is to give up the center and then play against it. Seidman, as Black, played the more traditional *3 . . . Q – R4* against me in the 1958–9 US Championship, which continued: *4* P – Q4, N – KB3;

5 N – B3, N – B3; 6 P – Q5!? (possibly an improvement over the usual 6 B – QN5), N – QN5; 7 B – N5+, P – B3 (more crucial is 7 . . . B – Q2; 8 B×B+, N×B; 9 P – QR3, N – KB3; 10 P×N, Q×R; 11 O – O, Q – R3; 12 R – K1 with a terrific attack. Not 12 . . . O – O – O?; 13 N – K5); 8 P×P, P×P; 9 B – R4, B – R3? (9 . . . B – Q2 is necessary); 10 P – QR3!, R – Q1; 11 B – Q2, Q – KB4; 12 P×N, R – Q3; 13 B – N3, N – K5; 14 R×B, R×B; 15 Q – B1, N×N; 16 P×N, R – Q3; 17 O – O, Black resigns.

4 P – Q4   P – KN3!?

The idea is to reserve the option of developing the KN to KR3 followed by N – B4 with pressure on the QP. After the game Robatsch told me he'd enjoyed excellent results with this system.

5 B – KB4!   . . .

Against the pedestrian 5 N – B3 (or 5 B – QB4, B – N2; 6 N – B3, N – KR3), B – N2; 6 P – KR3, N – KB3 (not 6 . . . N – KR3; 7 P – KN4! Sokolsky) White holds no more than a minimal edge.

5 . . .   B – N2

On 5 . . . N – KR3; 6 B – K5!, P – KB3; 7 B – KB4 messes up Black's Pawns.

6 Q – Q2!   . . .

Ignoring the "threat." Weak is 5 N – N5, N – QR3 followed by . . . P – QB3, etc. (Bronstein–Kholmov, USSR 1959). And 5 N – B3, N – KR3 would permit Black the setup he is striving for.

ROBATSCH

Position after 6 Q – Q2

FISCHER

6 . . .   N – KB3

Stymied, Black can no longer play N – KR3.

The main line is 6 . . . Q × P; 7 Q × Q, B × Q; 8 N – N5, B – N3 (forced); 9 N × P+, B × N; 10 B × B with the two Bishops and all the chances. Another possibility is 6 . . . B × P?; 7 O – O – O, N – QB3; 8 B – QN5, B – Q2; 9 N – Q5! (not 9 B × N?, B × B; 10 Q × B?, Q × Q; 11 R × Q, B × P), P – K4; 10 N – KB3 and Black will never get out of the opening alive.

7 O – O – O   P – B3

Better is 7 . . . N – Q4; 8 B – K5 (8 B – KR6!?, B × B; 9 Q × B, N × N ruptures White's Pawns), O – O; 9 P – KR4, P – KR4; 10 KN – K2 with a clear advantage but no forced win.

8 B – KR6   O – O?

Castling into it—with a vengeance. Black should strive to castle long with 8 . . . B × B; 9 Q × B, B – B4.

9 P – KR4   Q – R4
10 P – R5!   . . .

The attack plays itself. My experience with this line dates back to the Dragon-slaying days (see game 2).

ROBATSCH

Position after 10 P – R5

FISCHER

10 . . .   P × P

Horrible, but Black must keep the R-file closed one way or another. On 10 . . . R – Q1; 11 P × P, BP × P; 12 B × B, K × B; 13 Q – R6+, K – N1; 14 N – B3 – KN5 is slaughter.

Or *10* . . . N × P; *11* B – K2, N – B3; *12* B × B, K × B; *13* Q – R6+, K – N1; *14* P – KN4!, R – Q1; *15* P – N5, N – R4; *16* B × N, P × B; *17* R × P, B – KB4 (or *17* . . . Q – KB4; *18* P – N6!, Q × NP; *19* R – KN5); *18* P – N6! wins.

On *10* . . . B – B4; *11* P – B3 (threatening P – KN4), B × B (*11* . . . P × P?; *12* Q – N5 wins); *12* Q × B, P × P?; *13* Q – N5+, K – R1; *14* B – Q3 wins a piece.

11 B – Q3   . . .

It's important to exclude Black's Bishop from KB4.

11 . . .   **QN – Q2**

Not *11* . . . B – B4?; *12* Q – N5.

12 KN – K2   . . .

Taking advantage of the lull to bring out the reserves.

12 . . .   **R – Q1**
13 P – KN4!   **N – B1**

On *13* . . . N × P; *14* QR – N1! (threatening both P – B3 and/or R × N+) wins at least a piece. Black hopes to hang on by clustering minor pieces around his King.

14 P × P   . . .

Now the open KN-file becomes the new base of operations.

14 . . .   **N – K3**
15 QR – N1   **K – R1**

Also hopeless is *15* . . . K – B1; *16* B × B+, N × B; *17* Q – R6, N – N5; *18* Q × RP.

16 B × B+   **N × B**
17 Q – R6   **R – KN1**

On *17* . . . N – K3; *18* N – B4! forces mate.

18 R – N5   **Q – Q1**

On *18* . . . N – B4; *19* R × R+, N × R; *20* Q – B8 followed by R – N1 is tasty.

19 KR – N1   . . .

ROBATSCH

Position after 19 KR – N1

FISCHER

19 . . .   N – B4

Blundering a piece. But Black is completely tied up, and it's a pity he didn't allow the prettier finish after *19* . . . Q – B1; *20* P – Q5!, B – Q2 (if *20* . . . P×P; *21* N×P, N×N; *22* Q×P mate); *21* P – Q6!, N – B4; *22* Q×Q, QR×Q (or *22* . . . KR× Q; *23* B×N, P – KR3; *24* P×P, KR – QN1; *25* R – N7, B×B; *26* R×P, etc.); *23* B×N, R×R; *24* R×R, P – KR3; *25* P×P, R – QN1; *26* R – N3!, B×B; *27* R – B3 winning a piece.

20 B×N   **Black resigns**

42 Unzicker [*W. Germany*] - Fischer

VARNA OLYMPIC 1962

SICILIAN DEFENSE

Playing by ear

This game illustrates the hazard of trying to rely solely on
natural talent, without detailed knowledge of the latest
opening innovations. Seldom is a chess master so drastically
punished, as is Unzicker here, for failing to do his homework.
Disastrously pursuing a line with which Tal had just barely
survived against Fischer, Unzicker blunders further through
apparent unfamiliarity with Geller's improvement (15
K – R1!). That had previously defeated Fischer at Curaçao.
Unzicker simply puts his trust in "natural moves" and drifts
into a constrained position, allowing Fischer to penetrate
neatly on the weakened squares. The early decision, on move
26, comes as a surprise only to Unzicker.

1	P – K4	P – QB4
2	N – KB3	P – Q3
3	P – Q4	P×P
4	N×P	N – KB3
5	N – QB3	P – QR3
6	B – K2	. . .

On and off, White resorts to this solid and still respected system
(championed by Smyslov) whenever the sharper tries fail.

6 . . .   P – K4

Black's expectation in this Najdorf Variation is that his control
of important central squares, with possibilities of Q-side expansion,
will more than compensate for the slight weakness of his backward
QP.

                        7 N – N3   B – K3

To provoke P – KB4 – 5, weakening White's KP. For the non-committal 7 . . . B – K2 see game 4.

                        8 O – O   QN – Q2
                        9 P – B4   Q – B2
                       10 P – B5   B – B5
                       11 P – QR4   . . .

To hinder . . . P – QN4.

                       11 . . .   B – K2

Better than 11 . . . R – B1?; 12 P – R5, B – K2; 13 B × B, Q × B; 14 R – R4!, Q – B2; 15 B – K3, P – R3; 16 R – B2 with a bind. (Schmid–Evans, Varna 1962.)

                       12 B – K3   O – O

FISCHER

Position after 12 . . .
O – O

UNZICKER

                       13 P – R5   . . .

A critical alternative is 13 P – N4, P – Q4!; 14 P × P (if 14 P – N5, P – Q5! or 14 N × P, N × N; 15 P × N, N – B3; 16 P – Q6?, B × P; 17 B × B, Q × B; 18 Q × B?, Q × P+; 19 K – R1, Q – K5+), B – N5; 15 P – N5, B × N; 16 P × N, B × NP; 17 P × P, KR – Q1; 18 R – N1, B – B6. White's Pawns are overextended and his King is exposed.

                       13 . . .   P – QN4

Too passive is 13 . . . P – R3; 14 P – N4, N – R2; 15 B – B2 followed by P – R4.

14 P×P e.p.	N×NP
15 B×N?	. . .

At Curaçao 1962, Geller had found the right line: *15* K – R1!, KR – B1; *16* B × N, Q × B; *17* B × B, R × B; *18* Q – K2, R – N5; *19* R – R2! and Black is hard-pressed to defend his QRP, but *19* . . . P – R3!; *20* KR – R1, B – B1; *21* R × P, R × R; *22* R × R, Q – N2; *23* N – R5, Q – B2; *24* N – N3, Q – N2 (ZUCKER-MAN) = .

15 . . .	Q × B+
16 K – R1	B – N4!

Intending . . . B – B3 followed by . . . P – QR4.

17 B × B	. . .

White has already dissipated his theoretical advantage. He should settle for *17* N × B, P × N; *18* Q – Q3 with opposite colored Bishops.

17 . . .	P × B
18 N – Q5	N × N
19 Q × N	R – R5!

Avoids conceding the QR-file and puts pressure on the KP.

20 P – B3	Q – R3

FISCHER

Position after 20 . . .
Q – R3

UNZICKER

21 P – R3	. . .

It's hard for White to hit upon a constructive plan. At Curaçao 1962, Tal played against me *21* QR – Q1, R – B1; *22* N – B1, P – N5; *23* N – Q3!? (White's in a bad way anyhow), P × P; *24* P × P and now R × BP (instead of my . . . R – R4 lemon) wins

outright. If *25* N×P, P×N; *26* Q×P (*26* Q – Q8+, B – B1!),
B – N5!; *27* Q×R, Q×R+! (KMOCH).

21	. . .	R – B1
22	KR – K1	P – R3!

A handy *luft*, as becomes apparent later.

23	K – R2	B – N4
24	P – N3?	. . .

Creating more K-side weaknesses. Better is *24* QR – Q1.

24	. . .	Q – R2!
25	K – N2	R – R7
26	K – B1	. . .

What else? On *26* R×R, Q×R; *27* R – K2, R×P!

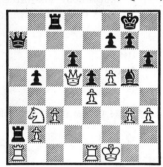

FISCHER

Position after 26 K – B1

UNZICKER

Now Black has a decisive shot.

26	. . .	R×BP!

White resigns

On *27* R×R (*27* P×R?, Q – B7 mate), R – B6+; *28* K – K2,
R – B7+; *29* K – Q3, Q×R; *30* R – QR1, Q×P wins. Black's
first rank is no longer vulnerable since the King can escape to
R2 on the check.

43 Fischer - Reshevsky *[U.S.A.]*

USA CHAMPIONSHIP 1962-3

SICILIAN DEFENSE

The missing link

Many critics have dubbed this the "12th game" of the unfinished match, which had ended in a 5½–5½ tie. It is as adventurous and as bitterly contested as their earlier ones.
This time Reshevsky is well prepared for Fischer's opening, countering forcefully and equalizing without difficulty.
However, instead of maintaining tension, he strives inconsistently for simplifications, forcing an exchange of Queens which leaves him with a strategically weak ending. Working with simultaneous threats on both wings, Fischer, despite the reduction in material, succeeds in exploiting several of his opponent's targets (backward Pawns on open files).
Reshevsky defends this passive position with his usual tenacity, but is unable to prevent an eventual breakthrough.

1	P – K4	P – QB4
2	N – KB3	P – Q3
3	P – Q4	P × P
4	N × P	N – KB3
5	N – QB3	P – QR3
6	P – KR3	P – KN3

A good reaction. So is 6 . . . P – QN4 (see game 40).

By transposing into a Dragon Variation, Black hopes to render P – KR3 useless, since in the normal Yugoslav Attack White will be forced to advance this Pawn again, thereby losing a tempo.

7	P – KN4	B – N2
8	P – N5!?	. . .

Consistent, but perhaps premature. However, no other method offers more: e.g., *8* B – K3, O – O; *9* P – N5, N – K1! Or *8* B – N2, O – O; *9* O – O, N – B3 =.

8 . . .   N – R4!

On 8 . . . KN – Q2; 9 B – K3, N – QB3; 10 Q – Q2 Black is
slightly bottled up.

9 B – K2   P – K4

I had intended to answer 9 . . . N – QB3!? with 10 N – N3
(and not 10 N × N, P × N; 11 B × N, P × B; 12 Q × RP, R – QN1
with good compensation for the Pawn).

10 N – N3   . . .

Bad is 10 N – B5, P × N; 11 B × N, P – B5 shutting out White's
QB.

10 . . .   N – B5
11 N – Q5   . . .

11 B – N4, N – B3; 12 N – Q5 might transpose to the game.

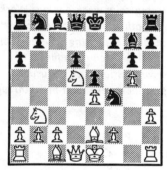

RESHEVSKY

Position after 11 N – Q5

FISCHER

Objectively speaking, White has no opening advantage.

11 . . .   N × N

Instead of simplifying so readily, Black could try to exploit the
weakened K-side. Tal says more "logical" is 11 . . . O – O;
12 P – KR4, P – B4 (or the interesting Pawn sac 12 . . . N –
Q2!?; 13 N × N, P × N; 14 Q × P, B – K4).
    Another possibility is 11 . . . N × B (not 11 . . . N × P?;
12 B – K3 and the threat of B – N6 wins material); 12 Q × N,
B – K3=.

12 Q × N   N – B3

Tal gives the dubious sac 12 . . . B – K3!?; 13 Q × NP,

N – Q2; but *14* B – K3 keeps the upper hand. But there's no need for Black to gamble. His position is basically sound.

13 B – N4   B × B

Tal gives *13 . . .* P – B4; *14* P × P *e.p.* (if *14* P × P, N – K2!; *15* Q – Q3, P × P; *16* B – R5+, N – N3, etc.), Q × P; *15* B × B, R × B; *16* P – QB3, R – B2; but after *17* B – K3 followed by O – O – O White stands better.

14 P × B   Q – B1 !

With the double threat of *15 . . .* Q × P and/or *. . .* N – N5.

15 Q – Q1   . . .

On *15* Q × P, Q × P; *16* Q – Q3, R – Q1; *17* Q – K2, Q – N7; *18* R – B1, P – R3 Black wrests the initiative.

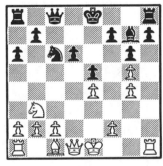

RESHEVSKY

Position after 15 Q – Q1

FISCHER

15 . . .   N – Q5 ?

Apparently intent on simplifying at all cost, Reshevsky steers for an inferior ending. Tal gives *15 . . .* Q – K3; *16* B – K3, O – O – O =.

A Bulgarian magazine gives the sharp *15 . . .* P – Q4!? as best, since it dissolves the backward QP immediately. The tactical justification shows up after *16* P × P (if *16* Q – K2 or P – QB3, P – Q5), N – N5; *17* P – QB3 (if *17* O – O, N × BP; *18* R – N1, O – O foils White's strategy), Q – B5! and now there are two main lines:

A] *18* P × N?, Q – K5+; *19* K – Q2, R – Q1; *20* K – B3, B – B1!; *21* P – R3 (if *21* N – B5, B × N; *22* P × B, R × P wins), R – B1+; *22* K – Q2 (not *22* N – B5?, B × N; *23* P × B, R × P+; *24* K – N3, Q – B5 mate), B – K2! with a continuing attack.

B] *18* R – R3, N × QP (if *18 . . .* Q – K5+; *19* K – B1, N – B7?; *20* N – Q2 wins); *19* Q – K2, Q – B2=.

16	P – QB3	N × N
17	P × N	Q – K3
18	R – QR5!	P – B3?

Leads to a lifeless ending. Better chances are offered by *18 . . .* O – O (or *18 . . .* P – N4; *19* Q – Q5, Q × Q; *20* P × Q, K – Q2); *19* R – Q5, QR – Q1 followed by *. . .* P – B4.

19	Q – Q5!	Q × Q

Not *19 . . .* Q × P?; *20* Q × NP, O – O; *21* P × P.

20	R × Q	K – Q2
21	P × P	B × P
22	P – N5	B – K2
23	K – K2	. . .

Now it's clear that Black's game is, at best, barely tenable. Both his QP and KRP are ugly weaknesses exposed on open files.

23	. . .	QR – KB1
24	B – K3	R – B1
25	P – N4	. . .

More accurate possibly is *25* P – QB4, K – B2; *26* P – N4 and Black has constantly to worry about breaks with P – B5, P – N5, or even P – B4.

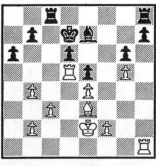

RESHEVSKY

Position after 25 P – N4

FISCHER

25 . . .   P – N4!?

Many annotators criticized this because it creates a fresh weakness (the QRP). But if Black just waits he ultimately should get squeezed to death after K – Q3 followed by P – QB4, etc. Reshevsky apparently feels more comfortable living with his new weaknesses, rather than with the uncertainties which would be created after an eventual P – QB4.

26 R/5 – Q1 . . .

White cannot keep Q5 under control indefinitely. In order to make progress, the Rooks must strike at the backward RPs.

26 . . . K – K3
27 R – R1 R – B3
28 R – KR3 . . .

On 28 R – KR4?, P – KR4! eliminates the weakness.

RESHEVSKY

Position after 28 R – KR3

FISCHER

28 . . . B – B1

28 . . . P – Q4!? loses a Pawn but offers a slight ray of hope: e.g., 29 P × P+, K × P; 30 R/1 – R1, K – B5; 31 R × P, R × R; 32 R × R, R – K3; 33 K – Q2 (33 K – B3?, P – K5+!; 34 K – B4, K – N6), K – N6; 34 K – Q3, K × P; 35 K – K4!, B – B1 (if 35 . . . K × P; 36 K – Q5, R – Q3+; 37 K × P, B – B1; 38 R – B7+!, K – N6; 39 R – B8, B – K2; 40 R – K8, R – Q2; 41 K – K6 wins a piece); 36 R – R8, B – N2; 37 R – KN8, R – K2; 38 R – QB8! followed by R – B6 should win.

29 R/1 – R1 R – B2

Now on 29 . . . P – Q4?; 30 P × P+, K × P; 31 R × P, R × R; 32 R × R, K – B5; 33 R – KB7, R – B1; 34 R – B6, K – N6; 35 R × RP, K × P; 36 B – Q2, etc.

30 R – R4! . . .

The critical position. Black is virtually in *zugzwang*. The Rook on R4 serves a valuable function, as will become apparent.

    30 . . .   P – Q4

On *30 . . . R – B5* (if *30 . . . R – B2; 31 R – R1); 31 P – B3, R – B2; 32 K – B2!, P – Q4; 33 R – R1, R – B3; 34 P×P+, K×P; 35 R – Q1+, K – K3; 36 R – Q8* should win.

    31 R – R1!   . . .

Reshevsky doubtlessly underestimated this interpolation. He probably expected *31 P×P+, K×P; 32 R – Q1+, K – K3; 33 R – Q8, B – N2!*

    31 . . .   R – B3

On *31 . . . P×P; 32 R×P+, K – Q4; 33 R – N6* wins.

    32 P×P+   K×P
    33 R – Q1+   K – K3

The merit of the Rook on R4 is that it prevents the King from entering at QB5.

    34 R – Q8   K – B4

With Black's Rook on B3 (instead of B2, as before) he no longer has the reply . . . B – N2. And on *34 . . . R – B2; 35 R – R8* is decisive.

    35 R – R8   R – K3
    36 R – R3!   . . .

RESHEVSKY

Position after 36 R – R3

FISCHER

    36 . . .   B – N2

Equally useless is *36 . . . K – N5; 37 R – N3+, K – R4; 38*

R – B3, B – N2; *39* R×R, B×R; *40* R – B8, B – N2; *41* R – B7.
Or *36* . . . K – K5; *37* R – B3, B – N2; *38* R×R, B×R; *39*
R – B8, B – N2; *40* R – B7, B – R1; *41* P – B3+, K – Q4; *42*
R×P, R – K1; *43* K – Q3.

37	R×R	B×R
38	R×P	R – K1
39	R – B7+	K – N5

Or *39* . . . K – K5; *40* P – B3+, K – Q4; *41* K – Q3 wins.

40	P – B3+	K – N6
41	K – Q3?	. . .

A buzz began to circulate in the playing hall and I wondered
what it was all about. Later they told me *41* K – B1! (threatening
B – B2+) forces at least the win of a piece. Of course the text
move also wins, but it takes ten moves longer.

41	. . .	P – K5+

Throwing another Pawn to the winds in order to get the Bishop
into play. On *41* . . . R – QB1; *42* B – B5 also is easy.

42	P×P	R – Q1+
43	B – Q4	K – N5
44	R – B1	B – K4

On *44* . . . K×P; *45* R – N1+, K – B5; *46* R×P, etc.

45	K – K3	B – B2

After *45* . . . B×B+; *46* P×B, K×P; *47* P – K5 the center
Pawns are irresistible.

46	R – N1+	K – R5
47	K – B3	R – Q2

Or *47* . . . R – B1+; *48* B – B6, K – R6; *49* R – R1+, B –
R7; *50* P – K5, R – K1; *51* K – K4, etc. The rest is silence.

48	P – K5	R – B2+
49	K – K4	R – B4
50	P – K6	B – Q1
51	B – B6!	B×B
52	P×B	R×P
53	K – Q5	R – B7
54	R – K1	Black resigns

44 Fischer - Fine [U.S.A.]

NEW YORK 1963: Skittles Game

EVANS GAMBIT

Shock treatment

Having become one of the leading players in the world, Fine quit chess at the height of his career (1945) to become a practising psychoanalyst; but he has lost none of his love for the game and little of his brilliance. The following is one of seven or eight offhand games played at his home in New York. As far as can be ascertained, Dr. Fine very nearly held his own.

Here, departing for the first time from his beloved Ruy Lopez, Fischer employs the daring gambit introduced by Captain Evans a century ago. This ploy has all but disappeared from the arena. Fine, although the author of several opening manuals, is understandably rusty, and he gets caught in a vise from which he never escapes. Fischer uncorks a sparkling finish in seventeen moves.

1	P – K4	P – K4
2	N – KB3	N – QB3
3	B – B4	B – B4
4	P – QN4!?	B × P

Safer is *4 . . . B – N3*, but that is hardly the way to refute the gambit.

5	P – B3	B – R4

For *5 . . . B – K2* see game 50.

6	P – Q4	P × P

6 . . . P – Q3; 7 O – O (better is *7 Q – N3*), *B – N3* is the famous Lasker's Defense, which put the Evans out of commission last century.

7 O–O   . . .

FINE

Position after 7 O – O

FISCHER

7 . . .   P × P

"A little too greedy." (*MCO*, 10th Ed.)

7 . . . B – N3; *8* P × P, P – Q3 leads to the so-called "normal variation" which is tenable. After 7 . . . P – Q3; *8* Q – N3 (Walter's Attack) someone played Q – Q2 against me at an exhibition (Davis College 1964); *9* P × P, B – N3; *10* B – QN5, K – B1!; *11* P – Q5, N – R4 and Black saves the piece.

8 Q – N3   Q – K2

More usual is *8* . . . Q – B3; *9* P – K5, Q – N3; *10* N × P, KN – K2; and now either *11* N – K2 or B – R3 leads to complicated positions which Tchigorin, for example, thought were playable for Black.

9 N × P   . . .

FINE

Position after 9 N × P

FISCHER

9 . . .   N – B3?

On *9* . . . B × N; *10* Q × B, P – B3 (if *10* . . . N – B3; *11* B – R3, P – Q3; *12* P – K5, N – K5; *13* Q – N2 and against N ×

KP; *14* N×N, Q×N; *15* KR – K1! wins a piece); *11* B – R3,
P – Q3; *12* B – Q5!, B – Q2; *13* QR – N1, O – O – O; *14* N – Q4
is crushing.

The best defense follows an old analysis from Freeborough and
Rankin (1893): *9* . . . Q – N5!; *10* B×P+, K – Q1; *11* B – N5+
(if *11* B×N?, Q×Q! holds), KN – K2; *12* N – Q5, Q×Q; *13*
P×Q, B – N3 (*13* . . . B – N5! looks better); *14* KR – B1, P –
KR3; *15* R×N, P×B; *16* N×B, BP×N; *17* R×NP, etc.

10 N – Q5!	N×N

Necessary is *10* . . . Q×P; but *11* N – N5 produces a violent
attack.

11 P×N	N – K4

On *11* . . . N – Q1; *12* B – R3 is decisive (*12* . . . P – Q3;
13 Q – N5+).

12 N×N	Q×N
13 B – N2	Q – N4

FINE

Position after 13 . . .
Q – N4

FISCHER

14 P – KR4!	. . .

Deflecting the "overloaded" Queen.

14 . . .	Q×RP

On *14* . . . Q – R3; *15* Q – QR3 (threatening KR – K1+)
wins. Or *14* . . . Q – N5; *15* KR – K1+, B×R (if *15* . . .
K – Q1; *16* Q – K3, B – N5; *17* Q – R6!!, P×Q; *18* B – B6+,
B – K2; *19* B×B+, K – K1; *20* B – N5+!, K – B1; *21* B×P+,
Q – N2; *22* R – K8+!!, K×R; *23* B×Q wins); *16* R×B+,
K – Q1; *17* Q – K3, Q×P; *18* P – N3! and Black's Queen must
relinquish its guard of K2.

15	B×P	R – KN1
16	KR – K1+	K – Q1

16 . . . B × R; *17* R × B+ leads to the same finale.

        17 Q – KN3!   **. . .**

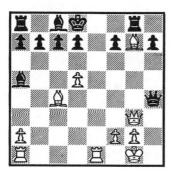

FINE

Position after 17 Q – N3

FISCHER

       17 . . .   **Black resigns**

17 . . . Q × Q; *18* B – B6 mate.

45 Fischer - Bisguier [U.S.A.]

NEW YORK STATE OPEN CHAMPIONSHIP 1963

TWO KNIGHTS' DEFENSE

Ghosts

Steinitz, nicknamed "the Austrian Morphy" (although two styles could hardly be more dissimilar), apparently exercises a great influence on Fischer, who has restored several of his pet lines to prominence. One of these is the bizarre 9 N – R3!?, found wanting at the turn of the century, and perhaps best left there.

Bisguier appears unimpressed, regaining his gambit Pawn with a strong initiative. But he misses several opportunities to gain an advantage and is gradually outplayed. Just at the critical moment, when the chances are roughly equal, he commits the same kind of gross oversight that had doomed Fischer against Spassky (game 18). He suffers the same fate.

1 P – K4 . . .

Best by test.

1 . . . P – K4
2 N – KB3 N – QB3
3 B – B4 . . .

The last time I played this move in a tournament was when I was 12, at the 1955 US Junior Championship.

3 . . . N – B3!?

Steinitz considered this to be an unsound sacrifical continuation!

4 N – N5 . . .

Tarrasch branded this a "duffer's move" and Panov called it "primitive." But there is no other way for White to try for an advantage. *4 P – Q3* is tame. And after *4 O – O, N × P; 5 N – B3,*

N×N; 6 QP×N, Q – K2! White has no compensation for the Pawn. Finally, 4 PQ4 leads to the Max Lange attack.

        4 . . .   P – Q4
        5 P×P   N – QR4

5 . . . N – Q5!? (FRITZ) and 5 . . . P – N4!? (ULVESTAD) are both interesting but unsound. On 5 . . . N×P; 6 P – Q4! (6 N×P!? is the "Fried Liver Attack") is so strong that 5 . . . N×P is practically extinct.

        6 B – N5+   P – B3
        7 P×P   P×P
        8 B – K2   P – KR3
        9 N – KR3!?   . . .

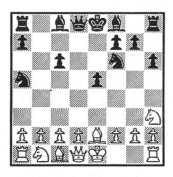

BISGUIER

Position after 9 N – KR3

FISCHER

To my knowledge, this is the first time that this move had been employed in Grandmaster chess for over seventy years. It is one of Steinitz's many unique opening contributions. The famous cable match game in 1891 between Steinitz and Tchigorin, which ended in a victory for Black, apparently caused the chess world to shy away from this variation.

        9 . . .   B – QB4

A] 9 . . . B – Q3 (STEINITZ) might be worth investigating. If 10 P – Q4 (TCHIGORIN), then . . . P – K5 (FISCHER).

B] 9 . . . B – KB4 is too crude: 10 O – O, Q – Q2; 11 R – K1, B×N; 12 P×B, Q×RP; 13 B – B1 and Black is busted, e.g., 13 . . . Q – N5+?; 14 Q×Q, N×Q; 15 P – KR3 wins a piece (STEINITZ).

C] 9 . . . P – N4; 10 P – Q3, P – N5; 11 N – N1, B – QB4; 12 N – QB3 effectively wards off the threats (12 . . . Q – N3 is answered by 13 N – R4!).

10 O – O   . . .

Played by Steinitz in the 6th game of his second match with Tchigorin in 1892. Better is *10* P – Q3!, O – O; *11* N – B3, R – K1; *12* O – O, B×N; *13* P×B, Q – Q2; *14* B – N4, N×B; *15* P×N, etc., as I played vs. Radoicic here in a later round.

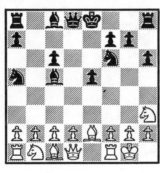

BISGUIER

Position after 10 O – O

FISCHER

10 . . .   O – O

Dr. Gottschall, in the 1892 *Deutsche Schachzeitung*, suggests *10* . . . P – N4, remarking it strange that a player as aggressive as Tchigorin did not chance it. Gottschall gives *11* K – R1, P – N5; *12* N – N1, N – K5; *13* B×P!, N×P+; *14* R×N, B×R and, although Black has won the exchange, prefers White's practical chances.

After *10* . . . P – N4; *11* K – R1, P – N5; *12* N – N1, N – K5 let us suppose White tries to avert material loss with *13* P – N4 (of no avail is *13* Q – K1, Q – Q5; *14* B – Q1, N×P+; *15* R×N, Q×R; *16* Q×P+?, B – K3), N×P+ (or Gottschall's *13* . . . B×BP; *14* P – Q3, Q – R5; *15* P×KN, B – N6; *16* N – KR3 [if *16* P – KR3, P×P; *17* P×P, R – KN1], B×P!; *17* K×B, P – N6+; *18* K – N1, B×N, etc.); *14* R×N, B×R; *15* P×N, Q – R5!; *16* Q – B1, B – N6; *17* P – KR3, R – KN1 with a crushing attack.

11 P – Q3   B×N

This certainly seems an improvement over the aforementioned Steinitz–Tchigorin match game which continued: *11* . . . N – Q4 (Gottschall's *11* . . . N – R2 also merits attention); *12* P – B4, N – K2; *13* K – R1, B×N; *14* P×B, N – B4; *15* P – B4, P×P; *16* B×P, N – K6; *17* B×N, B×B; *18* N – B3 and White won easily with his Q-side majority.

12 P×B	Q – Q2
13 B – B3	. . .

A difficult choice. I rejected *13* K – N2 since this was the square I had reserved for my Bishop. On *13* B – N4, N×B followed by . . . P – B4 gives fair attacking chances.

13 . . .	Q×RP

So Black regains the Pawn, but I have faith in my two Bishops.

14 N – Q2	. . .

It would be a mistake to play for the win of a Pawn by *14* B – N2, Q – R5!; *15* Q – K1, KR – K1!; *16* Q×N, N – N5; *17* P – KR3, B×P+; *18* R×B (if *18* K – R1, Q – N6), Q×R+; *19* K – R1, P – K5!; *20* P×N (if *20* P×P, R×P), P×P with a winning attack.

14 . . .	QR – Q1

Not *14* . . . P – K5?; *15* N×P, N×N; *16* B×N, B – Q3; *17* P – KB4, etc.

15 B – N2	Q – B4

The Queen is forced off the R-file. On *15* . . . Q – R5?; *16* N – B3, Q – R4; *17* Q – K1 wins a Pawn.

16 Q – K1	. . .

Perhaps better is *16* Q – B3 with possibilities of a slightly favorable ending.

16 . . .	KR – K1
17 N – K4	B – N3
18 N×N+	. . .

I was worried about the maneuver . . . N – Q4 – KB5. But sharper is *18* P – N4, N – N2; *19* P – N5.

18 . . .	Q×N
19 K – R1	P – B4

Stronger is *19* . . . P – N4 preventing White's break on KB4 once and for all. Then by bringing his Knight to KR5! Black could get a good game.

20 Q – B3!	. . .

Serves the double purpose of preventing . . . P – B5 and of enforcing P – KB4. For all the good it does, Black's Bishop on QN3 might just as well be a Pawn for the rest of the game.

BISGUIER

Position after 20 Q – B3

FISCHER

| 20 . . . | N – B3 |

Too late now is *20 . . . P – N4?; 21 P – B4!*

| 21 P – B4 | N – Q5 |
| 22 Q – B4 | . . . |

To prepare P – B3, driving the Knight away from Q5. I didn't like the looks of *22 P×P, Q×P; 23 B – B4, Q – K7*, etc.

| 22 . . . | Q – N3 |

Intending . . . Q – R4 followed by . . . N – B4. (Not *23 . . . Q – K3; 24 Q – R4, Q – Q2?; 25 Q×Q, R×Q); 25 P – B3, N – B7; 26 B – B6!*

| 23 P – B3 | . . . |

After the game a kibitzer suggested *23 B – K4, Q – R4; 24 P – B5,* but this allows Black to turn the tables by *24 . . . Q – K7; 25 R – KN1, N – B6!*

| 23 . . . | N – B4 |

On *23 . . . N – K7; 24 P – B5, Q – B3 (24 . . . Q – R4?; 25 B – B3!); 25 B – K3, N – B5; 26 B – K4* is tremendous.

| 24 P×P | . . . |

After *22 B – K4, Q – R4* just who has got the attack is not quite clear!

24 . . .   R × KP
25 B – B4   . . .

25 Q – B4 turns out badly after B – B2!; 26 B – K4, Q – R4!

25 . . .   R – K7

Black is playing for an advantage. 25 . . . N – K6; 26 B × N, R × B is absolutely equal.

26 B – K4   . . .

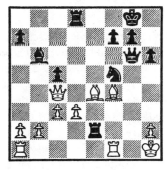

BISGUIER

Position after 26 B – K4

FISCHER

The critical position.

26 . . .   R × NP?

A pity that just when the game was getting interesting, Black had to make this terrible mistake.

Correct is 26 . . . R – K1! (threatening . . . R/1 × B). Bad would be 27 R – KN1, Q – R4; 28 QR – KB1, N – K6!; 29 Q – N5, R × B; 30 P × R, N × R; 31 Q – K8+ (if 31 R × N, Q – N5 wins), K – R2; 32 R × P+, K × R; 33 B – K5+, Q × B; 34 Q × Q+, P – B3; 35 Q – K7+, K – N3; 36 Q – K8+, K – N4 escaping the perpetual and should win.

After 26 . . . R – K1! therefore, the best White has is 27 B – B3 (to prevent . . . Q – R4), R × P; 28 QR – K1 with even chances, owing to the Bishop pair.

27 B – K5!   . . .

Bisguier slumped and his chest collapsed, as he saw that Black cannot avert the loss of a piece.

27 . . .   R – K1
28 R × N   R × B
29 R × R   Black resigns

46 Fischer - Benko [U.S.A.]

USA CHAMPIONSHIP 1963–4

PIRC-ROBATSCH DEFENSE

Romp

Chess Life, *January 1964, reported:*
"In the later stages of the tournament some of Fischer's opponents did almost as much to guarantee his 11–0 score as Bobby did. The building tension worked to Fischer's advantage . . . On Monday, December 30, Fischer won his last game of 1963—defeating Paul Benko with a neat little combination, after Benko had shown some suicidal tendencies in the management of his defense."

And so, in twenty-one moves, another Grandmaster is demolished. Benko misses a chance to simplify (on move 15) in order to reach an inferior but possibly tenable ending. This is fortunate for the reader, who otherwise would be cheated of White's scintillating 19th move. That alone is worth the price of admission!

1	P – K4	P – KN3
2	P – Q4	B – N2
3	N – QB3	. . .

3 P – QB4, P – Q3; *4* N – QB3 transposes to a King's Indian. An unorthodox try is *3* P – KR4!?

3	. . .	P – Q3
4	P – B4	. . .

Sharpest. Another build-up is *4* B – K3, N – KB3; *5* P – B3, etc.

4	. . .	N – KB3
5	N – B3	O – O
6	B – Q3	. . .

An improvement over *6* B – K2 which I played against Korchnoi

at Curaçao 1962. That game continued: 6 . . . P – QB4; 7
P×P, Q – R4; 8 O – O, Q×P+; 9 K – R1, N – B3; 10 N – Q2,
P – QR4!; 11 N – N3, Q – N3; 12 P – QR4, N – QN5; 13 P – N4,
B×P! with a big advantage.

6 . . .   B – N5?

Preparing to sac the "minor exchange." Interesting is Valvo's
6 . . . N – R3!?; 7 P – K5, P×P; 8 BP×P, N – Q4; 9 N×N,
Q×N about equal. (Bisguier–Benko, match 1964.)
The book gives 6 . . . QN – Q2; 7 O – O (7 P – K5 is best),
P – K4; 8 QP×P, P×P; 9 P×P, QN×P; 10 N×N, Q – Q5+;
11 K – R1, Q×KN; 12 B – KD4, Q – QB4 with a tenable game.
Fischer-Perez, Havana 1965 continued: 6 . . . N – B3!?;
7 P – K5, P×P; 8 BP×P, N – Q4 (Spassky's 8 . . . N – KN5
or maybe even . . . N – KR4 is better); 9 N×N, Q×N; 10
P – B3, B – N5; 11 Q – K2! with a pull.

7 P – KR3   B×N
8 Q×B   . . .

I overheard someone explaining this game to a beginner: "You
take off the Knight here, another piece comes out to replace it, so
Black hasn't really stopped White's development . . ."

8 . . .   N – B3
9 B – K3   P – K4

On 9 . . . N – Q2; 10 P – K5 keeps Black cramped.

10 QP×P   P×P
11 P – B5   . . .

Already threatening to obtain a winning bind with P – KN4 - 5·

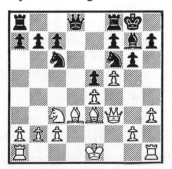

BENKO

Position after 11 P – B5

FISCHER

11 . . .   P × P

Best. My original note said: "If immediately *11* . . . N – Q5;
12 Q – B2, P × P; *13* P × P with a quick crush in sight." This verdict
was later confirmed in Bednarski–Kraidman, Tel Aviv 1964, which
continued: *13* . . . P – N4; *14* O – O, P – B4; *15* N – K4, P –
B5; *16* N × N+, Q × N; *17* B – K4, QR – Q1; *18* P – B3, KR – K1;
19 K – R1, K – R1; *20* QR – K1, P – N5; *21* P × N, P × P; *22*
B – B1, P – Q6; *23* P – QN3, B – R3; *24* B × B, Q × B; *25* B – B3,
R × R; *26* Q × R, P – B6; *27* Q – K7! and White won in ten more
moves.

12 Q × P   . . .

After *12* P × P, P – K5! Black gets good counterplay.

12 . . .   N – Q5

Benko is willing to gamble a Pawn to drive White's Queen from
its dominating post. *12* . . . : Q – Q2 is safer, however.

BENKO

Position after 12 . . .
N – Q5

FISCHER

13 Q – B2   . . .

I was tempted to accept the dare with *13* Q × P!, N – N5; *14*
Q × B+!, K × Q; *15* P × N with threats all over the place. For
example, if *15* . . . N – K3; *16* P – K5, R – R1; *17* B – R6+,
K – N1; *18* N – K4 wins. But *15* . . . N – B3 is hard to crack.

13 . . .   N – K1

More active than *13* . . . N – Q2; *14* O – O – O, N – B4; *15*
K – N1 followed by N – K2 and P – B3 driving out the Knight.
Now with . . . N – Q3 pending, Black threatens either to break

with . . . P – KB4 or, in some lines, to advance with . . . P – QB4 – 5.

14 O – O . . .

An alternative is *14* O – O – O, N – Q3; *15* N – K2. I thought White's King would be safer after the text—the drawback is the K-side Pawns can no longer safely advance.

14 . . . N – Q3

Sharp! I had expected *14* . . . P – QB3; *15* N – K2 after which Black must either exchange his only well-placed piece or allow White's Knight to scramble to KN3 followed by R5 or KB5.

15 Q – N3 . . .

The only way to sustain the initiative. On *15* N – Q5, P – KB4; *16* B × N, N × P!; *17* B × N, P × KB wins a Pawn. And after *15* N – K2, P – KB4 gives Black active counterchances.

15 . . . K – R1

On *15* . . . P – KB4; *16* B – R6, Q – B3; *17* B × B, Q × B; *18* Q × Q+, K × Q; *19* P × P, N/3 × P; *20* QR – K1, QR – K1; *21* N – K4 with a comfortable edge, but certainly no forced win.

16 Q – N4 . . .

To prevent . . . P – KB4.

16 . . . P – QB3

Too passive. Black should seize the opportunity for *16* . . . P – QB4!

17 Q – R5 . . .

Threatening *18* B × N, P × B; *19* P – K5.

17 . . . Q – K1?

Either *17* . . . N – K3 or . . . P – QB4 is essential.

18 B × N P × B

19 R – B6! . . .

The *zwischenzug* Benko missed. He had expected *19* P – K5, P – KB4!

BENKO

Position after 19 R – B6

FISCHER

A bolt from the blue!

19 . . .   K – N1

Forced. On *19 . . . P × N (or . . . B × R); 20* P – K5 mates.

20 P – K5   P – KR3
21 N – K2!   . . .

Black was hoping for *21* R × N, Q × P! and he survives to an ending.

21 . . .   Black resigns

There is no defense to the threat of R × N. On *21 . . .* N – N4; *22* Q – B5 wins. Or *21 . . .* B × R; *22* Q × P forces mate.

47 Fischer - Bisguier *[U.S.A.]*

USA CHAMPIONSHIP 1963–4

RUY LOPEZ

The Indian sign?

Bisguier is the one Grandmaster who consistently obtains decent positions against Fischer, only to throw them away for no apparent reason. Out of something like a dozen encounters, he has squeezed but a single draw.

Here is the only game in which Bisguier is outplayed from the start. Still, he does catch Fischer napping and nearly escapes. Describing his sensations before the game, Bisguier wrote:

"For the first time I was really in doubt as to what Bobby would play against me as White . . . I was hoping to play the Black side of the King's Gambit or the Two Knights' Defense, but he 'surprised' me with the Ruy Lopez . . . taken by surprise I was not so prepared or comfortable as I would like to have been. Now that Bobby has added psychology to his arsenal of weapons he is a much more dangerous opponent than ever before."

1	P – K4	P – K4
2	N – KB3	. . .

In a previous round, against Evans, I had hazarded a King's Gambit: *2* P – KB4, P×P; *3* B – B4, Q – R5+; *4* K – B1 and White won only after some uneasy moments.

2	. . .	N – QB3
3	B – N5	P – QR3
4	B – R4	N – B3
5	O – O	B – K2
6	R – K1	P – QN4
7	B – N3	O – O
8	P – B3	P – Q3

Bernstein tried the Marshall Attack against me in the 1959–60 US Championship, and an interesting struggle developed: *8 . . . P – Q4!?; 9* P × P, P – K5 (in place of the usual . . . N × P); *10* P × N, P × N; *11* Q × P, B – KN5; *12* Q – N3, B – Q3; *13* Q – R4, R – K1; *14* P – B3, B – B4; *15* P – Q4, B × P +; *16* K × B, N – N5 +; *17* K – N3, Q × Q +; *18* K × Q, R × R; *19* P × N, R × B; *20* P × B, R – Q1; *21* P – R4! White won shortly.

9	P – KR3	N – QR4
10	B – B2	P – B4
11	P – Q4	Q – B2

For *11 . . .* N – Q2 see game 38.

12	QN – Q2	N – B3
13	P × BP	. . .

The Rauzer Attack. White gives up the center in order to exploit Black's weakened squares on Q5 and KB5.

13	. . .	P × P
14	N – B1	R – Q1

Risky. Better is the usual *14 . . .* B – K3; *15* N – K3, QR – Q1; *16* Q – K2, P – N3, etc.

15	Q – K2	N – KR4

An old line rehabilitated by Reshevsky against Bronstein at Zurich 1953. If now *15 . . .* B – K3; *16* N – K3, P – N3; *17* N – N5, B – QB1; *18* N – Q5!, N × N; *19* P × N, B × N (*19 . . .* R × P; *20* Q – B3!, B – K3; *21* N × B, P × N; *22* Q – N4!); *20* B × B, R × P; *21* QR – Q1 with a plus (LIPNITZSKY).

16	P – KN3!	. . .

Bronstein's move—after first interpolating *16* P – QR4, R – N1.

BISGUIER

Position after 16 P – KN3

FISCHER

This idea bankrupts Black's strategy. The slight weakening of the K-side is inconsequential, but Black's loss of time with his KN is.

Actually the sharpest continuation is *16* P – QR4! as I played against Eliskases at Mar del Plata 1960 (I simply forgot to interpolate it here), which continued: *16 . . .* R – N1; *17* P×P, P×P; *18* P – KN3!, P – N3; *19* P – R4!, B – K3; *20* N – K3, P – B5; *21* N – N5, B×N; *22* P×B, N – R4; *23* N – N4, B×N; *24* Q×B, N – N6; *25* B×N, P×B; *26* B – K3 with a great advantage.

16 . . .		P – N3

Simply *16 . . .* N – B3 may be best. Then on *17* P – KR4, P – R3; *18* N – K3, B – K3.
16 . . . B×P is bad owing to *17* N – N5, KB×N (if *17 . . .* QB×N; *18* Q×N, B×N; *19* B×B, P – B3; *20* B×P!, P×B; *21* K×B White's better); *18* B×B, N – B3 (not *18 . . .* B×N?; *19* B×R); *19* B×N, P×B; *20* N – K3 White has more than enough for the Pawn

17 P – KR4!		. . .

Bronstein's *17* K – R2 and Weinstein's *17* K – N2 are time-consuming and hence weaker.

When I told Bronstein (at Mar del Plata 1960) that the text was a tremendous improvement over his game with Reshevsky, he replied: "Of course. After seven years one must find an improvement."

17 . . .	B – K3
18 N – K3	P – B3

Probably best. *18 . . .* P – B5; *19* N – N5! is similar to the quoted game with Eliskases.

19 N – Q5!		. . .

Of course! Chess is a matter of timing. Given another move or two Black would be able not only to defend himself against this invasion, but even try for the initiative.

BISGUIER

Position after 19 N – Q5

FISCHER

19 . . .   Q – N2

Prudent. "Winning" the Pawn would allow White's Bishop-pair
to enter the game with powerful effect: e.g., *19 . . .* B × N; *20*
P × B, R × P; *21* P – B4!, N – Q5; *22* N × N, R × N; *23* P × P, P × P;
24 Q × NP and now Eliskases recommends *24 . . .* P – B5 but
I fail to see how this improves matters since *25* B – K3, R – N1;
26 Q – R4, R – QN5? is answered by *27* Q – K8+.

20 N × B+   Q × N

White has the two Bishops—or a "half point" advantage.

21 N – R2   . . .

This Knight is also bound for Q5.

21 . . .   N – N2
22 N – N4   P – B5
23 Q – B3!   . . .

Winning the second "minor exchange." On *23 . . .* R – KB1;
24 N – K3 the Knight is ready to pounce on Q5, especially after
Black's Rook has been deflected from the Q-file.

23 . . .   B × N
24 Q × B   N – K3
25 P – R5?   . . .

More accurate is *25* B – K3 (*25 . . .* N – B4?; *26* B × N,
Q × B; *27* Q – K6+, K – N2; *28* QR – Q1 penetrates decisively).

25 . . .   K – R1!

Alert. I had expected *25 . . .* P – N4; whereupon *26* B – K3
is even more devastating than before.

26 K – N2! . . .

On *26* P × P, R – KN1 White is in trouble!

26 . . . P – N4

Forced—eventually. On *26* . . . R – KN1; *27* R – R1, P × P? (*27* . . . P – N4 is better); *28* Q × P, N – B5+; *29* B × N, P × B; *30* P – K5!, R – N2; *31* P × P, Q × P; *32* B × P wins.

27 B – K3 N – B5+!

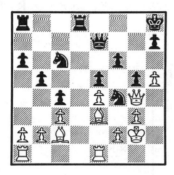

BISGUIER

Position after 27 . . .
N – B5+

FISCHER

28 K – R2! . . .

28 P × N?, NP × P threatening *28* . . . R – KN1 as well as *28* . . . P × B regains the piece advantageously.

28 . . . N – Q6
29 B × N P × B?

Now the advanced soldier must fall. Exchanging a pair of Rooks would make it more difficult, but White still maintains his grip after *29* . . . R × B; *30* KR – Q1, QR – Q1; *31* R × R, P × R (*31* . . ; R × R?; *32* Q – B8+, N – Q1; *33* Q × RP); *32* R – Q1, R – Q2. *33* R – Q2 threatening a winning bind with B – B5.

30 KR – Q1 R – Q2

On *30* . . . P – N5; *31* R – Q2, P × P; *32* P × P, Q – R6; *33* QR – Q1, Q × BP; *34* Q – K6, K – N2; *35* P – R6+! wins.

31 R – Q2 N – R4

A useless excursion, but there was no good defense. Strangely enough, Black's difficulty stems from his third move and its consequent weakening on QN3. If the Pawn were still on QR2 (preventing a later B – N6) he might well hold.

On *31* . . . QR – Q1; *32* QR – Q1, Q – B2; *33* B – N6, R – QN1; *34* B – B5, QR – Q1; *35* Q – B3 picks up the QP at leisure.

32 P – N3   Q – Q3

Not *32* . . . R – QB1?; *33* R × P!

33 QR – Q1   R – K1

On *33* . . . QR – Q1; *34* R × P, Q × R; *35* R × Q, R × R; *36* B – N6!

34 R × P   Q × R

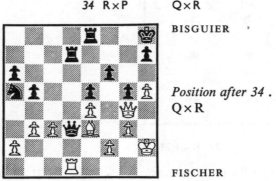

BISGUIER

Position after 34 . . .
Q × R

FISCHER

Black is braced to give up his Queen for two Rooks and keep control of the crucial Q-file.

35 Q × R!   Black resigns

A devastating X ray. After *34* . . . Q × Q; *35* R × Q it's just a matter of time. E.g., *35* . . . R – K3; *36* K – R3 followed by K – N4 – B5, etc.

48 R. Byrne *[U.S.A.]* - Fischer

USA CHAMPIONSHIP 1963–4

GRUENFELD DEFENSE

The brilliancy prize

K. F. Kirby, editor of the South African Chess Quarterly, *summed up the astonishment and admiration of the chess world when he wrote:*

"The Byrne game was quite fabulous, and I cannot call to mind anything to parallel it. After White's eleventh move I should adjudicate his position as slightly superior, and at worst completely safe. To turn this into a mating position in eleven more moves is more witchcraft than chess! Quite honestly, I do not see the man who can stop Bobby at this time . . ."

And one can add nothing to Byrne's own words:

"And as I sat pondering why Fischer would choose such a line, because it was so obviously lost for Black, there suddenly came 18 . . . N×B. This dazzling move came as the shocker . . . The culminating combination is of such depth that, even at the very moment at which I resigned, both grandmasters who were commenting on the play for the spectators in a separate room believed that I had a won game!"

1 P – Q4	N – KB3
2 P – QB4	P – KN3
3 P – KN3	P – B3
4 B – N2	. . .

In the 1962–3 US Championship we reached the same position, but Byrne continued *4* P – Q5, P – QN4!; *5* P×BP, NP×P; *6* P×P+, QN×P; *7* B – N2, R – QN1; *8* N – KB3, B – KN2; *9* O – O, O – O=. Black's weak QBP is compensated for by pressure on the open QN-file.

4 . . .	P – Q4
5 P×P	. . .

5 Q – N3 maintains more tension.

5 . . .	P×P
6 N – QB3	B – N2
7 P – K3	. . .

Benko–Fischer, US Championship 1962-3, continued: *7* N – B3,
O – O; *8* N – K5 (if *8* O – O, N – K5!=), B – B4; *9* O – O, N –
K5; *10* Q – N3, N – QB3; *11* Q×QP, N×QN; *12* P×N, Q×Q;
13 B×Q, N×N; *14* P×N, B×P with a draw shortly.

7 . . .	O – O
8 KN – K2	N – B3
9 O – O	P – N3
10 P – N3	. . .

It's hard for either side to introduce an imbalance into this
essentially symmetrical variation.

Deadeye equality also ensues after *10* N – B4, P – K3; *11*
P – N3, B – QR3; *12* R – K1, R – B1; *13* B – QR3, R – K1; *14*
QR – B1, etc. (Stahlberg–Flohr, Kemeri 1937.)

10 . . .	B – QR3
11 B – QR3	R – K1
12 Q – Q2	. . .

A good alternative is *12* R – B1.

A kibitzer later suggested *12* P – B4?! to prevent . . . P – K4.
But after *12* . . . P – K3 followed by . . . B – KB1 and eventual doubling on the QB-file, Black gets an advantage.

12 . . .	P – K4!

I was a bit worried about weakening my QP, but felt that the
tremendous activity obtained by my minor pieces would permit
White no time to exploit it. *12* . . . P – K3 would probably lead
to a draw.

13 P×P	. . .

Passive is *13* QR – B1, P×P (if *13* . . . R – QB1; *14* KR –
Q1, P – K5; *15* P – B3! is tenable); *14* P×P, R – QB1; *15* P – B3,
although Black has difficulty breaking through.

13 . . .	N×P

FISCHER

Position after 13 . . .
N × P

BYRNE

14 KR – Q1? . . .

Add another to those melancholy case histories entitled "the
wrong Rook." Correct is *14* QR – Q1! Originally I gave the following "refutation": *"14 . . .* N – K5; *15* N × N, P × N; *16* B × P,
Q × Q; *17* R × Q, N – B5; *18* B × R, N × R; *19* R – Q1, N – B5;
20 P × N (best), R × B regaining the Pawn with a big endgame
advantage." But Averbakh found a hole in my analysis with *20*
B – B6! (instead of *20* P × N which I had carelessly given as "best"),
N × B; *21* B × R, B × N; *22* R – Q7 and White is the one who wins
instead of Black!

I spent an evening just staring at the position after *14* QR – Q1,
trying everything, unwilling to let my brilliancy go down the drain.
The more I looked, the more I liked White's game! For example,
14 . . . R – QB1 (*14 . . .* N – Q6 is refuted by Q – B2); *15*
N × P, N × N; *16* B × N, B – Q6; *17* B – N2, R – B7; *18* Q × R!
kaput. No better is *14 . . .* Q – Q2; *15* Q – B2 followed by
R – Q2 and KR – Q1 (if *15 . . .* R – QB1; *16* Q – N1!).

Another try which just falls short is *14* QR-Q1, Q – B2; *15* Q –
B1!, N – K5!? (otherwise *16* Q – N1 consolidates); *16* N × P!,
Q × Q; *17* N × Q, B × R; *18* B × N, B – R6; *19* N – K7+, K – R1;
20 B × R, R × B; *21* P – B4 keeping the extra Pawn. Indeed, how
does Black even equalize, let alone sustain the initiative?

Finally I found *14 . . .* Q – B1!—the only move to keep the
pressure. Now on *15* N × P, N × N; *16* B × N, R – Q1; *17* P – B4,
R × B!; *18* Q × R, B – N2!; *19* Q – Q8+ (if *19* Q – Q2, Q – R6!;
20 N – Q4, N – N5; *21* KR – K1 [or *21* N – B2, P – KR4 with a
strong attack], N × KP! should win), Q × Q; *20* R × Q+, R × R;
21 P × N, B × P with a better ending. And on *15* R – B1, Q – Q2!;
16 QR – Q1, QR – Q1 Black has finagled a precious tempo, since

his Queen is on Q2 instead of Q1. After *14 . . . Q – B1!* relatively best is *15 B – N2* (if *15 Q – B1, N – K5; 16 N × P, B × N; 17 B × N, K – R1!* wins the Exchange. One possible line is *18 Q × Q, QR × Q; 19 N – K7, R – B2; 20 R – B1, R – Q2; 21 KR – K1, B – B6!*) although Black keeps the initiative with Q – KB4.

14 . . .	N – Q6!	
15 Q – B2		. . .

There is hardly any other defense to the threat of . . . N – K5.

A] *15 N – Q4, N – K5; 16 N × N, P × N; 17 B – N2, R – QB1* with a powerful bind.

B] *15 N – B4, N – K5; 16 N × N, P × N* (not *16 . . . B × R?; 17 N – Q6*); *17 QR – N1, R – QB1; 18 N × N, B – B6!; 19 Q – K2, B × N; 20 Q – N4, P – B4; 21 Q – R3, B × R!; 22 R × Q, KR × R; 23 B – KB1, R – Q8; 24 K – N2, B – Q6!; 25 B × B, P × B* wins.

C] *15 P – B3, B – R3; 16 P – B4* (if *16 N – B4?, P – Q5!*), B – KN2! resumes the threat of . . . N – K5, only White has weakened himself in the interim.

15 . . .	N × P!

FISHER

Position after 15 . . . N × P

BYRNE

The key to Black's previous play. The complete justification for this sac does not become apparent until White resigns!

16	K × N	N – N5+
17	K – N1	N × KP
18	Q – Q2	. . .

Forced. Now on *18 . . . N × R; 19 R × N* White is all right again.

18 . . .	N × B!

Removing this Bishop leaves White defenseless on his light squares.

19	K×N	P – Q5!
20	N×P	B – N2+

The King is at Black's mercy.

21	K – B1	. . .

Equally hopeless is *21* K – N1, B×N+; *22* Q×B, R – K8+!; *23* K – B2, Q×Q+; *24* R×Q, R×R; *25* R – Q7, R – QB1; *26* R×B (if *26* B – N2, R – R8), R×N; *27* R – N8+, K – N2; *28* B – N2, R×P, etc.
Or *21* K – B2, Q – Q2!; *22* QR – B1, Q – R6; *23* N – B3, B – KR3; *24* Q – Q3, B – K6+; *25* Q×B, R×Q; *26* K×R, R – K1+; *27* K – B2, Q – B4! finis!

21 . . .	Q – Q2!

FISCHER

*Final Position after
21 . . . Q – Q2!*

BYRNE

White resigns

A bitter disappointment. I'd hoped for *22* Q – KB2, Q – R6+; *23* K – N1, R – K8+!!; *24* R×R, B×N with mate to follow shortly. Also *22* N/4 – N5, Q – R6+; *23* K – N1, B – KR3 and the curtain comes down.

49 Fischer - Steinmeyer [U.S.A.]

USA CHAMPIONSHIP 1963-4

CARO-KANN DEFENSE

A complex trap

While generally thought of as "one movers," some opening traps are deeper and more beautiful than others because falling into them requires a certain degree of skill. They might not attract and, if they did, might work for an amateur! Steinmeyer's concept beginning with 13 . . . Q – B5+ is both subtle and novel. The only trouble is that it meets with a smashing refutation. Instead of simplifying, as Steinmeyer hopes, his variation enmeshes him in complications. The nail in the coffin is 16 N – K5, after which Black's Queen can no longer be extricated without fatal loss of material.

	1 P – K4	P – QB3
	2 P – Q4	. . .

For 2 N – QB3, P – Q4; 3 N – B3 see game 16.

	2 . . .	P – Q4
	3 N – QB3	P × P
	4 N × P	B – B4

STEINMEYER

Position after 4 . . .
B – B4

FISCHER

5 N – N3   . . .

On tour (1964) I experimented with the weird 5 N – B5!? Most of my opponents countered with 5 . . . P – K4; 6 N×P, Q×P (if 6 . . . Q – N3; 7 N – B5, B×N; 8 P×B, Q×BP; 9 P – QB3 White's better. Fischer–Petrosian, five-minute game, Bled 1961); 7 Q×Q, P×Q; 8 B – Q3 with the better ending. Some replied with 5 . . . P – QN3; 6 N – R6, N×N; 7 B×N, Q – Q4! Still others played 5 . . . Q – B2; 6 B – Q3, B×B; 7 N×B, P – K3. White has more space, but only experience can tell whether he has the edge; however, the Knight on Q3 discourages the normal freeing maneuver . . . P – QB4 and /or . . . P – K4. At least it's something to break the monotony.

5 . . .	B – N3
6 N – B3	N – B3

More usual is the immediate . . . N – Q2 to prevent N – K5.

7 P – KR4	. . .

7 B – Q3 (if 7 N – K5, QN – Q2; 8 N×B, RP×N Black is solid), P – K3; 8 O – O, B – K2; 9 P – B4, O – O; 10 B×B, RP×B leads to equality. (Evans–Benko, US Championship 1962–3.)

7 . . .	P – KR3
8 B – Q3	. . .

White can try to exploit the order of Black's moves by 8 N – K5, but B – R2; 9 B – QB4, P – K3; 10 Q – K2, N – Q4! (not 10 . . . Q×P?; 11 N×KBP!); followed by . . . N – Q2 equalizes.
  8 P – R5, B – R2; 9 B – Q3, B×B; 10 Q×B, P – K3; 11 B – Q2, QN – Q2; 12 O – O – O, Q – B2; 13 N – K4 (Spassky – Petrosian, 13th match game 1966, continued: 13 Q – K2, O – O – O; 14 N – K5, N×N; 15 P×N, N – Q2; 16 P – KB4 with an edge), O – O – O; 14 P – KN3! (Geller-Petrosian, Moscow 1967), and now 14 . . . N×N (instead of . . . N – N5?); 15 Q×N, B – Q3 holds White to a minimal pull.

8 . . .	B×B
9 Q×B	P – K3
10 B – Q2	QN – Q2

Or 10 . . . Q – B2; 11 P – B4 (if 11 O – O – O, B – Q3; 12 N – K4, B – B5!; 13 N×N+, P×N is satisfactory), QN – Q2; 12 B – B3 (the whole idea is to prevent Black from swapping Bishops),

P - QR4!; *13* O - O!? (if *13* O - O - O, B - N5!), B - Q3; *14* N - K4 (Tal suggested *14* P - Q5!? mixing it up, but *14* . . . B × N! holds; not *15* P × KP?, N - K4; or *15* P × B, BP × P; *16* P × P, N × P; *17* B × NP, R - KN1; *18* Q - R7, N/2 - B3; *19* B × N, N × B; *20* Q × P, Q × P; *21* Q - Q2=), N × N; *15* Q × N, O - O=. (Fischer–Donner, Varna 1962.)

<table>
<tr><td>11 O - O - O</td><td>Q - B2</td></tr>
<tr><td>12 P - B4</td><td>. . .</td></tr>
</table>

STEINMEYER

Position after 12 P - B4

FISCHER

12 . . .	O - O - O

12 . . . B - Q3!; *13* N - K4 (if *13* N - K2, O - O - O; *14* K - N1, P - K4=), B - B5! leads to immediate simplifications.

13 B - B3!	. . .

Now Black no longer can force the exchange of Bishops.

13 . . .	Q - B5+?

The start of a faulty concept. After *13* . . . B - Q3 (on *13* . . . P - B4; *14* P - Q5!); *14* N - K4, B - B5+; *15* K - N1, N - K4!; *16* KN × N, B × N produces equality.

14 K - N1	N - B4?

He still has time to back out with *14* . . . Q - B2.

15 Q - B2	N/4 - K5

Now there is no turning back. On *15* . . . N/4 - Q2; *16* N - K5! is very strong: e.g., *16* . . . N × N; *17* P × N, N - Q2 (or *17* . . . N - N5; *18* R × R+, K × R; *19* R - Q1+, K - B1; *20* R - Q4); *18* R - Q4, Q × KP; *19* R × N!, etc.

STEINMEYER

Position after 15 . . .
N/4 – K5

FISCHER

16 N – K5!   . . .

A clear refutation. The Queen's retreat is cut off and the ancient weakness on Black's KB2 is etched more sharply than ever. Shamkovich–Goldberg, USSR 1961, continued with *16 B – R5?* which won only against inferior defense.

16 . . .   N×P

What else? *16 . . . N×N* loses to *17 P×N, Q×NP; 18 R – Q3, Q – B5; 19 R – B3, Q – K5; 20 N×KBP. And 16 . . . N×B+* is refuted by *17 P×N!, R – N1 (if 17 . . . N – N5; 18 N – R5!, Q – B4; 19 Q×Q, P×Q; 20 N×KBP); 18 R – Q3, P – KR4; 19 R – B3, Q – R3; 20 N×KBP,* etc.

17 QR – KB1!   Black resigns

Probably what Steinmeyer overlooked when he went into this whole mess. On *17 . . . Q×N; 18 R×N, Q – K6* (otherwise R – B3); *19 R – K2, Q – B5; 20 N×KBP* wins at least the exchange.

Motivated by my lopsided result (11–0!), Dr. Kmoch congratulated Evans (the runner-up) on "winning" the tournament . . . and then he congratulated me on "winning the exhibition."

50 Fischer - Celle [U.S.A.]

CALIFORNIA 1964: Exhibition Tour

EVANS GAMBIT

Tour de force

As one of ten simultaneous clock games played on tour, at Davis
College, this is a perfect example of the precept that if White
makes a slip in the opening he is punished by loss of the
initiative, while if Black makes a slip (since he is skating on
thin ice from the very start) it is likely to be fatal. 6 . . .
P – Q3 is the offender.

With 9 Q – R5 Fischer assumes a commanding control of
space, but faces a strong defense which compels him to offer a
piece in order to maintain pressure. Continuing with restraint
and circumspection, he builds up the attack with a series of
quiet developing moves—reminiscent of Morphy's famous
victory over the Duke of Brunswick at the Paris opera. When
the time is ripe, Fischer throws everything at Black's King,
including the proverbial kitchen sink. His show of brute force
is handsomely rewarded.

1	P – K4	P – K4
2	N – KB3	N – QB3
3	B – B4	B – B4
4	P – QN4!?	. . .

The Evans was already analyzed to death by the 'nineties. But it
still makes for enterprising chess.

4	. . .	B × P
5	P – B3	B – K2

Must be the trend. At least, on tour most players answered this
way. For 5 . . . B – R4 see game 44.

6	P – Q4	P – Q3?

A mistake is usually much more serious in these open games. Black must return the Pawn with 6 . . . N – QR4!; 7 N × P, N × B; 8 N × N, P – Q4!

7 P×P	N×P

On 7 . . . N – R4?; 8 B × P + !, K × B; 9 Q – Q5+, B – K3; 10 Q × N wins a Pawn. Or 7 . . . P × P; 8 Q – N3, N – R4; 9 B × P+, K – B1; 10 Q – R4 is strong.

8 N×N	P×N
9 Q – R5!	. . .

In an earlier exhibition game I played 9 Q – N3 but got nothing after 9 . . . B – K3!; 10 B × B, P × B; 11 B – R3!? (if 11 Q × KP, Q – Q3=), Q – Q6!

9 . . .	P – KN3
10 Q×KP	N – B3

On 10 . . . P – KB3; 11 Q – N5+!, P – B3?; 12 Q – N3, K – B1; 13 B × N! wins.

11 B – R3!　　. . .

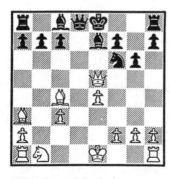

CELLE

Position after 11 B – R3

FISCHER

Incredible how Black is so completely immobilized by this one move!

11 . . .	R – B1

The only way to get relief. 11 . . . K – B1? works in all lines except 12 Q × N !

12 O – O	N – N5

12 . . . N – Q2 followed by . . . N – N3 might be better, but this certainly looked good at the time.

| 13 Q – N3 | B × B |
| 14 N × B | Q – K2! |

Apparently Black has freed his game. If now *15* N – B2, Q – K4 virtually forces an exchange of Queens. *15* N – N5 is rendered harmless by . . . N – K4. How's White to sustain the initiative?

15 B – N5+!   . . .

That's how. This forces Black to weaken himself on Q3, although White must sacrifice a piece to exploit it.

15 . . .   P – B3

On *15* . . . B – Q2; *16* Q × P (not *16* Q × N, P – QB3!).

CELLE

Position after 15 . . .
P – B3

FISCHER

16 N – B4!   Q – K3!

Some fascinating possibilities appear after *16* . . . P × B; *17* N – Q6+, K – Q1; *18* KR – Q1, B – Q2; *19* N × NP+, K – B1; *20* N – Q6+, K – Q1; *21* R – Q4!, N – K4; *22* QR – Q1, K – B2 (if *22* . . . P – N4; *23* N – B5, Q – K1; *24* Q × N!, Q × Q; *25* R × B+, K – K1 [if *25* . . . K – B1; *26* N – K7+! wins]; *26* R – K7+!, Q × R; *27* N – N7 mate); *23* P – B4, N – N5; *24* P – KR3, N – B3; *25* P – B5, K – N3; *26* Q – K3, K – B2 (after *26* . . . K – R3; *27* P – QR4 smashes Black); *27* R – B4+!, P × R (if *27* . . . K – Q1; *28* Q – B5 anyway); *28* Q – B5+, B – B3 (if *28* . . . K – Q1; *29* Q – R5 mate; or *28* . . . K – N1; *29* R – N1+); *29* N – N5+, etc.

Black may not have seen the mate, but he suspected the worst!

17 QR – Q1!   . . .

Piling on the pressure. White mustn't amateurishly rush in with *17* Q – B7, Q – Q2! forcing him to simplify by *18* N – Q6+,

K – K2; *19* N × B+, QR × N; *20* Q × Q+, K × Q, etc., and the advantage has evaporated.

              17 . . .   P × B

He might as well take it since after *17 . . .* B – Q2; *18* N – Q6+, K – K2; *19* B – B4 White wins a Pawn without any risk.

              18 Q – B7   B – Q2

Forced.

              19 N – Q6+   K – K2
              20 N – B5+!   . . .

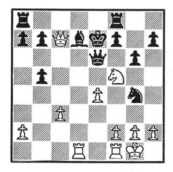

CELLE

Position after 20 N – B5+!

FISCHER

The attack needs fresh fuel. Material is not what counts now, but open lines. Black is forced to capture against his will. *20* . . . K – K1 is out because of *21* N – N7+. And *20* . . . K – B3; *21* R – Q6, P × N; *22* Q × B! wins outright.

              20 . . .   P × N
              21 P × P   QR – B1

On *20* . . . Q × BP; *21* Q – Q6+, K – Q1 (*21* . . . K – K1; *22* KR – K1+, B – K3; *23* Q – Q7 mate); *22* Q × R+, K – B2; *23* Q × R wins.

              22 R × B+!   Q × R
              23 P – B6+!   . . .

Originally I intended *23* R – K1+, N – K4; *24* R × N+, K – B3; *25* Q × Q, K × R; *26* Q × P+ with a won ending. But then I remembered Emanuel Lasker's maxim: "When you see a good move—wait—don't play it—you might find a better one."

23 . . .　　　　　N × P

Not *23* . . . K – K1?; *24* R – K1+, Q – K3; *25* Q × R mate.
Or *23* . . . K × P; *24* Q × Q.

24　R – K1+　　. . .

CELLE

Position after 24 R – K1+

FISCHER

Note the amusing piece configuration. All Black's pieces are
stepping on each other's toes.

24 . . .　　　　　N – K5

The only legal move!

25　R × N+　　　K – B3
26　Q × Q　　　　KR – Q1
27　Q – N4　　　. . .

Here I forgot Lasker's maxim. *27* Q – K7+ would have forced
mate in four.

27 . . .　　　　　**Black resigns**

5I Fischer - Smyslov [U.S.S.R.]

HAVANA 1965

RUY LOPEZ

Squeeze play

*Fischer competed in this Capablanca Memorial Tournament
by long-distance telephone, and his victory over the winner
is reminiscent of the famous Lasker–Capablanca duel at St.
Petersburg, 1914, where Black was also gradually constricted
and strangled.*

*Taken by surprise with an antiquated line (5 P – Q3),
Smyslov soon gets into trouble. He finds a way out, although
it burdens him with doubled King Pawns. After the subsequent
exchange of Queens he apparently underestimates White's
winning chances and permits himself to drift into a cramped
ending. Applying persistent pressure, Fischer makes gradual
inroads; the defensive task eventually proves too graet and
Smyslov buckles under the strain.*

1	P – K4	P – K4
2	N – KB3	N – QB3
3	B – N5	P – QR3
4	B – R4	N – B3
5	P – Q3	. . .

Steinitz's favorite, long abandoned, and the first time I've employed it in a tournament game.

5	. . .	P – Q3

A solid but passive reaction. An alternative is 5 . . . P – QN4;
6 B – N3, B – K2; 7 P – QR4, etc. Anderssen–Morphy, match
1858(!), continued: 5 . . . B – B4; 6 P – B3, P – QN4; 7 B – B2,
O – O; 8 O – O, P – Q4; 9 P×P, N×P; 10 P – KR3, P – R3

(Steinitz had a field day criticizing White's last two moves); *11*
P – Q4, P×P with a satisfactory game for Black.

SMYSLOV

Position after 5 . . .
P – Q3

FISCHER

             6 P – B3   B – K2

On *6* . . . P – KN3; *7* QN – Q2 (or Bronstein's B – KN5),
B – N2; *8* N – B1, O – O; *9* P – R4 opens fresh vistas.

             7 QN – Q2   O – O
             8 N – B1   . . .

One facet of White's strategy is to defer castling and possibly
institute a K-side attack with P – KR3, P – KN4, etc. Furthermore,
this Knight can be deployed to K3 or KN3 immediately without
having to waste a tempo (after having castled) with R – K1.

             8 . . .   P – QN4
             9 B – N3   P – Q4

Inconsistent, after having lost a tempo with . . . P – Q3.
Right is *9* . . . N – QR4; *10* B – B2, P – B4; *11* N – K3, R – K1;
12 O – O, B – B1 with equal chances.

             10 Q – K2   P×P

Opens the position prematurely. No better would be *10* . . .
P – Q5; *11* N – N3, P×P; *12* P×P, P – N5; *13* B – Q2. Black
should keep tension in the center with *10* . . . B – K3; *11*
N – N3 (if *11* N – N5, B – KN5; *12* P – B3, B – B1!; *13* P×P,
N – QR4!), P – R3.

             11 P×P   B – K3!

I was surprised that Smyslov was prepared to saddle himself
with doubled King Pawns, but surmised that it must be all right
since he doesn't do such things lightly. Anyway Black's game,
without this exchange, would remain permanently cramped.

>12 B×B   P×B
>13 N – N3   . . .

This Knight is undeniably misplaced here, but White intends to
castle and then regroup his pieces in order to bring maximum
pressure to bear on the doubled Pawns.

>13 . . .   Q – Q2

Some annotators suggested the obvious *13 . . . B – Q3* (followed by N – K2 – N3, etc.) but Black has no time for such
sophisticated strategy: e.g., *14 O – O, N – K2; 15 P – B4!, P – B3;
16 R – Q1*, winning material (if *16 . . . Q – B2; 17 N – N5*).

>14 O – O   . . .

During the game I was kicking myself for allowing the subsequent
exchange of Queens. Sharper is *14 P – QR4, QR – Q1* (if *14 . . .
P×P; 15 Q – B4, P – R6; 16 P – QN4*); *15 P×P, P×P; 16 R –
R6, P – N5; 17 O – O* and Black can no longer ease his burden
with *. . . Q – Q6*. So correct is *14 . . . P – N5!*

>14 . . .   QR – Q1

Suddenly Black's plan hit me! At first I thought he just wanted
to control the Q-file; but now I realized he was scheming to chop
wood.

>15 P – QR4   Q – Q6!

Of course! With the Queens gone, it's that much harder to
strike at Black's weaknesses.

>16 Q×Q   R×Q
>17 P×P   P×P
>18 R – R6!   . . .

Forcing Black's reply, and thus preventing the freeing maneuver
with *. . . B – B4. 18 B – K3* would be met by N – KN5.

18 . . .   R – Q3

SMYSLOV

Position after 18 . . .
R – Q3

FISCHER

19 K – R1!   . . .

The threat was *19 . . . N – Q5* forcing a favorable series of exchanges.

19 . . .   N – Q2

19 . . . P – N5; 20 P×P, N×NP; 21 R – R7, R – B3; 22 N×P, R – B7 would give Black active play for the Pawn.

20 B – K3   R – Q1

20 . . . P – N5 is still playable. Neither of us realized at this stage how essential this move was. I didn't want to weaken my QB3 and QB4 squares by playing P – QN4 to prevent it; and Smyslov didn't want to commit himself yet.

21 P – R3   . . .

More accurate is *21 P – N4*, from which I abstained for the reasons already mentioned.

21 . . .   P – R3
22 KR – R1   N/2 – N1
23 R – R8   R – Q8+
24 K – R2   . . .

On *24 R × R, R × R+; 25 K – R2, B – Q3* holds (*26 B – R7?, R – R8!*).

24 . . .   R × R
25 R × R   . . .

SMYSLOV

Position after 25 R × R

FISCHER

25 . . .   N – Q2?

When I spoke to Smyslov on the direct phone line immediately after the game, he congratulated me on a beautiful performance and attributed his loss to his reluctance to play . . . P – N5 at some point—and this is his last chance. After *25* . . . P – N5; *26* P × P, B × P; *27* N – B1 Black obtains much more freedom than in the actual game, and eliminates a weakness (his QNP) as well. Perhaps Smyslov feared that in this line White could maneuver his Knight to QB4; even so, this is hardly fatal.

26 P – N4!   . . .

Smyslov confessed that he felt Black was probably lost after this riposte. But the win is far from easy, and Black might later have improved upon his defense.

26 . . .   K – B2
27 N – B1   B – Q3
28 P – N3   . . .

Once and for all negating all possible combinations with . . . N – Q5.

28 . . .   N – B3
29 N/1 – Q2   K – K2
30 R – R6!   N – QN1

Very uncomfortable is *30* . . . K – Q2; *31* N – K1, N – QN1; *32* R – R5, K – B3.

31 R – R5!   . . .

Now White strengthens his bind by forcing . . . P – B3 which takes away another breathing space from Black's pieces.

31 . . .	P – B3
32 K – N2	N/1 – Q2
33 K – B1	. . .

Preparing to bring the King to K2 where it can support the N – K1 – Q3 maneuver.

SMYSLOV

Position after 33 K – B1

FISCHER

| 33 . . . | R – QB1 ? |

A surprise! I had expected the much stouter defense with *33 . . . N – K1!* (intending to exchange Rooks with *. . . N – B2* and *. . . R – QR1*). After *34 R – R6, R – B1; 35 N – N3, P – B4; 36 P × P, B × P!* Black can hold. And there is no time for *34 N – K1, N – B2; 35 N – Q3, R – QR1; 36 N – N3, R × R; 37 N × R, N – N1; 38 B – R7, N/2 – R3; 39 P – QB4, B – B2.*

The main line is *33. . . N – K1; 34 N – N3!, N – B2; 35 R – R7, R – QR1; 36 N – R5, N – N1; 37 R × R* (if *37 R – N7, K – Q2),* N × R; *38 B – R7, K – Q2; 39 N – N7.* It looks bad, but Black has chances to survive in the absence of a forced win.

| 34 N – K1! | N – K1 |

Too late now.

| 35 N – Q3 | N – B2 |
| 36 P – QB4! | P × P |

36 . . . R – QR1? is refuted by *37 P – B5!* winning a piece.

| 37 N × BP | . . . |

The ideal position! Finally White has ganged up on Black's venerable weakness—his Pawn on K4.

| 37 . . . | N – N4 |

On *37. . . R – QR1; 38 R × R, N × R; 39 N – R5, N – N1; 40 B – R7, K – Q2; 41 N – QB4* picks off the KP.

38 R – R6   . . .

Keeping Black tied up some more.

38 . . .   K – B3

38 . . . N – N1; *39* R – R8, N – B2; *40* N×B, K×N; *41*
B – B5+ wins.

39 B – B1!   B – N1
40 B – N2   . . .

Threatening P – B4.

40 . . .   P – B4

A desperate bid for counterplay.

41 N – N6!   . . .

41 R – R5! also has a nasty sting; for if *41* . . . P×P; *42*
N/4×KP! wins outright.

41 . . .   N×N
42 R×N   P – B5

On *42* . . . N – Q5; *43* N×BP, B – R2; *44* N – Q7+, K –
N4; *45* P – R4+, K – R4; *46* R – N7, R – B7; *47* R×B, R×B;
48 N×P, R×P; *49* R×P is decisive.

43 N – B5   P – B6 and Black resigns

SMYSLOV

Final Position after
43 . . . P – B6

FISCHER

White can win with *44* B – B1, N – Q5; *45* N – Q7+, K – K2
(if *45* . . . K – B2; *46* R×B, R×R; *47* N×R, N – N6; *48* B –
R3, P – B7; *49* N – B6, etc.); *46* N×B, N – N6; *47* R – N7+,
K – Q1; *48* R – Q7+, K – K1; *49* R×P!

52 Fischer - Rossolimo *[U.S.A.]*

USA CHAMPIONSHIP 1965-6

FRENCH DEFENSE

Peekaboo strategy

The MacCutcheon Variation gives rise to unusual positions where White is frequently obliged to forfeit the privilege of castling in order to try and wrest an advantage. After some slight but instructive opening inexactitudes on both sides, Rossolimo appears to achieve equality. Indeed, he is constantly on the brink of crashing through with a counter-attack against White's vulnerable King, although his own monarch is also stranded in the centre. After 13 . . . P – B4, which shores up his fortress, it's not clear just whose attack will come first.

In a theoretically important formation—a logical offshoot of this variation—Fischer unearths two fine moves (17 B – N5+ and 19 N – N1) to sustain his flagging initiative. Still, he is forced to wage a running battle, no sooner landing a blow than having to duck. Consequently, the outcome is in doubt until the very last punch.

1	P – K4	P – K3
2	P – Q4	P – Q4
3	N – QB3	N – KB3
4	B – N5	B – N5

The MacCutcheon Variation, giving rise to immediate complications. *4 . . . B – K2* or *. . . P × P* are tamer.

5	P – K5	P – KR3
6	B – Q2	. . .

6 P×N, P×B; 7 P×P, R – N1 leads to nothing.

6 . . .   B×N
7 P×B   . . .

Against Petrosian, at Curaçao 1962, I tried the ridiculous 7 B×N?, N – K5; 8 B – R5?? (if 8 B – N4, P – QB4; 9 P×P, N×KBP!; 10 K×N, Q – R5+), O – O (weaker is 8 . . . P – QN3; 9 B – N4, P – QB4; 10 B – R3, P×P; 11 Q×P, N – QB3; 12 B – N5); 9 B – Q3, N – QB3; 10 B – B3, N×B; 11 P×N, P – B3 and Black already had the initiative.

7 . . .   N – K5
8 Q – N4   P – KN3

More risky is 8 . . . K – B1; 9 P – KR4, P – QB4; 10 R – R3.

9 B – Q3   N×B
10 K×N   P – QB4

Producing a position well-known to theory, but never completely worked out. Not 10 . . . Q – N4+; 11 Q×Q, P×Q; 12 P – N4!

11 N – B3   . . .

ROSSOLIMO

Position after 11 N – B3

FISCHER

11 . . .   N – B3

According to *Modern Chess Openings*, 11 . . . Q – B2 is more accurate; the point being that 12 Q – B4 can be met by P – B4! 11 . . . B – Q2; 12 P×P deserves testing.

12 Q – B4   . . .

Possibly better is *12* QR – N1, restraining the development of Black's Q-side.

12 . . .   Q – B2

Better is the natural *12* . . . Q – R4 (if *12* . . . P – KN4; *13* Q – B6!, Q×Q; *14* P×Q, P – N5; *15* N – K5, P×P; *16* P×P, N×P; *17* P – KR3 with a better ending); *13* QR – N1 (if *13* KR – N1, P – N3; *14* P – QR4, B – R3; *15* B – N5, QR – B1; *16* P×P, P×P; *17* B×N+, R×B; *18* R – N8+, R – B1 holds), P – N3; *14* P×P, Q×BP; *15* N – Q4, N×N; *16* P×N, Q – R4+ with equality.

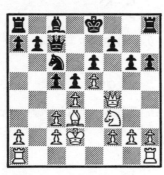

ROSSOLIMO

Position after 12 . . .
Q – B2

FISCHER

13 P – KR4   . . .

Sharper is *13* Q – B6!, R – KN1; *14* P – KR4, and if Q – R4 (. . . P – KR4 looks practically forced); *15* P – R5!, P×RP; *16* R×P, P×P; *17* QR – R1 yielding good attacking prospects.

13 . . .   P – B4!

Re-establishing parity.

14 P – N4   P×QP
15 P×P   N – K2?

After the game Rossolimo suggested *15* . . . B – Q2; but White keeps the better of it after *16* P×P, NP×P (if *16* . . . KP×P; *17* Q – N3, N – K2; *18* P – K6!, Q – R4+; *19* P – B3, B×P; *20* KR – K1 gives a powerful attack); *17* KR – N1, O – O – O; *18* R – N6. At least Black's King reaches safety in this line.

16 P×P   KP×P
17 B – N5+!   . . .

ROSSOLIMO

Position after 17 B – N5+

FISCHER

17 . . .	K – B1 ?

On *17 . . . N – B3* (if *17 . . . B – Q2; 18* B×B+, Q×B
19 P – K6!); *18* B×N+, P×B (*18 . . .* Q×B is again met by
19 P – K6!, B×P; *20* N – K5, Q – Q3; *21* N×P, Q×Q+; *22*
N×Q and the Knight beats the Bishop in the ending); *19* KR – N1,
etc.

Black's best chance, however, is to try and reach sanctuary with
17 . . . K – Q1!; 18 B – Q3, B – K3. White undoubtedly has the
initiative, but it's hard to get at the King.

18 B – Q3	. . .

Mission accomplished. Now Black's King is pinioned to the
K-side.

18 . . .	B – K3
19 N – N1!	. . .

The key move. This Knight is headed for KB4 where it can exert
maximum pressure on the KNP.

19 . . .	K – B2
20 N – R3	QR – B1 !?

Quite rightly, Rossolimo prefers active defense. After *20 . . .
QR – KN1*, White eventually triples on the KN-file (bringing his
Knight to KB4) with a crushing bind.

21 KR – KN1	. . .

ROSSOLIMO

Position after 21 KR – KN1

FISCHER

21 . . .   P – N3

This takes QR4 away from the Queen, eliminating any possible defenses there with check.

But Black also loses after *21* . . . Q – B6+; *22* K – K3, N – B3; *23* QR – N1, N – N5; *24* R × N!, Q × R; *25* P – R5, QR – KN1; *26* P × P+, R × P; *27* R × R, Q – K8+; *28* K – B3, K × R; *29* Q – R4!, Q – Q8+; *30* K – N2, R – KN1; *31* K – R2!

22 P – R5!   Q – B6+
23 K – K2   N – B3

On *23* . . . QR – KN1 (if *23* . . . P – KN4; *24* N × P+!, P × N; *25* Q × P, K – K1; *26* Q – B6, K – Q2; *27* B – N5+!, R – B3; *28* Q × R, Q × P+; *29* K – B1 wins); *24* P × P+, R × P (if *24* . . . N × P; *25* Q – B3); *25* Q – R4 is decisive.

24 P × P+   K – N2

No better is *24* . . . K – K2; *25* Q – R4+, K – Q2; *26* QR – Q1!, Q × P (*26* . . . N × P+?; *27* Q × N!); *27* N – B4!

25 QR – Q1!   N × P+

On *25* . . . Q × P; *26* K – B1!, Q × P; *27* R – K1, Q × Q; *28* N × Q, B – Q2; *29* N – R5+ wins.

26 K – B1   KR – K1
27 R – N3   . . .

Overprotecting the Bishop. After the hasty *27* Q – R4, N – B6!: *28* Q – B6+, K – N1; *29* B × P, N – R7+; *30* K – N2, Q – B6+; *31* K × N, Q × B holds!

27	. . .	N – B3
28	Q – R4	N × P

After *28* . . . Q × KP; *29* N – B4 contains too many threats.

29	N – B4	N – N5
30	N × B+!	R × N
31	B × P	Q – B5+
32	K – N1!	. . .

No credit for other moves!

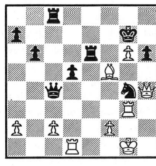

ROSSOLIMO

Final Position after
32 K – N1

FISCHER

32 . . .   Black resigns

If *32* . . . N × P; *33* Q × Q, R × Q; *34* K × N, R – B5+; *35* R – B3, etc.

A hard-fought game!

53 Portisch *[Hungary]* - Fischer

SANTA MONICA 1966

NIMZO INDIAN DEFENSE

Black magic

Here is one of the few instances when Fischer does not employ the fianchetto of his King's Bishop as a defense to the QP. By ignoring White's gambit on move nine he lays the groundwork for the positional trap (11 . . . Q–Q2) into which Portisch falls (14 Q×R). Normally, two Rooks for the Queen is a good trade—better than good when it produces a setting in which the scope and power of the Rooks may be formidable. But Portisch's judgment is faulty, he fails to take into account the weakness of his Pawns. This is one of the rare occasions when the Queen can run rampant, and she does.

Still, the question remains: how did Black manage to weave his spell? To achieve a winning endgame within fifteen moves, against a specialist with White in this opening, is an almost unheard of feat.

1	P – Q4	N – KB3
2	P – QB4	P – K3 !

To throw White off balance. I felt Portisch was just too well-versed in the K's Indian.

3	N – QB3	B – N5
4	P – K3	. . .

This has been fashionable for some time. Spassky's offbeat *4* B – N5 leads to no advantage after *4* . . . P – KR3; *5* B – R4, P – B4; *6* P – Q5, P – Q3; *7* P – K3, B×N+!; *8* P×B, P – K4, etc. The two Knights are better than the Bishops in such closed formations.

4 . . .   P – QN3!

Other moves have been analyzed to death.

5 N – K2   . . .

Reshevsky–Fischer, U.S. Champ., 1966, continued: 5 B – Q3,
B – N2; 6 N – B3, O – O (sharper is 6 . . . N – K5!; 7 O – O,
P – KB4 [or 7 . . . N×N!; 8 P×N, B×P; 9 R – N1, N – B3!
and White 'hasn't got enough for his Pawn]; 8 B×N, P×B; 9
N – Q2, B×N; 10 P×B, O – O; 11 Q – N4, R – B4!=. Gligorich–
Larsen, Havana 1967. Not 12 N×P?, P – KR4); 7 O – O, B×N
(. . . P – Q4 is an alternative); 8 P×B, B – K5; 9 Q – B2, and
now . . . B×N! (instead of 9 . . . B×B); 10 P×B, P – B4
would lead to an exciting positional struggle—two Knights vs.
two Bishops, but White's Pawn formation is shaky.

5 . . .   B – R3

Bronstein's active idea, trying to profit from White's last move.
I had adopted it with success in the 1966 U.S. Championship.
A very interesting try is 5 . . . N – K5!? as in the 1967 USSR
Championship. Taimanov–Levin continued 6 Q – B2, B – N2;
7 P – B3 (7 P – QR3 is better), and now instead of 7 . . . B×N+
(as in the game) 7 . . . N×N! 8 N×N (8 P×N, B – Q3!; 9 P – K4,
N – B3 with good play against White's doubled QBP), Q – R5+;
9 Q – B2, B×N+; 10 P×B, Q×Q+; 11 K×Q, B – R3! threatening . . . N – B3 – R4 with at least equality.

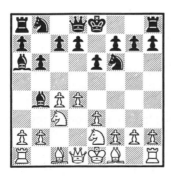

FISCHER

Position after 5 . . .
B – R3

PORTISCH

6 N – N3   . . .

Somewhat inconsistent. The whole point is to play 6 P – QR3

so that after *6 . . . * B × N+ (if *6 . . . * B – K2; *7* N – B4, P – Q4; *8* P × P, B × B; *9* K × B, P × P; *10* P – KN4! gives White a slight edge, as demonstrated in the 1954 Botvinnik–Smyslov match); *7* N × B White can avoid doubling his QBP. After *7 . . . * P – Q4; *8* P – QN3, O – O; *9* P – QR4, N – B3 I reached this position, as Black, twice in the 1966 U.S. Championship. Addison played *10* B – N2? and got the worst of it after *10 . . . * P × P; *11* P × P, N – QR4; *12* N – N5, P – B3; *13* N.– R3, Q – K2!; *14* Q – B2, P – B4; *15* B – K2 (finally), P × P; *16* P × P, KR – B1; *17* O – O, R – B3!; *18* B – KB3, N – Q4 and White's QBP falls. Evans chose *10* B – K2, P × P; *11* B – R3!, R – K1; *12* P – QN4, N – K2; *13* O – O? (*13* P – N5, B – N2; *14* O – O permits White to regain his Pawn with a tiny pull), N/2 – Q4; *14* R – B1, P – B3!; *15* B – B3, P – QN4; *16* P – R5, Q – B2; *17* Q – B2, QR – Q1; *18* KR – Q1, B – N2; *19* R – Q2, N × N; *20* Q × N, P – QB4!; *21* QP × P, B × B; *22* P × B, R × R; *23* Q × R, R – Q1; *24* Q – K1, R – Q6; *25* B – N2, N – Q4 and White soon collapsed.

6 . . .   B × N+!

Inferior is *6 . . . * O – O (not *6 . . . * P – Q4??; *7* Q – R4+); *7* P – K4, N – B3 (White keeps his initiative also after *7 . . . * P – B4; *8* P – Q5, P – Q3; *9* B – K2, P × P; *10* KP × P, B × N+; *11* P × B, QN – Q2; *12* O – O, R – K1; *13* Q – R4, etc. Portisch–Reshevsky, Santa Monica, 1966); *8* B – Q3!, P – Q4 (*8 . . . * N × QP?; *9* Q – R4 wins a piece); *9* BP × P, B × B; *10* Q × B, P × P; *11* P – K5, N – K5!; *12* P – QR3! with a clear advantage. Portisch–Spassky, Moscow 1967.

7   P × B   P – Q4
8   Q – B3   . . .

The whole idea is dubious. No better is *8* B – R3, P × P!; *9* Q – B3, Q – Q4; *10* P – K4, Q – B3 and White hasn't got enough for the Pawn.

Simply *8* P × P leads to level play. It is White's insistence on seeking the initiative that lands him in trouble.

8 . . .   O – O
9   P – K4!?   . . .

Right is *9* P × P, P × P (not *9 . . . * B × B?; *10* P × P!); *10* B × B, N × B; *11* Q – K2, Q – B1; *12* O – O, P – B4; *13* P × P, N × P;

14 P – QB4=. The text involves a gambit which Portisch probably had expected me to accept.

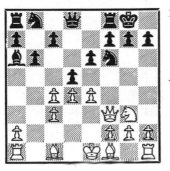

FISCHER

Position after 9 P – K4

PORTISCH

9 . . .   P×KP!

An improvement over *9* . . . P×BP!? which I had played against Saidy in the 1966 U.S. Champ.: *10* B – N5, P – R3; *11* B – Q2? (right is *11* P – KR4!, B – N2! *12* B×N, Q×B; *13* Q×Q, P×Q; *14* B×P. Or White might try to continue the attack with *12* N – R5!?, QN – Q2!—But not *12* . . . P×B?; *13* P×P, N×P; *14* N – B6+!! wins—Spassky), QN – Q2; *12* P – K5, N – Q4; *13* N – B5 (if *13* N – R5, Q – R5!), P×N; *14* P×N, R – K1!; *15* B×BP (or *15* O – O – O, P – B4), N×P!; *16* Q×Q, N×B+; *17* Q×R+, R×Q+; *18* K – Q1, N×B; *19* K×N, R – K7+with an easily won endgame.

10 N×P   N×N
11 Q×N   Q – Q2!!

The finest move in the game, far superior to the "natural" *11*. . . N – Q2; *12* B – Q3, N – B3; *13* Q – R4 with two Bishops and a beautiful development despite the doubled Pawns.

Black can well afford to give up two Rooks for a Queen (after *12* Q×R?, N – B3), as will soon become apparent. The text prepares . . . N – B3 – R4 hitting the "weakling," as Alekhine used to call that kind of a target.

12 B – R3   . . .

White gets the worst of it after *12* B – Q3, P – KB4; *13* Q – K2, N – B3, etc. Still, this was a prudent choice.

12 . . .   R – K1

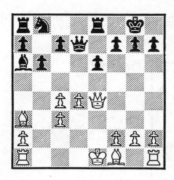

FISCHER

Position after 12 . . .
R – K1

PORTISCH

13 B – Q3 . . .

13 O – O – O seems more consistent, making a real fight of it. Such double-edged lines, however, are not to Portisch's taste.

13 . . . P – KB4
14 Q × R? . . .

Very bad judgment. White should resist temptation and try to hold on with *14* Q – K2. His doubled QBP, though weak, is not fatal. As the game goes, however, it is.

14 . . . N – B3
15 Q × R+ Q × Q
16 O – O N – R4
17 QR – K1 B × P

Too routine. Crushing is *17* . . . Q – R5! E.g., *18* B – N4 (if *18* B – B1, B × P; *19* B × B, Q × B should easily win), B × P; *19* B × B, N × B; *20* R × P, P – QR4; *21* B – K7, N – Q7!; *22* KR – K1, N – K5; *23* P – B3, Q × P! Curtains.

18 B × B . . .

If 18 B × P?, Q – R5 wins

18 . . . N × B
19 B – B1 P – B4
20 P × P . . .

White cannot hold the ending. If *20* P – Q5? Simply . . . P – K4.

20 . . . P × P
21 B – B4 P – KR3!

Preparing to expand on the K-side, which cannot be prevented.

22 R – K2 . . .

If *22* P – KR4, P – K4!; *23* B × KP, N × B; *24* P – B4, N – B6+!; *25* P × N, Q – R5 and White's Pawns are too loose.

22 . . .	P – N4
23 B – K5	Q – Q1
24 R/1 – K1	. . .

On *25* P – B4, N – Q7!; *26* KR – K1, N – K5 ties White up.

24 . . .	K – B2
25 P – KR3	P – B5
26 K – R2	P – R3

Taking care of details, so that the Pawn will not be within the Bishop's reach after *25* . . . Q – Q4; *26* B – N8, etc.

27 R – K4   Q – Q4!

The Queen is boss.

FISCHER

Position after 27 . . .
Q – Q4

PORTISCH

Black's superiority is obvious. He has some minor threats, and a major one which cannot be met. To the surprise of no one, *Sovietski Sport*, a Soviet newspaper, reported that Portisch had blundered and thrown away a perfectly even endgame.

28 P – KR4 . . .

After the comparatively better *28* R/4 – K2, Black wins more slowly with *28* . . . P – B6!; *29* P × P (or *29* R – K4, P × P followed by . . . N – Q7 wins), N – Q7, etc.

28 . . .   N – K6!

Wins the Exchange, as *29* P – B3 fails against . . . Q – Q7; *30* R – KN1, Q – KB7.

29	R/1 × N	P × R
30	R × P	Q × P
31	R – B3+	K – K1
32	B – N7	Q – B5
33	P × P	P × P
34	R – B8+	. . .

A check before dying.

34	. . .	K – Q2
35	R – QR8	K – B3
	White resigns	

The ominous presence of Black's RP is the deciding factor.

54 Fischer - Najdorf [Argentina]

SANTA MONICA 1966

SICILIAN DEFENSE

Najdorf's night off from the Najdorf

This game follows a loss (with Black) to Najdorf earlier in the tournament. Here, Najdorf adopts the Sicilian but not his Variation—perhaps because he had lost with it previously. (See game 40.) White soon launches a sharp line, a curious violation of principle involving three consecutive Bishop sorties before his other men have been developed. In relatively uncharted terrain, both players miss their way on move twelve. It then becomes a question of whether Najdorf's doubled center Pawns are a mass or a mess. Fischer proceeds to exploit his slight advantage with restraint, gradually building up pressure against Black's uncastled King. At the right moment he offers a stunning Pawn sacrifice (26 P–B5). Najdorf is compelled to decline, whereupon he lands in a hopeless endgame.

This forceful and resourceful performance typified Fischer's surge throughout the last half of the 2nd Piatagorsky Cup.

1	P – K4	P – QB4
2	N – KB3	N – QB3

Najdorf avoids the Najdorf Variation.

3	P – Q4	P × P
4	N × P	P – K3

4 . . . N – B3 obliges 5 N – QB3, which precludes the Maroczy Bind by P – QB4. Ever since ways of combatting the "Bind" have been found, it has become almost an obsession to abstain from 4 . . . N – B3, although the most that can be said for other moves is that some of them may be as good.

5 N – N5 . . .

Alekhine was of the opinion that *5* P – QB4 is best, but it has since been discovered that White cannot maintain any advantage after *5* . . . N – B3; *6* N – QB3, B – N5, etc.

5 . . . P – Q3
6 B – KB4!? . . .

Sharpest. Objectively speaking, it is probably best to establish an immediate Maroczy Bind with *6* P – QB4.

6 . . . P – K4

After *6* . . . N – K4!? *7* QN – R3! (Bronstein's idea) is best. But not Euwe's suggestion to win a Pawn by *7* Q – Q4, P – QR3; *8* N×P+??, B×N; *9* B×N because of *9* . . . Q – R4+! (ZUCKERMAN).

7 B – K3 N – B3

Black can avoid the doubling of his Pawns by *7* . . . P – QR3; *8* N/5 – B3, N – B3; *9* B – N5, B – K2. However, Najdorf may have been worried about *9* B – QB4! Fischer–Badilles, Manila 1967, then continued: *9* . . . B – K2; *10* N – Q5!, N×N; *11* B×N, O – O; *12* N – B3 with absolute control of Q5. After the text, *8* B – QB4 is met simply by *8* . . . B – K3! (but not *8* . . . N×P??; *9* Q – Q5, B – K3; *10* Q×N, P – Q4; *11* B×QP! and wins); *9* B×B, P×B; *10* P – QB4!, B – K2= (not *10* . . . N×P?; *11* Q – N4).

8 B – N5!? . . .

Another of Bronstein's ideas. The customary line was *8* QN – B3 and after . . . P – QR3; *9* N – R3 Black has 3 possibilities:
A] *9* . . . P – QN4; *10* N – Q5, N×N (or *10* . . . R – QN1; *11* N×N+, Q×N; *12* N – N1! with an edge for White); *11* P×N, N – K2; *12* P – QB4 with advantage.
B] Simagin gives *9* . . . B – K3; *10* N – Q5, B×N!; *11* P×B, N – K2; *12* P – QB4, N – B4 with harmonious development for all of Black's pieces. Or *10* N – B4, P – QN4; *11* N – N6, R – QN1; *12* N/6 – Q5, B×N; *13* P×B, N – K2 with a good game. But *13* N×B!? (instead of P×B) launches a promising gambit (*13* . . . N×P; *14* Q – B3, N – B4; *15* O – O – O).

c] Best is *9 . . . R – QN1!*; *10* B – KN5, P – N4=. Aronin–Taimanov, U.S.S.R. Champ., 1962. *11* N – Q5 is met by Q – R4+; forcing *12* B – Q2, then Q – Q1 and White has made no progress. On *13* N×N+, Q×N; *14* N – N1, P – N5! and White must regroup his forces.

NAJDORF

Position after 8 B – N5

FISCHER

The third consecutive Bishop sortie is well-motivated since White is threatening to double Black's KBP.

8 . . .   B – K3?

Also weak is *8 . . .* P – QR3; *9* B×N, P×B; *10* N/5 – B3, P – B4?; *11* Q – R5!, N – Q5; *12* B – B4, Q – B2; *13* N – Q2, N×P+; *14* K – K2, N×R (Bronstein–Polugaievsky, U.S.S.R. Champ., 1964); and now simply *15* R×N! must win out. Another try is *11 . . .* B – N2!? (instead of *. . .* N – Q5); *12* B – B4, O – O; *13* P×P, N – Q5; *14* B – Q3, R – K1; *15* B – K4! (not *15* P – B6? as in Estrin-Tcherepkov, Leningrad 1964). For instance, *15 . . .* P – Q4; *16* N×P, B×P; *17* B×B, Q×N; *18* N – B3, Q×NP?; *19* B – K4, N×P+; *20* K – K2, N – Q5+; *21* K – K3, etc.

But Black could equalize immediately with *8 . . .* Q – R4+!; *9* Q – Q2 (or *9* B – Q2, Q – Q1 draws), N×P; *10* Q×Q, N×Q; *11* B – K3 (R. Byrne suggests *11* N – B7+?, K – Q2; *12* N×R, N×B; *13* B – N5+, but after K – Q1!; *14* N – B3, B – Q2; *15* O – O – O, B – K2 White's straying Knight is soon lost), K – Q2; *12* N×RP, P – Q4, etc.

9 QN – B3   *. . .*

After *9* P – QB4, P – KR3!; *10* B×N, P×B Black's position is excellent.

9 . . .	P – QR3
10 B×N	P×B
11 N – R3	N – Q5

Other possibilities (all favoring White) are:

A] *11* . . . P – N4; *12* N – Q5!

B] *11* . . . B – K2; *12* B – B4!

c] *11* . . . P – B4?; *12* B – B4, B×B; *13* N×B, P×P; *14* QN×P, P – Q4; *15* Q×P!

12 B – B4?	. . .

Correct is *12* N – B4, and if . . . R – B1; *13* N – K3, B – R3 (if *13* . . . Q – N3 simply *14* R – QN1); *14* B – Q3, R – KN1; *15* Q – R5! snuffs out Black's initiative.

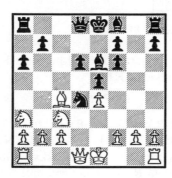

NAJDORF

Position after 12 B – B4

FISCHER

12 . . .	P – N4

Sharper is *12* . . . P – Q4!; *13* N×P (if *13* P×P, B×N; *14* P×KB, Q – R4), KB×N; *14* P×B, Q – R4+; *15* K – B1 (or *15* P – B3, B×N; *16* B×B, Q×P+; *17* K – B1, R – QB1! with advantage), O – O – O with active play: e.g., *16* P – QB3, then N – N4, etc.

13 B×B	. . .

Of course not the tempting *13* B – Q5?, P – N5.

13 . . .	P×B

All in all this exchange benefits Black since it enables him to protect his weak squares (Q4 and KB4). However if (as in the sequence) his central Pawn mass can be restrained, then it becomes merely a fixed target subject to constant pressure.

14 N – K2   N – B3

Black should get some scope for his pieces by *14* . . . N × N!; *15* Q × N, P – Q4. The check looming on KR5 is not to be feared.

15 N – N3   . . .

15 P – QB4 at once is met by Q – R4+.

15 . . .   Q – Q2?

Dr. Kmoch recommends *15* . . . P – Q4! Or *15* . . . Q – R4+!; *16* P – B3, P – N5; and if *17* N – B4, Q – B4.

16 P – QB4   N – Q5
17 O – O   P – N5

"Castling Q-side is a risk Black's insurance company would not permit him to take." (R. Byrne)

The text later enables White to use this NP to pry open the QR file (after P – QR3). Better is *17* . . . B – N2.

18 N – B2   N × N
19 Q × N   P – KR4
20 KR – Q1   P – R5
21 N – B1   R – KN1?

Better is *21* . . . P – R6; *22* P – N3, Q – B3 with reasonable play.

22 P – QR3!   P – R6
23 P – N3   P × P
24 R × RP   Q – B3
25 Q – K2!   P – B4

NAJDORF

Position after 25 . . .
P – B4

FISCHER

Hoping to trade his KRP for the KP in the event of *26* Q – R5+. But White now is ready to exploit Black's poor development.

26 P – B5!   . . .

More than a glancing blow. Black can know nothing about the imminent destruction of his compact mass of center Pawns.

26 . . .   **Q × KP**

26 . . . P × BP (if *26 . . .* Q × BP; *27* Q – R5+ followed by P × P, etc.); *27* Q – R5+, K – K2; *28* R/3 – Q3, P × P; *29* R/3 – Q2 is quite hopeless for Black.

27 Q × Q   **P × Q**
28 P × P   . . .

Black's game is in ruins—note his pathetic triplets on the K-file. The rest is technique.

28 . . .   **B – R3**

To prevent N – K3 – B4.

29 R – R5   **K – Q2**
30 R × KP   **B – N2**
31 R × P/4   **B × P**
32 N – K3   **P – R4**

A last gasp. Different people feel differently about resigning.

33 N – B4   **KR – N1**
34 R – R4   **K – B3**
35 R – R7   **B – Q5**
36 R – B7+   **K – Q4**
37 P – Q7   **P – R5**

NAJDORF

Position after 37 . . .
P – R5

FISCHER

38 N – N6+ . . .

Najdorf was probably hoping for *38* R – B8!, R×R; *39* N –
N6+, K – B4; *40* P×R=Q+?, R×Q; *41* N×R, P – R6 with
some practical chances. But we both overlooked the neat
Zwischenzug. 40 R – B1+!, K×N; *41* R×R! breaking all further
resistance.
The text is good enough, but prolongs the game.

38 . . .	R×N
39 R – B8	. . .

The point: on *39* . . . R/3 – N1 the Pawn queens with check.

39 . . .	R – Q3
40 R×R	R×P
41 R×P	P – K4
42 K – B1	R – QN2
43 P – B4!	K – K3
44 P×P	R – B2+
45 K – K2	R – B7+
46 K – Q3	B×P
47 R – K1!	Black resigns

NAJDORF

Final Position after 47
R – K1

FISCHER

After *47* . . . R – B4; *48* R – R5 (win by pin!), K – B3;
49 R/1×B, R×R; *50* R×R, K×R; *51* K – K3, K – B4; *52* K – Q4!
(but not *52* K – B3, K – N4; *53* P – N4??, K – R5! and draws),
K – N4; *53* K – K5, K – N5; *54* K – K4, K – N4; *55* K – B3,
K – B4; *56* P – N4+ followed by K – N3 wins.

55 Fischer - Bednarsky *[Poland]*

HAVANA OLYMPIC 1966
SICILIAN DEFENSE

The price of incaution

Once more Fischer rehabilitates his pet move (6 B – QB4) against his favorite Najdorf Variation, and it is remarkable that he should continue to win with such ease. In fact, his opponents do not seem to offer serious resistance. Young Bednarsky apparently is caught napping, improvises, and loses in just 22 moves!

Seeking active counterplay, Bednarsky blunders through bravado. He takes a tainted Pawn (9 . . . KN×P) and impetuously pursues the attack only to find himself in an ambush which, ironically, he had helped to construct. By move 12 Fischer obtains a formation at which he had had success even as a child. Naturally he wins, but the economy with which he does so is delightful.

1	P – K4	P – QB4
2	N – KB3	P – Q3
3	P – Q4	P×P
4	N×P	N – KB3
5	N – QB3	P – QR3
6	B – QB4	. . .

Here we go again!

6	. . .	P – K3

Probably best. White's Bishop is made to "bite on granite."

7	B – N3	. . .

Too slow is Bronstein's idea 7 P – QR3. E.g., Robatsch–Fischer, Havana 1965: 7 . . . B – K2; 8 B – R2, O – O; 9 O – O,

P – QN4; *10* P – B4, B – N2; *11* P – B5, P – K4 (Black is healthy as long as White can't exploit his hole on Q4); *12* N/4 – K2, QN – Q2; *13* N – N3, R – B1; *14* B – K3 (if *14* B – N5, R × N!; *15* P × R, N × P with advantage—Gligorich), N – N3; *15* B × N, Q × B+; *16* K – R1, Q – K6! (to prevent N – R5) with the better game for Black.

White would of course like to get in P – KB4 – 5 as swiftly as possible, but he must exercise some caution. The text is essentially a waiting move which narrows Black's options. After *7* P – B4 Black has the choice of . . . P – Q4, . . . P – QN4, or *7* . . . N × P; *8* N × N, P – Q4.

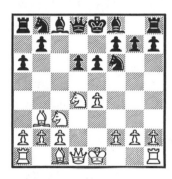

BEDNARSKY

Position after 7 B – N3

FISCHER

7 . . . QN – Q2

In order to reach QB4 with an attack on the Bishop as well as the KP. But *7* . . . P – QN4! is better (see game 17). An example of static White play is Garcia–Fischer, Havana Olympic, 1966: *8* P – QR3, B – K2; *9* B – K3, O – O; *10* O – O, B – N2; *11* P – B3, QN – Q2; *12* Q – Q2 (*12* B × P!? leads to rough equality), N – K4; *13* Q – B2, Q – B2; *14* QR – B1, K – R1!; *15* N/3 – K2, R – KN1!; *16* K – R1, P – N4!; *17* P – R3, R – N3; *18* N – N3, QR – KN1 (White is curiously helpless against the threat of . . . P – KR4 – N5. His normal break with P – KB4 is restrained by the silent Bishop on QN2); *19* N × P?, P × N; *20* B × KP, N × KP!; *21* N × N, R × B; White resigns.

After *7* . . . P – QN4 recent analysis indicates that Black's best plan is rapid development on the Q-side: *8* P – B4, B – N2; *9* P – B5, P – K4; *10* N/4 – K2, QN – Q2; *11* B – N5, B – K2. Now on *12* N – N3? (Correct is *12* B × N, N × B; *13* Q – Q3, R – QB1 with even chances—Fischer–Zuckerman, U.S. Champ.,

1966), R – QB1!; *13* O – O, P – KR4! White's in trouble, as indicated by the following examples:

A] *14* P – KR4, P – N5; *15* B × N, B × B; *16* N – Q5, B × P; *17* N × P!?, Q – N4; *18* P – B6, P – N3; *19* N – N7+, K – Q1; *20* R – B3, B – N6; *21* Q – Q3, B – R7+; *22* K – B1, N – B4; *23* R – R3!?, R – R5!; *24* Q – B3, N × B; *25* RP × N, R × R; *26* Q × R, B × N; *27* P × B, Q × P+; *28* K – K1, Q – B5 and since there's nothing left—but emptiness—White resigns. (R. Byrne–Fischer, Tunisia Interzonal, 1967.)

B] *14* B × N, N × B; *15* N – Q5, P – R5; *16* N × N+, P × N; *17* N – K2, B × P; *18* B – Q5, Q – N3+; *19* K – R1, B × B; *20* Q × B, R × P; *21* Q – Q3, Q – B3; *22* QR – B1, P – R6! White resigns. (Chocaltea-Gheorghiu, Bucharest 1967.)

8 P – B4!   N – B4

Too passive is *8* . . . B – K2; *9* Q – B3, O – O; *10* P – N4. Bad is *8* . . . P – QN4; *9* P – B5!, P – K4; *10* N – B6!, Q – B2; *11* N – N4! and White is ready to sit on Black once he occupies the hole on Q5.

9 P – B5!   . . .

Thematic. Bednarsky told me after the game he had reached this position before, as White, and he had continued *9* P – K5, P × P; *10* P × P, KN – Q2; *11* B – KB4 vs. Bogdanovich, E. Germany 1964. Obviously that approach is too tame.

9 . . .   KN × P!?

Playing with fire.

The question is whether *9* . . . P – K4 is sufficient. Apparently not, after *10* N/4 – K2, N × B (not *10* . . . QN × P?; *11* N × N, N × N; *12* Q – Q5, N – N4; *13* P – KR4); *11* RP × N, P – R3; *12* N – N3 followed by N–R5 with a bind. R. Byrne–Bogdanovich, Sarajevo 1967.

9 . . . B – K2 is steadier than the text (for *9* . . . N × B; *10* RP × N see note to White's 7th move in game 58). But White stays on top after *10* Q – B3, O – O; *11* B – K3. Now on *11* . . . P – Q4; *12* P × QP, N × B; *13* N × N!, P × BP (if *13* . . . N × P?; *14* O – O – O wins a Pawn); *14* O – O – O, etc.

10 P × P!   . . .

BEDNARSKY

Position after 10 P×P

FISCHER

10 . . .   Q – R5+?

Tempting, but suicidal. Black had two better tries:
A] *10* . . . B×P; *11* N×N, N×N; *12* N×B, P×N (not *12*
. . . Q – R5+; *13* P – N3, N×P; *14* B – N5!, Q – K5+;
15 K – Q2, N×R; *16* N – B7+, K – Q2; *17* N×R wins); *13*
Q – N4, N – B4; *14* B – K3! with a strong initiative.
B] *10* . . . P×P!; *11* N×N, N×N; *12* O – O, Q – K2!
(weaker is *12* . . . N – B4; *13* Q – N4—if *13* . . . N×B;
14 RP×N, P – K4; *15* Q – B3). White has good play for the Pawn,
but no forced win in view.

    11 P – N3   N×NP
    12 N – B3!   . . .

This twist is well known: e.g., from the Vienna *1* P – K4, P – K4;
2 N – QB3, N – KB3; *3* P – B4, P – Q4; *4* P×KP, N×P; *5* P – Q3,
Q – R5+; *6* P – N3, N×P; *7* N – B3, etc.
Only not *12* P×P+?, K – Q1; *13* N – B3, Q – K2+!

    12 . . .   Q – R4
    13 P×P+   K – Q1
    14 R – KN1   N – B4
    15 N – Q5!   Q×BP

Black's attack has boomeranged. Now his King gets caught in a
merciless crossfire.
On *15* . . . P – R3; *16* N – B4! picks off the Queen. No better
is *15* . . . N×B; *16* B – N5+, K – Q2 (or *16* . . . B – K2;
17 N×B!, N×N; *18* Q×P+); *17* N – K5+!

    16 B – N5+   K – K1
    17 Q – K2+!   . . .

By now I was hunting for bigger game than the paltry win of a Queen after *17* N – B6+, P × N; *18* B × Q+.

17 . . .	B –K3
18 N –B4	K – Q2
19 O – O – O	. . .

BEDNARSKY

Position after 19
O – O – O

FISCHER

One threat of course is *20* N – K5+.

19 . . .	Q – K1

Black is helpless. After *19* . . . N × B+; *20* RP × N, Q – K1; *21* KR – K1, B – N1; *22* Q – Q3 it's also quits. The only way for Black to last is to give up his Queen with *19* . . . B × B; *20* N – K5+, K – B2; *21* N × Q, B × N.

20 B × B+	N × B
21 Q – K4!	. . .

Centralization with a vengeance!

21 . . .	P – KN3
22 N × N	Black resigns

On *22* . . . Q × N; *23* Q × P+, K – K1; *24* KR – K1! wins everything.

56 Fischer - Gligorich *[Yugoslavia]*

HAVANA OLYMPIC 1966

RUY LOPEZ

The Fischer continuation

Fischer's surprising 4 B×N, a revival of Emanuel Lasker's Exchange Variation—the one he used at St. Petersburg in 1914 to defeat Alekhine and Capablanca, but which subsequently fell into desuetude because ways to equalize were rapidly discovered—drew from his opponent the obligatory response. However, Fischer's next move, regarded as inferior, and his sixth (the customary follow-up) prepared no one for the gambit which he introduced on move seven. Gligorich reacted with innocent appropriateness until move seventeen, then made a startling blunder that met with speedy retribution. Because, in the course of the tournament, Fischer had played and won two other games with this very same line (demonstrating in each case White's hitherto unsuspected potential), it was promptly dubbed "The Fischer Variation." Of course, sticklers will insist that it should be called the Fischer continuation of the Barendregt Variation.

1	P – K4	P – K4
2	N – KB3	N – QB3
3	B – N5	P – QR3
4	B×N!	. . .

A surprise! I had introduced this in an earlier game against Portisch (see note to Black's 6th). After sizing up Gligorich over-the-board, I decided he was ripe for a repeat performance.

4 . . .	QP×B

This recapture is so automatic that most annotators fail to comment on it. After *4 . . . NP×B; 5 P – Q4, P×P; 6 Q×P*

White maintains an enduring initiative. If *6* . . . Q – B3; *7* Q – Q3! (but not *7* P – K5, Q – N3; *8* O – O, B – N2; *9* P – K6?, BP × P; *10* N – K5, Q × P + !; *11* K × Q, P – B4+—an old trap).

                    5 O – O!   . . .

GLIGORICH

Position after 5 O – O

FISCHER

"The text poses more problems for Black than does an immediate *5* P – Q4, and Nimzovich is once more proved right in his pronouncement that the threat is stronger than its execution. Though White has sold his strong Bishop for a Knight, a Bishop which is usually Black's main strategical problem in many variations of the Lopez, there is no basic flaw in White's tactics. He has gained a tempo for development, somewhat spoiled Black's Pawn structure and revived the threat on Black's KP." (GLIGORICH).

The text was favored by Emanuel Lasker, Bernstein and also, in recent years, by the Dutch master Barendregt. I had been pondering it for a long time before deciding to include it in my arsenal.

                    5 . . .   P – B3!

"This position has not been seen frequently in the modern grandmaster praxis and, thanks to imaginative Fischer, we have to go back to the 19th century to find the alternatives for Black. It is not clear, however, that Black has any better way of defending the KP." (GLIGORICH).

Black can defend his KP in numerous ways. Let's look at the lemons first.

A] *5* . . . B – K2? (played by Reshevsky); *6* N × P!, Q – Q5; *7* N – KB3, Q × KP; *8* R – K1 (instead of *8* P – Q3? as in Malesic–Reshevsky, Maribor 1967) and it's doubtful Black can get out of the opening with equality. One example, *8* . . . Q – B4; *9*

P – QN3!, N – B3; *10* B – R3 (or *10* R – K5!), B – K3; *11* N – Q4, etc.

B] The ballet dancer Harmonist showed good sense by trying *5* . . . Q – B3 with the threat of . . . B – KN5 (against Schallopp in Frankfurt, 1887); but after *6* P – Q4, P×P; *7* B – N5!, Q – N3; *8* Q×P White can get a clear initiative.

C] *5* . . . B – Q3?; *6* P – Q4, P×P (not *6* . . . P – B3?; *7* P×P, P×P; *8* N×P!—or *6* . . . B – KN5; *7* P×P, B×N; *8* Q×B with a comfortable K-side Pawn majority, as in Schallopp–Blackburne, Frankfurt, 1887); *7* Q×P, P – B3; *8* QN – Q2!, N – K2; *9* N – B4, etc.

D] A reasonable try is Bronstein's *5* . . . Q – Q3!?; *6* P – Q3 (*6* N – R3? works well against *6* . . . B – K3?; *7* N – KN5, but *6* . . . P – QN4! strands the Knight), P – B3; *7* B – K3, P – QB4; *8* QN – Q2, B – K3; *9* Q – K2, O – O – O=. White has possibilities of breaking on the Q-side after P – QR3 followed by KR – N1 and P – QN4, but Black can probably prevent this expansion. So best is *5* . . . Q – Q3; *6* P – Q4, P×P; *7* N×P, etc.

E] The most ambitious continuation is *5* . . . B – KN5!?; *6* P – KR3, P – KR4!? (Em. Lasker used to win such positions for White after *6* . . . B×N; *7* Q×B. Hort–Kolarov, Poland 1967, continued: *7* . . . Q – B3; *8* Q – KN3, B – Q3; *9* P – Q3, Q – N3; *10* B – K3!?, Q×Q; *11* P×Q and White managed to grind out a win in the ensuing endgame); *7* P – Q3! (On *7* P – B3, Q – Q6!; *8* P×B, P×P; *9* N×P, B – Q3!; *10* N×Q, B – R7+ draws. A fantasy variation occurs after *8* Q – N3?, B×N; *9* Q×P, K – Q2; *10* Q×R, B×NP!; *11* K×B, R – R3!; *12* R – N1, R – N3+; *13* K – R2, R×R; *14* K×R, B – B4 with a winning attack), Q – B3; *8* QN – Q2! (Keres in his old book on the open games wrongly praises this whole line for Black, having considered only *8* P×B?, P×P; *9* N – N5, Q – R3; *10* N – KR3, Q – R5; *11* K – R2, P – KN3; *12* N – B3, P×N; *13* P – KN3, Q – K2 with advantage), N – K2 (now *8* . . . P – KN4 is met by *9* N – B4!, B×N; *10* Q×B, Q×Q; *11* P×Q, P – B3; *12* P – KR4!, P×P; *13* P – B4 with promising play for the Pawn. But not *9* R – K1?, B – K3; *10* P – Q4, P – N5; *11* N×P, P×P; *12* P – KN3, P – R7+; *13* K – N2, P – R5 with initiative); *9* R – K1! (or *9* N – B4!, B×N; *10* Q×B, Q×Q; *11* P×Q, N – N3; *12* B – K3, P – QB4; *13* P – QR4! White stands better and eventually won. Hort-Sliwa, Poland 1967), N – N3; *10* P – Q4!, B – Q3; *11* P×B, P×NP; *12* N – R2, R×N!; *13* Q×P!, R – R5; *14* Q – B5 and White is slightly better.

6 P – Q4　　　B – KN5!

Best. In our earlier game Portisch had tried 6 . . . P×P;
7 N×P!, P – QB4 (Portsich played the more sensible 7 . . . B –
Q3 in a subsequent event but it's still inferior after 8 Q – R5+!,
P – N3; 9 Q – B3, B × P + ?; 10 K × B, Q × N; 11 R – Q1!); 8 N – N3,
Q×Q (now 8 . . . B – Q3? is met by 9 N × P!); 9 R×Q, B – Q3
(the queer looking 9 . . . P – QN3 as a defensive try scored an
unmerited success in a Soviet women's tournament due to White's
passive play. But 10 B – B4, R – R2!; 11 N – B3, N – K2; 12
P – QR4! followed by P – R5 is almost decisive. 13 . . . P –
QR4? is impossible because of 14 N – N5! Polugaievsky's 9 . . .
B – Q2 offers defensive prospects); 10 N – R5!, P – QN4 (amusing
is 10 . . . B – N5?; 11 P – KB3, O – O – O??; 12 P – K5! and
Black resigns. Hort-Zelandinow, Havana 1967. Keres tried 10
. . . N – R3 but also failed to equalize after 11 B × N, P × B;
12 N – B4, B – K2; 13 N – B3, B – K3; 14 N – Q5. Bagirov–
Keres, Moscow 1967); 11 P – QB4, N – K2; 12 B – K3, P – B4;
13 N – B3, P – B5; 14 P – K5!, B×P; 15 B × QBP and Black's
disorganized position soon crumbled.

GLIGORICH

*Position after 6 . . .
B – KN5*

FISCHER

7 P – B3!　　　. . .

The text involves a gambit.

Curiously, this was Gligorich's own published suggestion when
he annotated his game against Lee at Hastings, 1965–6, which
had continued: 7 P×P, Q×Q; 8 R×Q, B×N! (Fischer–Smyslov,
Monaco 1967, went 8 . . . P×P?; 9 R – Q3!, B×N; 10 R×B,
N – B3; 11 N – B3, B – N5; 12 B – N5!, B×N; 13 P×B! [was
Black playing for the cheap trap 13 B×N?, B×P; 14 B×NP??,

B×R; *15* B×R, O – O – O!], R – KB1; *14* B×N, R×B; *15* R×R, P×R; *16* R – Q1! and White should have won the ending); *9* P×B, P×P; *10* P – KB4, N – B3; and now *11* N – B3! (instead of *11* P×P?, N×P; *12* B – K3, B – B4; *13* N – Q2, N×N; *14* B×B, O – O – O as in the game), B – Q3; *12* P×P, B×P; *13* N – R4! gives White the better of a probable draw.

So the best is *7* P×P!, Q×Q; *8* R×Q, B×N!; *9* P×B, P×P; *10* B – K3! followed by N – Q2 – B4 with pressure. If *10* . . . N – K2; *11* P – B4! keeps the initiative.

       7 . . .   P×P

An alternative is *7* . . . B – Q3 holding the center.

       8 P×P   Q – Q2

Black dares not accept the Pawn: *8* . . . B×N; *9* Q×B, Q×P; *10* R – Q1, Q – B5; *11* B – B4, etc. However, Gligorich said (in *Chess Review*) he had completely forgotten his Hastings analysis, which indicated Black's best as *8* . . . P – QB4!; *9* P – Q5, B – Q3.

       9 P – KR3!   . . .

"Putting the question to the Bishop." Nimzovich, Steinitz, Evans, and other theoreticians have pointed out the enormous value of kicking this Bishop before the pin becomes really troublesome. Here, White must exercise care since his KRP could easily become a potential target.

       9 . . .   B – K3

This natural retreat, which releases the tension, gives White too free a hand and is the subsequent cause of Gligorich's difficulties. Better is *9* . . . B – R4! as played against me by Jimenez in a later round. After *10* N – K5!, B×Q (bad is *10* . . . Q×RP; *11* P×Q, B×Q; *12* R×B, P×N; *13* P×P, B – B4; *14* K – N2 with a dangerous preponderance of center Pawns); *11* N×Q, K×N; *12* R×B Black should hold the ending, although he found a way to lose: *12* . . . R – K1; *13* P – B3 (*13* N – B3 is more accurate), N – K2; *14* N – B3, K – B1; *15* B – K3, P – KB4; *16* QR – B1, P×P; *17* P×P, P – KN3? (. . . N – N3 is correct); *18* B – B4!, B – N2; *19* P – Q5!, R – Q1; *20* N – R4!, KR – B1; *21* P – KN3, P – KN4? (cracking under the pressure—*21* . . . R – B2 is more sensible); *22* B×NP, R – B2; *23* K – N2, P×P; *24* P×P, K – N1; *25* R – K1, B – B1; *26* R – B1!, R – N2; *27*

B – B6, R – N1; *28* QR – K1, R – Q2; *29* P – Q6!, P × P; *30* B × N, B × B; *31* R – B7, resigns (if *31 . . .* R – K1; *32* N – N6, R – B2; *33* N – Q5).

10 N – B3	**O – O – O**
11 B – B4!	**. . .**

GLIGORICH

Position after 11 B – B4

FISCHER

11 . . .   N – K2?

More solid is *11 . . .* B – Q3!; *12* B × B, Q × B.

The critical line is *11 . . .* P – KN4!?; *12* B – N3, P – KR4; *13* P – Q5!, P × P; *14* R – B1! and now:

A] *14 . . .* B – Q3; *15* N – QR4!, K – N1; *16* N – B5, Q – K2; *17* N × P + !, P × N; *18* N – Q4, B – Q2; *19* Q – N3 +, K – R2; *20* R × P + !!, B × R; *21* B × B, B – N4 (if *21 . . .* Q – B4; *22* Q – K3! is the simplest win); *22* N – B6 + ! (Palacio), B × N; *23* Q – N6 + and mate next.

B] The fantastic win is *14 . . .* P × P; *15* N – QR4!, K – N1; *16* R × P!!, Q × Q; *17* R – B8 + !!!, K – R2 (or *17 . . .* K × R; *18* N – N6 mate); *18* B – N8 +, K – R1; *19* N – N6 mate.

12 R – B1	**N – N3**

Black has lost time in order to reach this inferior square.

13 B – N3	**B – Q3**
14 N – QR4!	**B × B?**

Yielding his QB4 permanently to the Knight.
Correct is *14 . . .* K – N1; *15* N – B5, Q – K2.

15 P × B	**K – N1**

Bad is *15 . . . P – N3; 16 P – Q5!, B – B2 (16 . . . P×P?; 17 N×P+); 17 Q – K2!*, etc.

16.	N – B5	Q – Q3
17	Q – R4!	. . .

GLIGORICH

Position after 17 Q – R4

FISCHER

17 . . .		K – R2??

Catastrophic. After *17 . . . B – B1; 18 R – B3 (18 . . . Q×P?; 19 N – K5, Q – R5; 20 N×BP+)*, Black might have hung on with *18 . . . N – B1!*

18	N×RP!	. . .

The finishing stroke.

18 . . .		B×KRP

Desperation! *18 . . . P×N; 19 R×P* costs Black's Queen to prevent mate.

19	P – K5!	. . .

The most forceful method.

19 . . .		N×P

Sheer desperation!! After *19 . . . P×P; 20 N – B5+, K – N1; 21 R – B3!* followed by R – R3 is most persuasive.

20	P×N	P×P
21	N – B5+	K – N1
22	P×B	P – K5

Never say die!

23	N × KP	Q – K2
24	R – B3	P – QN4
25	Q – B2	. . .

Time to consolidate. *25* Q – R6 also does the trick.

According to a Havana newspaper, some casual spectators who had just wandered in thought White had merely won two pieces for a Rook. Nobody could believe that Gligorich was playing on two pieces behind! The rude awakening came when—

25 . . .   Black resigns

57 Larsen *[Denmark]* - Fischer

MONACO 1967

KING'S INDIAN DEFENSE

Change of pace

Larsen, uncharacteristically, forces an early exchange of Queens so that he can spring a surprise in the resulting endgame. Fischer beats him to it (13 . . . P – N3) and proceeds to defend with meticulous care. It looks as if a draw must ensue, but Larsen presses. He is rebuffed, and again a draw seems imminent. Larsen senses no danger and, as if by inertia, continues to play for a win. As the game simplifies, the self-inflicted dark square weaknesses in the Dane's position gradually reveal themselves. By move thirty it becomes Fischer's turn to assume the initiative, and he probes these flaws judiciously. Thrown on the defensive, Larsen makes one or two reckless moves out of which Fischer constructs elegant combinations. Thus, what begins as a barren endgame is transformed into an exhibition of chess sensibility and virtuosity.

1	P – Q4	N – KB3
2	P – QB4	P – KN3
3	N – QB3	B – N2
4	P – K4	P – Q3
5	B – K2	. . .

Larsen had won some good games with *5* N – B3, O – O; *6* B – K3, but after *6* . . . P – K4! (which no one seems to have played) White gets no advantage. *7* B – K2, N – B3 transposes into well-known modern lines. And *7* P – Q5, N – N5; *8* B – N5, P – KB3; *9* B – R4, Q – K1 gives Black dynamic play. Now *10* P – KR3, N – R3; *11* P – KN4!?, P – KB4 is too risky for White. Finally on *7* P×P, P×P; *8* Q×Q, R×Q; *9* N – Q5(?), N – R3! gives Black the better ending.

```
5 . . .        O – O
6 N – B3       P – K4
7 O – O        N – B3
```

FISCHER

Position after 7 . . .
N – B3

LARSEN

```
8 B – K3       . . .
```

A bit of a surprise. I had expected *8* P – Q5, N – K2; *9* N – K1, N – Q2; *10* N – Q3, P – KB4; *11* B – Q2. Now I had in mind *11* . . . P – B4!; *12* P – B3, P – B5! (but not *12* . . . N – KB3?; *13* P – KN4!, P – B5; *14* P – KR4! and Black's K-side counterplay is completely stymied) with active chances. Larsen–Najdorf, Santa Monica 1966, had continued: *11* . . . N – KB3?; *12* P – B3, P – B5!; *13* P – B5!, P – KN4; *14* R – B1, N – N3; *15* P × P, P × P; *16* N – N5, R – B2; *17* Q – B2!, N – K1; *18* P – QR4 and White came first on the Q-side since Black's attack never got off the ground.

```
8 . . .        R – K1!
```

The cleanest way to equalize. Najdorf found this move after some painful experiences with *8* . . . N – KN5 in his match vs. Reshevsky. The main point is that *9* P – Q5, N – Q5! levels.

```
9 P × P        P × P
10 Q × Q       N × Q
```

A dubious improvement over *10* . . . R × Q! as played by Reshevsky in his match with Benko. After *11* B – N5 Black must not play R – Q2? (after which Benko's *12* B – Q1!! followed by B – QR4 was very strong), but *11* . . . R – B1! solves all his problems.

```
11 N – QN5     N – K3
12 N – N5      R – K2
13 KR – Q1     . . .
```

Larsen is attempting to improve on Reshevsky–Fischer, Santa Monica 1966, which continued: *13* N×N, B×N; *14* P – B3, P – B3; *15* N – B3, R – Q2; *16* KR – Q1, B – B1; *17* K – B2, P – N3; *18* P – QN3, R – N2; *19* N – R4, N – Q2; *20* N – N2, P – QN4 with an eventual draw.

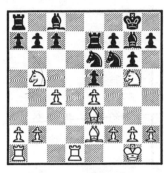

FISCHER

Position after 13 KR – Q1

LARSEN

13 . . .   P – N3!

In my 9th match game with Reshevsky, 1961, I tried *13 . . . P – B3!?* Larsen told me he had intended *14* N×P!? (instead of *14* N×N, B×N; *15* N – B3, R – Q2=), B – Q2; *15* N×N, B×N; *16* P – B3. But after *16 . . . R* – Q2! (threatening . . . R – Q5) Black has fair play for the Pawn, considering that the Knight is stranded on R7.

The book text was an improvement that I had hatched some time ago.

14 P – B5!?   . . .

Typically, Larsen adopts an enterprising continuation. He should settle for *14* N×N, B×N; *15* P – B3 with a draw in view. By overestimating his chances, he gradually drifts into a losing position.

14 . . .   N×BP

Naturally not *14 . . . P×P?; 15* N×N, B×N; *16* B×P, R – Q2; *17* P – B3 wins.

15 R – Q8+   B – B1

No better is *15 . . . R – K1; 16* R×R+, N×R; *17* B×N, P×B; *18* B – B4! Or *15 . . . N – K1?; 16* B×N, P×B; *17* N×QBP, R×N; *18* R×N+, B – B1; *19* N×RP!

16 N×QRP   R×N

On *16* . . . B – N2; *17* R × R, B × R; *18* P – B3 White has a
slight pull despite his misplaced Knight. After *18* . . . P – B3;
19 N – B8, R – N2; *20* R – Q1 maintains some pressure.

17 R × B   . . .

White recovers his Pawn with even chances.

FISCHER

Position after 17 R × B

LARSEN

17 . . .   K – N2

Black wisely resists the temptation of *17* . . . N/4 × P??;
18 N × N, N × N; *19* B – KR6. But even more accurate than the
text is *17* . . . P – R3!; *18* N – B3, K – N2; *19* B × N, P × B;
20 B – Q3 completely neutralizing any initiative for either side.

18 P – B3   N – K1
19 P – QR3(?)   . . .

Larsen's reluctance to simplify will soon backfire. Correct is
19 B × N!, P × B; *20* R – N8 with theoretical winning chances
because of the passed QRP. But it would be difficult to make
headway because of the opposite colored Bishops.

19 . . .   N – Q3
20 R – Q8   . . .

Optimistic as ever! *20* R – N8, N – Q2; *21* R – Q8, N – N2;
22 R – B8, N – Q3 would lead to a draw by repetition.

20 . . .   P – R3
21 N – R3   N – K3
22 R – N8   R – K1
23 R × R   N × R

FISCHER

Position after 23 . . .
N × R

LARSEN

"Now White's initiative is over and the position is even but by no means drawish. There is a lot of play." (KMOCH).

White's dark squares, notably his Q4, are weak. But it's still not too serious.

        24 B – QN5   . . .

Pointless. White should start bringing his Knight into the game via B2. He can't prevent . . . B – B4, gaining control of the dark squares. Of course not *24* P – QN4?, B × P.

        24 . . .   N – Q3
        25 B – KB1   N – N2!
        26 N – B2   B – B4!
        27 B × B   N/2 × B
        28 R – Q1   P – R4!

To keep the Knight out of KN4. This "prophylactic" thrust would have gladdened Nimzovitch's heart. Not *28* . . . N – Q5?; *29* N – N4, P – KB3; *30* P – B4!

        29 R – Q5   . . .

Larsen still has illusions, but his game is fast deteriorating. More prudent is *33* N – Q3, N × N; *34* B × N, N – Q5; *35* K – B2. White probably should hold the ending despite Black's creeping pressure.

        29 . . .   K – B3
        30 P – KR4   K – K2!
        31 B – B4   . . .

The Pawn is poisoned: *31* R × P?, P – QB3 folllowed by . . . N – Q2 (or . . . P – B3). The mission of the Rook has failed, but no serious harm has been done.

31 . . .	P – QB3
32 R – Q2	N – Q5!

Finally the Knight has gained this dominant outpost.

33 K – B1	. . .

The more active *33* N – Q3 is preferable. Now Black's tactical threats begin to proliferate.

33 . . .	P – B4!
34 P – QN4	. . .

Meets with a still sharper counter thrust. *34* N – Q3 offered a better chance for survival. After the text White's QRP is weakened. Not *34* P × P, N × P/4 with the double threat of . . . N – K6+ or . . . N × P (and if *35* R – K2?, N – N6+).

34 . . .	P – QN4!
35 B – N8	. . .

35 P × N, P × B clearly wins for Black. And *35* B × P? is refuted by . . . N/4 – N6.

35 . . .	P × P!

FISCHER

Position after 35 . . .
P × P

LARSEN

Fixing White with another weakness.

36 P × P	. . .

Not *36* P × N, P – K6; *37* R × N (if *37* R – Q3, P × N; *38* K × P, R – R1; *39* B – R2, P – N5—or *37* R – R2?, P × N; *38* K × P, K – B1!), P × R; *38* N – Q3, R × P; *39* K – K2, R – B6, etc.

36 . . .	N – Q2
37 R – Q3	R – R3!

Threatening . . . N – B7 which, if played immediately, could have been met by R – QB3.

38 R – QB3   P – B4!

FISCHER

Position after 38 . . .
P – B4!

LARSEN

This surprising combination apparently confused Larsen, who was in time-pressure.

39 P – N4?   . . .

The last blunder. On *39* P×P, P – N5!; *40* R – B1! (not *40* P×P, R – R8+), there's still a lot of fight. If *40* . . . R×P (or *40* . . . P×P; *41* B – R2); *41* P – B6, N – N3.

39 . . .   P – B5

This protected passed Pawn is just too strong. Not *39* . . . N – B3; *40* R × P!

40	P×P	P×P
41	B – Q5	N – KB3
42	R – KN3	N×B
43	P×N	R – KB3
44	K – N2	. . .

The sealed move. White is completely tied up. On *44* K – N1?, N – K7+ wins. Or if *44* K – K1, R – B5 mops up.

44	. . .	N – B4
45	R – R3	R – N3+
46	K – B3	N – Q5+
47	K – K3	. . .

On *47* K – K4, K – Q3 White is in *zugzwang*. If *48* R – R2 (to prevent . . . R – N7), R – N6.

47	. . .	R – N7
48	R – R1	K – Q3
49	N – K4+	K×P
50	N – B3+	K – K3
51	R – QB1	. . .

White has to prevent . . . R – QB7 as then the Knight cannot move because of . . . R – K7 mate.

51	. . .	R – KR7
52	P – R4	R – R6+
53	K – B2	N – N6
54	K – N2	N×R
55	K×R	P×P
56	N×P	N – K7
57	P – N5	P – B6
58	P – N6	P – B7
59	N – B5+	K – Q4

FISCHER

Position after 59 . . .
K – Q4

LARSEN

60	N – N3	. . .

White can choose his own end. If *60* N – Q3 (or *60* P – N7, P – B8=Q; *61* P – N8=Q, Q – R8 mate), N – B5+; *61* N×N+, P×N; *62* P – N7, P – B8=Q; *63* P – N8=Q, Q – R8 mate.

60	. . .	K – B3
61	K – N2	K×P

White resigns

58 Fischer - Geller [U.S.S.R.]

SICILIAN DEFENSE

Flawed masterpiece

After Fischer dropped this miniature (his third loss in a row to Geller) Kurajica concluded: "He just cannot play against Geller." Another Yugoslav, Trifunovich, opined at greater length:

> Geller is one of the best-prepared players in the world as to opening theory, and Fischer cannot be superior in that respect . . . Fischer [as White] chose a very sharp and modern variation . . . playing to win in the early stage of the game, as he usually does, and successfully, against weaker opponents. Fischer played better and attained a superior position, but it was very difficult to find the right solution over-the-board . . . There was his mistake . . . He has to impose a hard positional game, playing without pretensions for a win in the very opening.

Nowhere but in the notes that follow have the above errors been answered. Were it not for a momentary lapse (P – QR3?), Fischer would have won this little gem on move twenty—despite his critics.

1	P – K4	P – QB4
2	N – KB3	P – Q3
3	P – Q4	P×P
4	N×P	N – KB3
5	N – QB3	N – B3
6	B – QB4	P – K3

There is no apparent refutation to Benko's roguish 6 . . . Q – N3!? Saidy ventured it against me in the 1967 U.S. Champ. After 7 N – N3, P – K3; 8 O – O, B – K2; 9 B – K3, Q – B2; 10 P – B4, O – O; 11 B – Q3 it's a mutually hard game. Also see game 11.

GELLER

Position after 6 . . .
P – K3

FISCHER

7 B – K3 . . .

7 B – N3 cuts down Black's options. Fischer–Dely, Skopje, 1967, continued: 7 . . . P – QR3; *8* P – B4!, Q – R4 (*8* . . . N – QR4; *9* P – B5!, N×B; *10* RP×N, B – K2; *11* Q – B3, O – O; *12* B – K3, B – Q2; *13* P – KN4, P – K4; *14* N/4 – K2 with a crush in sight: Fischer–Bielicki, Mar Del Plata 1960. *8* . . . Q – B2; *9* P – B5!, N×N; *10* Q×N, P×P; *11* P×P, B×P; *12* O – O yields White a strong attack); *9* O – O!, N×N? (a better try is *9* . . . P – Q4; but after *10* N×N!, P×N; *11* P – B5! White's on top. If *11* . . . P – Q5?; *12* N – K2, P – K4; either *13* N – N3 or *13* Q – Q3 retains the advantage. Also on *11* . . . B – K2; *12* P – K5, N – Q2; *13* P×P, P×P [or *13* . . . N×P; *14* B – KB4!]; *14* Q – N4. Finally, *11* . . . B – B4+; *12* K – R1, O – O may be tenable); *10* Q×N, P – Q4 (*10* . . . Q – B4; *11* Q×Q, P×Q; *12* P – QR4! puts Black in an excruciating bind); *11* B – K3!, N×P (if *11* . . . N – N5; *12* K – R1!, N×B; *13* Q×N, P×P; *14* Q×P!, B – K2; *15* QR – K1 and mate is lurking in the wings: e.g., *15* . . . P – KN3; *16* N – Q5!, B – Q1; *17* Q – K5, O – O; *18* N – K7+! wins. Slightly more accurate, but still bad, is *11* . . . P×P; *12* N×P, B – K2; *13* N – Q6+, etc.); *12* N×N, P×N; *13* P – B5!, Q – N5 (if *13* . . . P×P; *14* P – N4!, B – K3 [*14* . . . Q – N5; *15* B – R4+!, P – N4; *16* Q – Q5! wins]; *15* P×P, B×B; *16* RP×B, Q – N5; *17* R – R4!, Q×Q; *18* R×Q and Black is in a curiously hopeless predicament: e.g., *18* . . . B – K2; *19* R×P, K – B1; *20* P – B6!!, B×P; *21* R×B!, P×R; *22* B – R6+ and mates); *14* P×P, B×P; *15* B×B!, P×B; *16* R×B+!, Q×R; *17* Q – R4+!, resigns. On *17* . . . P – N4; *18* Q×KP, R – Q1; *19* Q – B6+!, R – Q2; *20* R – Q1, Q – K2; and now *21* B – N6! (Dely) (About the only move that doesn't win is *21* B – N5?, O – O!)

7 . . .   B – K2

Too routine. Black should start quicker action on the Q–side.
More reasonable is 7 . . . P – QR3; 8 B – N3, Q – B2; 9 Q – K2
(or 9 P – B4), P – QN4; 10 O – O – O, N – QR4 (10 . . . B – N2
is also possible, whereupon White might reply 11 P – B3).

8 B – N3   . . .

Against Pascual, in a clock exhibition game at Davoa (Philip-
pines) 1967, I essayed 8 Q – K2, P – QR3; 9 O – O – O, Q – B2;
10 B – N3, B – Q2; 11 P – N4, N × N; 12 B × N (Fishy. Better is
12 R × N), P – K4; 13 P – N5, P × B; 14 P × N, P × N; 15 P × B,
P × P+; 16 K – N1, K × P? (. . . B – K3 equalizes); 17 Q – R5!,
P – KN3; 18 Q – R4+, P – B3; 19 P – K5!, P × P; 20 P – B4,
P – K5; 21 Q – R6, QR – K1; 22 R – Q4, K – Q1; 23 KR – Q1,
K – B1 (the beauty part is 23 . . . R – K2; 24 B – K6!!, R × B;
25 Q – N7, mopping up); 24 R × B, Q × R; 25 R × Q, K × R;
26 Q – N7+, K – Q3; 27 Q × QNP, P – K6; 28 Q – N6+, resigns.

8 . . .   O – O
9 Q – K2   . . .

Preparing Q-side castling and disallowing the reply . . . N –
KN5, which would be the case after 9 Q – Q2.

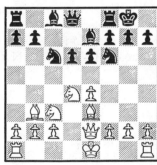

GELLER

Position after 9 Q – K2

FISCHER

9 . . .   Q – R4

Geller's attempt to improve on the customary 9 . . . P – QR3;
10 O – O – O, Q – B2; 11 P – N4, N × N; 12 R × N!, P – QN4
(Tal gives 12 . . . P – K4; 13 R – B4!, Q – Q1; 14 P – N5,
N – K1; 15 R × B!, R × R; 16 P – KR4, N – B2; 17 Q – N4
followed by P – R5, with a terrific attack); 13 P – N5, N – Q2;
14 Q – R5, N – K4; 15 P – B4, N – B3; 16 R – Q3, N – N5;
17 R – Q2, R – Q1; 18 P – B5, P – N3; 19 P × NP, RP × P; 20

Q – R4, N – B3; *21* Q – N3, N – K4; *22* P – KR4, B – N2; *23* P – R5, P – N5; *24* P×P, N×P; *25* QR – R2, P×N; *26* B – Q4, P – K4; *27* R – R8+!!, N×R; *28* P – N6!, B – KB3; *29* P×P+, K – B1; *30* R – R7! and White wins. (Velimirovich–Nikolich, Belgrade 1964.)

$$10 \quad O-O-O \quad . \ . \ .$$

10 O – O also comes into consideration.

$$10 \ . \ . \ . \qquad N\times N$$

Apparently Geller rejected *10 . . .* B – Q2; *11* N/4 – N5!, N – K1; *12* B – KB4, P – QR3; *13* N×P, N×N; *14* B×N, B×B; *15* R×B, Q – N4+; *16* Q – Q2, Q×P; *17* KR – Q1, B – K1; *18* Q – B4 with good pressure.

$$11 \quad B\times N \qquad B-Q2$$

Black cannot afford to go Pawn-snatching with *11 . . .* Q – N4+?; *12* K – N1, Q×P?; *13* KR – N1!, Q – R6 (if *13 . . .* Q×RP; *14* R – R1, Q – B5; *15* QR – N1!, P – K4 [or *15 . . .* P – KN3; *16* B – K3, Q – K4; *17* R – N5]; *16* B – K3, B – N5; *17* Q – K1, Q – B6; *18* R – N3 wins the Queen); *14* P – K5, N – K 1 (on *14 . . .* P×P; *15* Q×P carries too many threats); *15* P×P, B×P; *16* B×P!, N×B; *17* R×B and it's not a game any more. But interesting is *12 . . .* P – K4 (instead of *. . .* Q×P); *13* P – KR4, Q×NP; *14* QR – N1, B – N5; *15* R×Q!, B×Q; *16* N×B, P×B; *17* N×P with advantage. (If *17 . . .* N×P; *18* P – KB3! followed by N – B5.)

$$12 \quad K-N1 \qquad . \ . \ .$$

GELLER

Position after 12 K – N1

FISCHER

A critical position. White's immediate threat is *13* B×N.

12 . . . B – B3

In a later round Sofrevsky tried to improve against me with
12 . . . QR – Q1, but got into trouble after *13* Q – K3! Black
now rejected a dangerous Pawn sac which must be examined
very carefully: *13* . . . P – QN4!? But *14* P – QR3! (not *14* B × P,
R – R1 with active play), P – N5; *15* P × P, Q × P; *16* B × P, Q –
N2; *17* Q – N6!, Q – R1; *18* P – B3 and Black has no good way
to prosecute his attack. Consequently, Sofrevsky chose *13* . . .
P – QN3; *14* B × N!, P × B? (Black should reconcile himself to
the loss of a Pawn after *14* . . . D × D; *15* R × P, B – B1); *15*
N – Q5!!, KR – K1 (if *15* . . . P × N; *16* R × P, Q – R3; *17*
R – KR5! wins—*17* , , B – N5; *18* Q N3, etc.); *16* N × D+
(*16* Q – R6! is a quicker kill), R × N; *17* R × P, R – QB1; *18* Q –
Q4, B – K1?; *19* Q × BP, resigns.

13 P – B4 QR – Q1

If *13* . . . P – K4; 14 B – K3!, B × P (not *14* . . . N × P?;
15 N × N, B × N; *16* B – Q2 wins); *15* N × B, N × N; *16* Q – B3
with advantage.

14 KR – B1 . . .

I already had in mind the ensuing sacrifice. Also strong is *14*
P – N4—not to mention Trifunovich's post-mortem suggestion
14 P – B5!, P × P (not *14* . . . P – K4; *15* B – B2, P – Q4?;
16 P × P, N × P; *17* N × N, B × N; *18* Q × P wins a piece); *15* P × P,
KR – K1; *16* Q – B2 with positional pressure.

14 . . . P – QN4

On *14* . . . P – Q4; *15* P – K5, N – K5; *16* P – B5! maintains
the initiative.

15 P – B5!! . . .

The die is cast. I didn't want to lose a tempo playing it safe with
15 P – QR3.

15 . . . P – N5
16 P × P! P × N
17 P × P+ K – R1

Not *17* . . . R × P; *18* B × R+, K × B; *19* Q – B4+, P – Q4;
20 Q × B, etc.

18 R – B5!   Q – N5

On *18* . . . Q – B2 I had intended *19* QR – KB1 (threatening
R × N). If then *19* . . . N – Q2 (or on *19* . . . N × P; *20*
Q – N4 is bitter); *20* R – KR5! (threatening R × P+) is decisive.

19 Q – B1!   . . .

A hard move to find—it took around 45 minutes. The threat of
R × N must be attended to.

19 . . .   N × P

A fighting defense. *19* . . . N – Q2 loses immediately to
20 R – KR5, N – K4; *21* Q – B5, P – KR3; *22* Q – N6!!, R × P
(*22* . . . N × Q allows *23* R × P mate); *23* B × N, etc. On *19* . . .
R × P; *20* B × BP wins. And *19* . . . B × P gives White the pleasant
choice of *20* R × N or *20* R – QN5.

Objectively best is *19* . . . N – N5. But after *20* B × P (*20*
R – KR5, B – Q2! holds), Q – N2 (if *20* . . . Q × P; *21* R – Q4!);
21 Q – B4 with three Pawns for the piece and a winning attack
in the offing.

GELLER

Position after 19 . . .
N × P

FISCHER

20 P – QR3?   . . .

Losing! A couple of hours after the game it occurred to me
that White has a problem-like win after *20* Q – KB4!! (with the
threat of R – KR5). Black has no adequate defense:

A] *20* . . . P – Q4; *21* Q – K5, N – B3; *22* R × N, B × R; *23*
Q × B!

B] *20* . . . N – Q7+; *21* R × N, P × R; *22* P – B3!!, Q × KB;
23 B × P+!, K × B; *24* Q – N4+, K – R1; *25* Q – Q4+ and mates.

C] *20* . . . P × P; *21* R – KR5! (threatening B × P+), N – B6+

(if *21* . . . B – KB3; *22* Q – B5, P – KR3; *23* R×P+!, P×R;
24 Q – N6!! forces mate); *22* K×P, N×R+ (or *22* . . . R×P;
23 Q×R, N×R+; *24* K – N1!!, Q×B; *25* R×P+!!, K×R; *26*
Q – R5 mate); *23* K – B1, R×P (forced); *24* B×R! (*24* Q×R??,
B – N4+), and Black has no satisfactory answer to the threat of
25 R×P+, K×R; *26* Q – B5+ and mates. If *24* . . . B – Q2;
25 B×P+ wins Black's Queen.

20 . . .		Q – N2
21 Q – KB4		B – R5!!

I didn't see it! Moreover, the strength of this resource didn't
become fully apparent to me for another two moves.

22 Q – N4		. . .

Also futile is *22* Q – R6, B – KB3; *23* R×B, B×B.

22 . . .		B – KB3!
23 R×B		B×B!

GELLER

Final Position after
23 . . . B×B

FISCHER

At long last I saw the point of Geller's clever defense. As I was
studying *24* R – B4, it suddenly dawned on me that *24* . . .
B – R7+ was curtains. So—

24 White resigns

After *24* P×B, N×R! is the quietus. It is not enough to be a
good player, observed Dr. Tarrasch; you must also play well.

59 Kholmov *[U.S.S.R.]* - Fischer

SKOPJE 1967

KING'S INDIAN DEFENSE

The erring Bishop

In order to restrain Black from creating complications, Kholmov employs an unpretentious system. But he posts his Bishop prematurely on QR3, then penetrates ambitiously with 11 B – Q6. Fischer, with the routine 11 . . . Q – R4, promptly refutes. It is instructive to observe how, from now on, he creates an unhealthy climate wherever the Bishop seeks lodging. His Queen returns to QR6 on no less than three separate occasions, prompting one annotator to inquire, dryly, whether he was perhaps inventing perpetual motion. As early as move twelve it became apparent to both players that White was lost. However, Kholmov did his best to avert the inevitable for another twenty moves.

Fischer (with White) had lost to Kholmov in their only previous encounter, played via telephone to Havana in '65. Here, Fischer's victory brought him first place, a half point ahead of Geller.

1	P – Q4	N – KB3
2	N – KB3	P – KN3
3	P – KN3	B – N2
4	B – N2	O – O
5	O – O	P – Q3
6	N – B3	. . .

A straightforward but essentially passive development. The idea is to avoid creating a weakness with P – QB4; however, a drawback is White can no longer dominate the center with a Pawn-wedge.

6 . . .   QN – Q2

More flexible than *6 . . . P – Q4* which I adopted against Ivkov at the Piatagorsky Cup, 1966. That game continued *7 N – K5, P – B3; 8 P – K4*, and now Black could have equalized easily with *. . . P × P* (instead of *. . . B – K3?*); *9 N × KP, N × N; 10 B × N, B – R6* (not *10 . . . P – QB4? 11 Q – B3!*); *11 R – K1, N – Q2*, etc.

7 P – N3   . . .

A normal continuation, although it is dubious that White's Bishop is effective once posted on QN2 or QR3. This system is characterized by Pawn symmetry and quiet play with drawing tendencies. But a draw is precisely what I could not afford in this crucial encounter.

8 P – K4, P – K4 also presents Black with no opening problems.

7 . . .   P – K4
8 P × P   . . .

Dissipating the central tension. Black has no trouble getting play after *8 P – K4, P × P; 9 N × P, R – K1.*

8 . . .   P × P
9 P – K4   . . .

"The turbulent complications of the normal K's Indian can hardly arise, and the position can already be evaluated as even." (TRIFUNOVICH).

9 . . .   R – K1
10 B – QR3   . . .

Better is *10 P – QR4, P – QR4; 11 B – QR3*, whereupon the Bishop will be immune from eventual attack after *. . . Q – R4.*
"Even so early, White is on the wrong track. The Bishop has nothing to seek on the QR3 – KB8 diagonal. Yet, while it is easy now to condemn this move, till now it has often been adopted by White with never a harsh word. The punishment which ensues, however . . . is more severe than any this commentator has observed hitherto. *10 B – N2* is correct." (TRIFUNOVICH).

10 . . .   P – B3

"Black invites the Bishop to seize a strong position." (TRIFUNOVICH).

11 B – Q6?   . . .

Kholmov consumed over half an hour on this mistake. The idea is to keep Black bottled up while exerting pressure on the KP. The only trouble with the move, however, is that it loses. As Tarrasch wrote: "When you don't know what to do, wait for your opponent to get an idea—it's sure to be wrong!" *11* Q – K2 was indicated.

11 . . .   Q – R4!

This normal freeing maneuver is now devastating.

12 Q – Q3   . . .

What else? *12* P – QN4, Q – R6 leaves White in the same predicament.

FISCHER

Position after 12 Q – Q3

KHOLMOV

Black now has a shot which wins two pieces for a Rook; or, as it turns out, a lowly Pawn (which proves fatal).

12 . . .   R – K3!

Springing the trap! White cannot avoid material loss. Geller, who was tied with me for the lead, had displayed great interest in my game—up to now. When he saw this position, he smiled wryly. I never noticed him looking at the game again.

13 P – QN4   . . .

No matter how White wriggles and squirms, he cannot escape the fate in store for him. After *13* N – K2 Black has the pleasant choice of either . . . N×P or . . . N – K1—both of which win a Pawn.

After the game Kholmov told me he had originally intended *13* N – KN5, R×B; *14* Q×R, Q×N; *15* Q – K7 with active play

However, he saw (too late) that simply *14 . . . P – KR3!* squelches all such illusions.

13 . . .	Q – R6!

Renewing the ancient threat of . . . R × B.

14 B – B7	. . .

The wandering Bishop hopes to receive succor. But, in so doing, it must abandon protection of the QNP.

14 . . .	Q × NP

Perhaps White was hoping for *14 . . . N – K1; 15 B – R5, P – N3; 16 QR – N1!, P × B; 17 R – N3, N – B4!; 18 P × N, Q × BP; 19 KR – N1* where Black's technical difficulties are great.

15 QR – N1	Q – K2!

A cute tactical point. *15 . . . Q – B1?* loses the exchange after *16 N – KN5* (if the Rook retreats, then White's Bishop returns to Q6). Now *16 N – KN5* is refuted by N – B4. For all practical purposes the game is over.

16 KR – Q1	N – K1
17 B – R5	. . .

No rest for the weary.

17 . . .	R – Q3
18 Q – K2	R × R ch
19 Q × R	B – B1
20 N – Q2	. . .

Bad—as is everything else. *20 B – N4, Q – B3; 21 B × B, N × B* leaves White a Pawn behind with his weak squares still showing.

20 . . .	Q – R6!

Winning even more material.

21 N – B4	Q – B4
22 B – B1	P – QN4
23 N – Q2	. . .

23 B – N4 drops a piece to Q – Q5.

23 . . .	Q – R6!

This curious shuttle has proved White's undoing.

24	N – N3	N – B4
25	B × P	. . .

Desperation. After *25* B – Q8, N – K3!; *26* B – R5, N – Q3 Black wins as he pleases.

25	. . .	P × B
26	N × P	Q – R5

FISCHER

Position after 26 . . .
Q – R5

KHOLMOV

27	N × N	. . .

Perhaps White had intended *27* Q – Q5, but Q × KP! spells *finis.*

27	. . .	Q × B
28	Q – Q5	R – N1
29	P – QR4	B – R6!

Quickest.

30	Q × P	R – B1
31	N – Q3	Q × P
32	N – K1	P – QR3
	White resigns	

The Knight has no good square. If *33* N – Q4, B – N2. Or *33* N – QB3, Q – B5. Finally, *33* N – R7, R – B2; *34* R – R1, Q – Q2; *35* R × P, R × N; *36* R × R, Q × R; *37* Q × N, Q – R8 delivers the mate.

Afterwards, Geller tried to offer my opponent some sympathy. I overheard a dismayed Kholmov telling him that I had "seen everything!" This game was particularly sweet because it was my first win against a Russian in almost a dozen tries (since game 52)—and my first with Black since 1962 (Korchnoi at Curaçao).

60 Fischer - Stein [U.S.S.R.]

INTERZONAL, SOUSSE 1967

RUY LOPEZ

When champions meet

> On his ninth turn Black varies the routine sparring but the
> game proceeds innocuously until Fischer veers with 14 P –
> QN4, intensifying the struggle. If, in the ensuing slugfest,
> Stein can be said to have made an error, it is the strategic
> one of so pressing on the Q-side as to allow White to become
> entrenched on the opposite wing. Fischer's prosecution of the
> attack is crowned by a brilliant offer of a piece (29 B × P)
> which the Soviet champion declines. Had Fischer then renewed
> the sacrifice, the end would have come sooner. In his detailed
> notes Fischer refers to this oversight, reveals some important
> thoughts on the Ruy, pinpoints "the losing move"
> (21 . . . N – N3), criticizes a second subtle mistake of his
> own (26 N – B3), and offers a possible defense for Stein
> (28 . . . B – B3), which other commentators have failed to
> note.
>
> It is unfortunate that this interesting and most instructive
> game was expunged from the official records due to Fischer's
> withdrawal before having completed half his playing schedule.

1 P – K4   . . .

I have never opened with the QP—on principle.

1 . . .   P – K4

I had expected the Sicilian, with Stein's favorite accelerated
Dragon (2 . . . P – KN3). I suspect that the Russians "group-
think" before important games to decide which openings will
upset their opponents psychologically.

2 N – KB3   N – QB3
3 B – N5   P – QR3

Possibly Stein was braced for *4* B × N, as in game 56.

        4 B – R4   . . .

Relieving the suspense.

        4 . . .   N – B3
        5 O – O   B – K2
        6 R – K1   P – QN4
        7 B – N3   P – Q3

In the event the reader is interested in what I may have had in mind against the Marshall Attack, he is referred to my game against Spassky at the Piatagorsky Cup, 1966, which continued: *7* . . . O – O; *8* P – B3, P – Q4; *9* P × P, N × P; *10* N × P, N × N; *11* R × N, P – QB3; *12* P – N3!?, B – Q3; *13* R – K1, N – B3; *14* P – Q4, B – KN5; *15* Q – Q3 (*15* P – B3 might be better), P – B4; and now *16* B – B2! (instead of P × P?) allows Black insufficient compensation for his Pawn.

        8 P – B3   O – O
        9 P – KR3   . . .

For *9* P – Q4 see game 36.

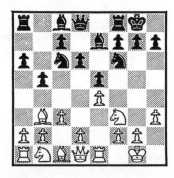

STEIN

Position after 9 P – KR3

FISCHER

        9 . . .   B – N2

A rare side line. *9* . . . N – QR4; *10* B – B2, P – B4 is a better-known sequence. The text is somewhat passive and commits the Bishop perhaps prematurely. Usually Stein continues *9* . . . N – Q2; *10* P – Q4, B – B3; then *11* P – QR4 is slightly better for White.

The line chosen in the game comes to resemble Breyer's Defense

(9 . . . N – N1; *10* P – Q4, QN – Q2; *11* QN – Q2, B – N2; *12* B – B2!, R – K1; *13* P – QN4, P×P; *14* P×P, P – QR4; *15* P×P, P – B4)—see note to White's 17th move.

10 P – Q4	N – QR4

Believe it or not, this Knight is headed for Q2! Black may prefer the shorter route with *10 . . . N – N1*; but experience has shown that after *11* P×P, P×P; *12* Q×Q, Black is obliged to recapture with his Bishop, which interferes with his development and produces endgame difficulties.

11 B – B2	N – B5

Unsound is *11 . . .* P×P; *12* P×P, P – Q4; *13* P – K5, N – K5; *14* N – B3, P – KB4; *15* P×P e.p., B×P; *16* N×N, P×N; *17* B×P, B×B; *18* R×B, P – B4; *19* P – Q5 and Black remains a Pawn down.
Another possibility is *11 . . .* P×P; *12* P×P, P – B4; but White holds the edge with 12 QN – Q2. On *11 . . .* P – B4 immediately, White replies *12* QN – Q2, retaining the option of P – Q5, locking in Black's Bishop on QN2.

12 P – QN3	N – N3
13 QN – Q2	. . .

Not *13* P×P, P×P; *14* Q×Q, QR×Q; *15* N×P, N×P!=.

13 . . .	QN – Q2

Black's 5th move with this Knight! *13 . . .* P×P; *14* P×P, P – B4 seems more active.
Stein-Lutikov, Moscow 1966 continued *13 . . .* R – K1?; *14* N – B1? and Black equalized easily. However, White should vary with *14* P×P, P×P; *15* N×P, B – Q3; *16* N/5 – B3, B×P (*16 . . .* N×P; *17* N×N, B×N; *18* B – N5! busts Black); *17* N×B, N×N; *18* Q – Q3! (White can't win a piece because his Queen hangs at the end after . . . B – R7ch), with initiative.

14 P – QN4!	. . .

Prevents . . . P – B4 and prepares a dominating build-up with *15* B – N2 followed by P – B4. The routine continuation *14* B – N2 (Keres-Gligorich, Zurich 1959) gives nothing.

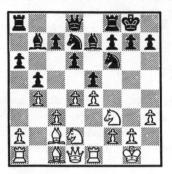

STEIN

Position after 14 P – QN4

FISCHER

14 . . .   P×P

Stein makes his bid for active counterplay even though it
involves abandoning his "strong point" (KP). If *14 . . . P
– QR4; 15 N – N3!* and Black might find himself in straightened
circumstances after the Knight reaches QR5.

15 P×P   P – QR4

On *15 . . . P – B4; 16 NP×P, P×P; 17 P – Q5* White's
steamroller in the center is more formidable than Black's Q-side
majority.

16 P×P   P – B4

Inferior would be *16 . . . R×P; 17 P – Q5!, P – B4; 18
P×P e.p., B×P; 19 N – Q4*, after which White, among other
things, goes to work on the isolated QNP.

17 P – K5!   . . .

This identical position was reached by transposition, with
Black's Rook on K1, in Ciric-Robatsch, Beverwijk 1967, which
continued: *17 B – N2, Q×P; 18 P – QR4, P – N5; 19 N – B4,
Q – B2; 20 P – K5, P×KP; 21 P×KP, N – Q4; 22 KN – Q2,
N/2 – N3* and now Spassky's recommendation of *23 P – K6!* is
unpleasant for Black. (See note to Black's 9th move.)

17 . . .   P×KP

Another line of defense is *17 . . . N – K1* with the idea of
eliminating both of White's center Pawns. "The consequences
are very ramified, and there is some danger that Black may fall
to recover White's Pawn on its QR5 or may lose his own on QN4,

or both. The text is more active but also more dangerous for Black's King." (KMOCH).

| 18 | P×KP | N – Q4 |
| 19 | N – K4 | N – N5! |

The idea is to force the Bishop to retreat and thereby hem in White's QR. On *19 . . . R×P; 20* N/4 – N5!, P – R3; *21* Q – Q3!, P – N3; *22* N – K6! wins.

| 20 | B – N1 | R×P |
| 21 | Q – K2! | . . . |

Increasing the pressure. Not *21* P – K6, P×P; *22* N/4 – N5? (or *22* N/3 – N5, B – Q4; *23* N×RP, R – B4! holds), QB×N!; *23* N×B, B – B3 wins.

STEIN

Position after 21 Q – K2

FISCHER

One can sense the storm looming against Black's King.

21 . . .   N – N3?

Quite possibly "the losing move." It is better to reserve this Knight for the defense of the K-side. More prudent is *21 . . . R – K1!* with *. . . N – B1* in the offing. *22* R – Q1, Q – B2 leads to nought. And *22* P – K6 leads to no demonstrable advantage after P×P; *23* N/4 – N5, KB×N; *24* N×B, N – B1; *25* Q – R5, P – N3, etc.

22 N/3 – N5!   . . .

Now the threats are beginning to jell.

22 . . .   QB×N!

Forced, because if *22 . . . P – R3; 23* N – R7!! stands Black up. On *23 . . . R – K1 (23 . . . K × N; 24 N × P* dis.+ followed by N × B leads to a small fork); *24* N/7 – B6ch!, B × N (*24 . . .* P × N; *25* Q – N4+, K – R1; *26* N – Q6!, B × N; *27* Q – B5!, K – N2; *28* B × P+ leads to mate); *25* N × B+, Q × N (again if *25 . . .* P × N; *26* Q – N4+, K – B1; *27* B × P+, K – K2; *28* P – K6!, K – Q3; *29* Q – N3ch, K – B3; *30* B – K4+, N/5 – Q4; *31* P × P, R – KR1; *32* B × N+wins); *26* P × Q wins the Exchange. Also insufficient is *22 . . .* P – N3; *23* P – K6!, P – B4; *24* N – B7! followed by B – N2 with a crushing attack.

> **23** Q × B   P – N3
> **24** Q – R4   P – R4
> **25** Q – N3!   . . .

Now White threatens *26* N – K6!, B – R5!; *27* N × Q, B × Q; *28* N – N7, R – R2; *29* N × P. After Black's next move, this variation fails against *29 . . .* B × P.

Impetuous would be *25* P – N4??, Q – Q5.

> **25 . . .**   N – B5!
> **26** N – B3?   . . .

More forcing is *26* P – K6!, P – B4; *27* N – B3 (not *27* N – B7, R × N!; *28* P × R+, K × P; *29* B × P!, P × B; *30* Q – KB3, K – N3; *31* P – N4, Q – Q4 and a draw appears likely), K – N2; *28* Q – B4, R – KR1 transposing into the game (but not *27 . . .* R – B3; *28* B – N5, K – R2; *29* B × R, B × B; *30* B × P!, P × B; *31* QR – Q1, N – Q4; *32* P – K7!, B × P; *33* R × N is decisive). This order of moves would prohibit the defense mentioned in the note to Black's 28th: after being forced to play *26 . . .* P – B4, Black loses his options.

At this stage the power failed. In the dark I began to worry about *26 . . .* N – Q6! (if *27* R – Q1, N × B! and White has nothing). Then the lights came on again and I saw clearly that *26 . . .* N – Q6? was crushed by *27* B × N!, Q × B; *28* B – N5! and White penetrates decisively on the weak dark squares.

> **26 . . .**   K – N2
> **27** Q – B4   R – KR1
> **28** P – K6!   . . .

"This blow rocks the remnants of the tower around the Black King." (GLIGORICH).

STEIN

Position after 28 P – K6

FISCHER

28 . . .   P – B4

Much stiffer resistance (taking advantage of White's inaccurate 26th move) is offered by *28 . . . B – B3!* (not *28 . . . P – B3; 29 N – R4). 29 P×P, B×R (29 . . . Q – Q3?; 30 P – B8=Q+!, K×Q; 31 Q – K4, Q – Q2; 32 B – N5!, R – R3; 33 B×B, R×B; 34 N – K5!* winning a Pawn and eventually the game); *30 P – B8= Q+!. Q×Q; 31 Q – QB7ch, K – N1; 32 B×P, N – Q4 (if 32 . . . R – QR3; 33 R – K8!); 33 Q – N7, N – B3; 34 B – B4* (threatening *35 N – N5* and *B – B7+), R – KR2!* White now appears to have nothing better than *35 B×Rch, N×R; 36 Q – Q5ch, Q – B2* (worse is *36 . . . K – R1?; 37 Q×RP!); 37 Q×Qch, K×Q; 38 R×B* with chances by virtue of the extra Pawn. But this would be a tough ending to win!

29 B×P!   Q – KB1

The only reasonable way to decline the sacrifice. On *29 . . . B – Q3; 30 P – K7!, B×Q* (or *30 . . . B×P; 31 Q – N3, R – QR3; 32 N – N5,* etc.); *31 P×Q=Q, R×Q; 32 B×B, P×B; 33 B – B7!* (R. Byrne).

Kmoch suggests that "Leonidas might even have better taken a chance and faced the storm by playing *29 . . . P×B.*" But the Bishop is tabu, for White wins quickly with *30 Q – N3ch.* Black now has two defenses which fail:

A] *30 . . . K – B1; 31 Q – N6, Q – K1* (if *31 . . . N – Q3; 32 N – K5!); 32 B – R6+, R×B; 33 Q×R+, K – N1; 34 N – N5.*
B] *30 . . . K – R2; 31 N – N5ch!, B×N; 32 B×B, Q – Q6* (if *32 . . . Q – QN1; 33 Q – R4!, K – N3; 34 B–B6*—or *32 . . . Q – K1; 33 QR – Q1, R – R2; 34 R – Q8!, Q×R; 35 B×Q, R×B; 36 P – K7, R – K1; 37 R – K6!, R/1×P; 38 Q – N6+,*

K – R1; *39* Q – B6ch, R – N2; *40* Q – R6+ and mates); *33* Q – B7+, K – N3; *34* Q – B7+!, K × B; *35* Q – N7+, K – B5; *36* QR – Q1!, etc.

STEIN

Position after 29 . . .
Q – KB1

FISCHER

30 B – K4?   . . .

Littlewood indicates *30* N – R4! as a quick win for White. He's right. The main line is *30 . . .* B × N; *31* Q × B, Q × B (if *31 . . .* Q – B3; *32* Q – N3!—or *31 . . .* P × B; *32* Q – N5+, K – R2; *33* P – K7, Q – K1; *34* R – K6!); *32* Q – K7+, K – N1; *33* Q – Q8+, K – N2; *34* Q – B7+, K – N1; *35* P – K7, etc.

30 . . .   Q × Q
31 B × Q   R – K1?

Stein's post-mortem suggestion of *31 . . .* R – QR3 is met by *32* QR – Q1, R × P; *33* R – Q7 (threatening N – N5), etc.

But the best try is *31 . . .* R × P! On *32* QR – Q1, R – QR2 holds. And if *32* R × R, N × R; *33* N – K5, P – N4; *34* B – N3 maintains the initiative, but Black has drawing chances.

Black, however, was in extreme time-pressure.

32 QR – Q1   R – R3
33 R – Q7   . . .

Even more convincing is *33* B – N7!, R – R2; *34* R – Q7.

33 . . .   R × KP
34 N – N5   R – KB3

Costs the Exchange. But no better is *34 . . .* R – R3; *35* B – N1, K – B3; *36* N – K4+, K – B2; *37* N × P, etc.

35 B – B3!   R × B

Of course *35 . . . K – B1* is refuted by *36 N – R7+.*

36	N – K6+	K – B3
37	N × R	N – K4
38	R – N7	B – Q3
39	K – B1	. . .

Puts an end to all effective resistance. White's material superiority must tell.

STEIN

Position after 39 K – B1

FISCHER

39	. . .	N – B7

A pretty point is revealed after *39 . . . N × B; 40 R × R, N – Q7+; 41 K – K2, B × N; 42 R – B8+, K – N4; 43 R × B, K × R; 44 K × N,* resigns.

40	R – K4	N – Q5
41	R – N6	R – Q1
42	N – Q5+	K – B4
43	N – K3+	. . .

The sealed move seals Black's fate, Not only is White an Exchange ahead, but his attack still rages.

43	. . .	K – K3

Equally hopeless is *43 . . . K – B3; 44 B – K2, P – N5; 45 P – B4,* followed by *B – B4.*

44	B – K2!	. . .

"The double threat of *45 P – B4* and *45 B × NP* clears the last stone from the road to victory." (KMOCH).

44	. . .	K – Q2
45	B × P+	N × B

46	R×N	K – B3
47	P – QR4	B – B2
48	K – K2	P – N4
49	P – N3	R – QR1
50	R – N2	R – KB1
51	P – B4	. . .

The beginning of the end.

51	. . .	P×P
52	P×P	N – B2
53	R – K6+	N – Q3

If 53 . . . B – Q3; 54 R – B6! is powerful.

54	P – B5	R – QR1
55	R – Q2!	R×P
56	P – B6	Black resigns

On 56 . . . R – KB5; 57 N – Q5 wins the house. A stubborn fight!

BOBBY FISCHER'S TOURNAMENT AND MATCH RECORD

(Born: March 9, 1943)

Event	Year	Place
Brooklyn Chess Club Championship . .	1955	3rd–5th
USA Amateur Championship, New Jersey	1955	minus score
USA Junior Championship, Nebraska . .	1955	10th–20th
Greater New York City Championship .	1956	5th–7th
Manhattan Chess Club, "A" Reserve . .	1956	1st
USA Amateur Championship, New Jersey	1956	21st
USA Junior Championship, Philadelphia .	1956	1st
USA Open Championship, Oklahoma . .	1956	4th–8th
Canadian Open Championship, Montreal .	1956	8th–12th
Eastern States Championship, Washington	1956	2nd
Rosenwald Trophy Tournament, New York	1956–7	8th
Log Cabin Open Championship, New Jersey	1957	6th
Western Open Championship, Milwaukee .	1957	7th
USA Junior Championship, San Francisco	1957	1st
USA Open Championship, Cleveland . .	1957	1st
Eight-game match with Cardoso, New York	1957	6–2 (won)
New Jersey Open Championship . . .	1957	1st
North Central Championship, Milwaukee	1957	6th
USA Championship, New York . . .	1957–8	1st
Interzonal, Portoroz	1958	5th–6th
Four-game match with Matulovich, Belgrade	1958	2½–1½ (won)
USA Championship, New York . . .	1958–9	1st
Mar del Plata, Argentina	1959	3rd–4th
Santiago, Chile	1959	4th–7th
Zurich, Switzerland	1959	3rd–4th
Candidates' Tournament, Yugoslavia . .	1959	5th–6th
USA Championship, New York . . .	1959–60	1st
Mar del Plata, Argentina	1960	1st
Buenos Aires	1960	13th
Reykjavik, Iceland	1960	1st
Olympic Team Tournament, Leipzig . . 1st board	1960	high scorer (finals)

USA Championship, New York . . .	1960–1	1st
Sixteen-game match with Reshevsky, New York and Los Angeles (unfinished) . .	1961	$5\frac{1}{2}$–$5\frac{1}{2}$
Bled, Yugoslavia	1961	2nd
Interzonal, Stockholm	1962	1st
Candidates' Tournament, Curaçao . . .	1962	4th
Olympic Team Tournament, Varna. . . 1st board	1962	high scorer (prelims)
USA Championship, New York . . .	1962–3	1st
Western Open, Michigan	1963	1st
New York State Open Tournament . .	1963	1st
USA Championship, New York . . .	1963–4	1st
Capablanca Memorial, Havana, Cuba . .	1965	2nd–4th
USA Championship, New York . . .	1965–6	1st
Piatagorsky Cup, Los Angeles . . .	1966	2nd
Olympic Team Tournament, Havana . . 1st board	1966	2nd high scorer
USA Championship, New York . . .	1966–7	1st
Monaco	1967	1st
Skopje, Yugoslavia	1967	1st
Interzonal, Sousse	1967	withdrew while leading
Israel	1968	1st
Yugoslavia	1968	1st

INDEX TO OPENINGS

(Numbers refer to games)

LIST OF OPPONENTS

(Numbers refer to games)